THE RISE OF MODERN WARFARE

From the Age of Mercenaries through Napoleon

H. W. KOCH

THE RISE OF
MODERN
WARFARE

From the Age of Mercenaries through Napoleon
H. W. KOCH

CRESCENT BOOKS
New York
 A Bison Book

Copyright © 1981 by Bison Books Limited

All rights reserved.

This 1982 edition is published by Crescent Books, distributed by Crown
Publishers, Inc.

First published in Great Britain by Bison Books Limited

Printed in Hong Kong

Library of Congress Cataloging in Publication Data

Koch, H. W. (Hannsjoachim Wilhelm), 1933–
    The Rise of Modern Warfare

    Originally published: 1st American ed.
Englewood Cliffs, N.J.: Prentice-Hall, ©1981.
    Includes index.
    1. Military art and science – History.
2. Military history, Modern. I. Title.
U39. K6 1982   355′.009′03   82-10596
ISBN 0-517-39340-9

h g f e d c b a

CONTENTS

French knights embarking for a Crusade (miniature, fourteenth century).

CHAPTER I
THE RISE OF ABSOLUTISM

History is the continuous flow of events: fundamental changes rarely happen suddenly. Absolutism has been defined by the great German historian Otto Hintze as 'the epoch of militarism' in Europe, but there are ample reasons to doubt whether this definition was true at the time Hintze wrote it, namely at the turn of the twentieth century. Absolutist power and the changes it brought to the art of war were not the products of sudden upheaval but the results of gradual change.

Such gradual change is demonstrated by the growth of the word for armed conflict be that war, *guerre* or *Krieg*. Certainly the Indo-Germans, who from 2000 BC had begun to divide into different tribal units, had neither a word for armed conflict nor one for peace. However, the fact that they were a warring people is shown by archeological finds – the weapons found in their burial places and the scars marking their skeletons. The later Germanic tribes had no common word for war, although they had established quite a reputation for their fighting skills. Anthropological studies have suggested that the deepest emotional roots of war are fear and anxiety of what is alien. Even a comparatively modern language, such as Latin, equates the stranger or alien with the enemy in the word *hostis*. Blood is the carrier of power and life, for it contains the soul and the spirit; the carriers of common blood assumed that, in the case of bloodshed, their very life substance had been impaired, which

they could strengthen only by shedding the blood of the enemy. Thus by war their life substance, their *hamingja*, would be restored, and the balance of their world regained. This is the origin of the blood feud. Primitive war is retribution against the sin committed against a member of one's own 'blood group,' but since entire families and tribes are involved, both organization for war and solidarity are prerequisites, as is the principle of undisputed leadership.

Among primitive tribes, conflict took place within the context of superhuman and divine powers. This was indicated by preparatory rituals before breaking camp and during the march. These rituals played an important, even a decisive, part in primitive warfare because victory was in the first place an emotional and psychological achievement. Victory was the purification of one's own blood. Booty and other material advantages played a secondary role.

These rituals were, in some ways, the precursors of psychological warfare. The enemy was ambushed if he was considered a law-breaker or criminal, whereas battle in the form of attack and defense took place on mutually-agreed holy ground. It was the gods who sat in judgment. Combat could take the form of a duel between the two leaders, two appointed warriors or the two opposing groups; the result meant total victory or defeat. Pursuit was unknown, and the defeated tribe willingly submitted to slavery under the victor.

Almost all primitive tribes developed different words for armed conflict. Germanic words like *Feud, Fehde, Hader, Orlog, Hiltia* and *Wig* all meant much the same thing. *Feud* and *Fehde* derive from the west-Germanic *Faih-itho,* meaning hostility; *Hader* is from *Hathu*; *Hiltia* means duel; *Wig* had the Indo-Germanic root of *Uik*, meaning to be bold and strong; and *Orlog* comes from the Old High German *Urluigi*, meaning lawless condition, one who has broken the law, or war against him who has broken the divine law, the *Leugh*, or, in its modern English form, the law. The word *Orlog* made a temporary disappearance at the end of the Middle Ages since practically all the wars against the breakers of divine law had come to an end.

The Middle High German *Kriec* derives from the Old High German *Chrec*, and at that time had nothing to do with war. In the Middle Ages the most commonly used word for armed conflict was *strit*, from which the English word 'struggle' and the German *Streit* are derived, the basic connotation being movement and uproar. *Wearra*, from which the English 'war' comes, has much the same meaning; it is also the root for the French *guerre* and for the Italian, Spanish and Portuguese *guerra*, all originally meaning the same thing – uproar and confusion. The German word *Kampf* comes from the Latin *campus*, meaning field or fight. In other words, despite the multitude of expressions used to indicate war, its outcome was considered a judgment of God.

This was also the case among the Romans, where it was up to the *festialis*, an assembly of 20 priests, to proclaim the *bellum iustum*, the just war. Only from the days of Caesar onward was the just war perverted into the *Pax Romana*, and, following the precedent of Alexander the Great, the *Pax Romana* was equivalent to the idea of Empire. Whoever opposed the *Pax Romana* was an enemy of the Empire and was to be destroyed, and those who submitted and accepted unquestioningly the power of the Caesars were accepted within the fold of the Empire.

Nevertheless the concept of a just war was not abandoned. It is one of the central subjects discussed in Saint Augustine's *De Civitate Dei (City of God)*. The concept of the just war and the defense of the state of God preoccupied a whole host of writers right into the Middle Ages. War could be conducted only on divine premises: *Dieus le veult!* ('The Lord wishes it') could be the only motto. This trend of thought provided a line of continuity, from Saint Augustine through the Visigoth Isidor of Seville to the Vienna deacon Johann von Seffner, who in 1386 wrote that the only just war was the Emperor's war to defend his heritage or expel the enemy.

Only with the decay of the feudal order in the sixteenth century, and the rise of the sovereign state as a concept in international law, according to the analysis of Hugo Grotius (1583–1645), did war become a legal conflict decided by force of arms. This was in a period of vehement religious wars where

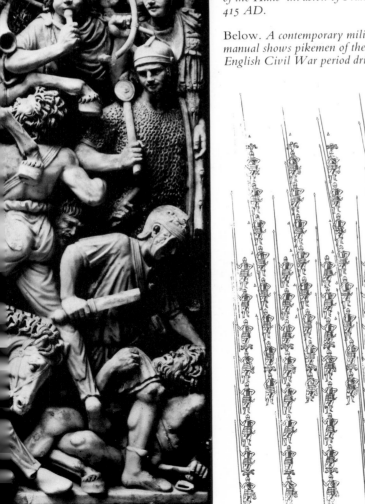

Left. *Mêlée between Roman soldiers and barbarians.*

Right. *This romanticized nineteenth century engraving gives a good idea of the terrifying impact of the Huns' invasion of France in 415 AD.*

Below. *A contemporary military manual shows pikemen of the English Civil War period drilling.*

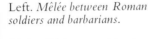

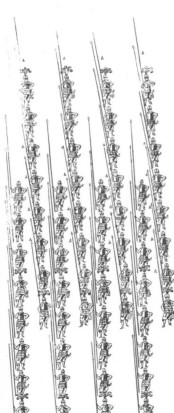

Above left. *The French employ primitive artillery against the walls of Tunis.*

Above right. *Fight between English and French during the Hundred Years' War.*

Right. *A French sword of 1375–1400.*

Below. *Roman legionaries (German print, nineteenth century).*

a creed supplied the pretext, at least, for the satisfaction of baser motives. Nevertheless, war among the European nations has remained an ethical problem to the present day. In the Marxist view of causation in history, ethical considerations are replaced by class interests.

The awakening of national consciousness among the peoples of Europe, by no means a process limited to the nineteenth century, while nominally preserving the concept of the just and unjust war, allowed war to become the people's war in which no individual could avoid involvement. In our own age the last fences of civilization have been broken down and the age of total war ushered in, culminating in a *Kriegsbild* which has no possible outcome except the ultimate destruction of mankind.

War in its earliest stages contained the seeds of all modern forms of war: armed conflict, confrontation in economic and other non-military arenas, and psychological warfare. Therefore one can define war as a collective form of struggle between tribes, nations or organized political groups, involving the use of all military, psychological and economic weapons. It is fought by the young adults of the opposing forces, who are trained in the use of arms (or weapons systems) and organized into military groups. Conflict is engaged until the will of one antagonist has been imposed upon the other.

In much the same way as the concept of war in its modern form did not emerge overnight, absolutism, the theory and the reality, also took time to develop.

In essence, medieval Europe was based on a federal structure. Feudalism, in many different and diluted forms, was one of the social and military instruments which made this federalism work. The acceptance of the Roman Catholic faith, one and indivisible, as well as the acceptance of the Emperor of the Holy Roman Empire of the German peoples as the successor to the imperial traditions of the Roman Empire was its basis. Any attack upon the Emperor or the Church inevitably shook the federal basis upon which the whole edifice rested. Some of the major examples which prove the point are the Investiture Contest in the eleventh century in Germany, the Great Schism, and the end of the Hohenstaufen dynasty.

The major problem of medieval government was one of communication, because the territorial units under the control of one dynasty were generally too large to be directly administered by it, and any weakness at the center of government led to the strengthening of the feudal or territorial lord. Territorial states and the concept of territorial sovereignty ultimately emerged from these feudal territories.

In 1300 the argument between the Holy Roman Emperor and the King of France still revolved around the divine rights which the French King claimed for himself, and which were previously preserved for the Emperor. By the fourteenth century, Renaissance Italy began to produce political theories which would shatter a united Christendom into millions of pieces, and vitally undermine the Roman Catholic Church. On the crest of the Promethean wave, Renaissance man recognized himself as the source and creative principle of political order. The state was a work of art, created and shaped by man. This was very much the view of Machiavelli: according to him, whether it was a princely state or a republic, the state on earth was an end in itself. Virtue, justice, order and religion were instruments in the hands of the state to be used and applied whenever necessary. Niccolo di Machiavelli and other contemporary theorists paved the way for analysis of the state without recourse to any theory of divine origin. One of Machiavelli's central concepts was that of *virtù*, which he interpreted as the quality which bound and integrated the individual to his or her state. It defined the maximization of the individual's resources, be they material, intellectual, artistic or military, for the sake of the state – virtue to the point of self-sacrifice.

As yet this was theory – in practice it was limited to the Italian city states which Machiavelli had taken as his test cases and the city states of early history. Machiavelli did not prophesy the decay of the feudal system: that was already long under way. The apex of the feudal pyramid, the ruler, was in serious

Above. *A knight's sword, probably French, circa 1340. It has a heavy double-edged blade, and the grip would once have been covered with wood or leather.*

Left. *David slays Goliath, watched by legionaries of the later Roman Empire. (Greek psalter, tenth century).*

Nach wenigh Predication
Die Caluinsche Religion

Das bildens sturmen fiengen an
Das nicht ein bildt dauon bleib stan

Kap Monstrantz, kilch, auch die altar
Und weß sonst dort vor handen war,

Zerbrochen all in kurtzer stundt
Gleich gar vil leuten das ist kundt.

Anno Dnj. M. D. LXVI. XX Augusti

Above. *Soldiers plunder a church in 1579 during the French Wars of Religion.*

Below left. *The Duke of Parma's victorious Spaniards enter Antwerp in August 1585, after a lengthy siege.*

trouble, a crisis which shattered the previously hierarchic and uniform structure of medieval feudalism, and which was symbolized by the downfall of the Hohenstaufens and the exile of the papacy in Avignon. It was precipitated by the invention of firearms and the rise of the cash nexus. The old order gradually dissolved and made way for new forms of organization.

The sovereign power of France grew out of the debris of medieval feudalism and the country was emerging as a centralized national state. In Germany, on the other hand, particularist forces dominated over the Imperial central power and ensured that a German national state did not emerge for another 500 years. If one looks at this process more closely, the pattern seems to be much the same throughout Europe. As the feudal pyramid decayed, the powers existing between the apex and base were the first to triumph – the kings, dukes, margraves, princes and counts, who all held control of territory they could effectively administer. For a long time it remained uncertain who would prevail. In France there seemed every chance that the feudal lords would prevail, the potential outcome being Flemish, Burgundian and Breton states. In Germany the problem was more complex since there the royal crown was burdened with the responsibility and historical legacy of the Imperial crown. Like the Pope in the ecclesiastical field, so the Holy Roman Emperor in a secular, sat almost next to God, and it would at that time have been almost unthinkable to give up the sacred

Imperial crown in favor of the national royal crown. Therefore the liege lords gained power in Germany in much the same way as in France. But, centuries later, in France and in England after the Wars of the Roses, the royal crown was to gain the overriding power.

At first it seemed as though Europe would transform itself into a series of properties owned by the most powerful families. However, marriage contracts, legacies and so forth created overnight power agglomerates, which were unstable because the constituent parts had little or nothing to do with one another. True, the dynasties did their utmost to fuse their territories into one nation. But for the outcome of the Hundred Years' War, France and England might have become united under one dynasty. Similar combinations would have been possible in central Europe.

The essential criterion was whether a territory could be effectively administered and defended. With the decay of feudalism it was the territorial lord who hired the mercenaries. He conducted the war and under his leadership all suffered the same fate, feared the same enemy and shared identical economic interests. The fate of his family deeply affected the mercenaries' fortunes. The question of a male heir affected not only the royal family, but the entire country – against the backcloth of the Wars of the Roses the question of a male successor was just as important to the English nation as it was to Henry VIII. To maintain the dynasty's position, the king or prince courted the popularity of his subjects. Balduin IV of Flanders always walked around with an axe to pass sentence and execute on the spot any vassal guilty of a transgression against the people.

Historiography was drawn into this process. The princes employed their own historians whose task was to elevate the prince and his ancestors, and to describe the historical development of the territory and its achievements. That most of it was pure fiction disturbed only interested parties – in point of fact, fiction was necessary as sources were scarce. Much could be scored if the ancestry could be allegedly traced back to Charlemagne. Artists fulfilled a similar function – for instance, at the court of Burgundy, painters, from the brothers van Eyck to Rogier van der Weyden, were engaged to paint visual images of the illustrious past of their rulers.

This kind of propaganda by itself would have amounted to little if ideological ideals had not existed at the same time upon which to found the national state. To reawaken Italians to their imperial past, Cola di Rienzo invoked the imperial traditions of ancient Rome; the Italians were the true heirs of the empire and not the barbarian usurpers from Germany or France. His attempts were in vain, at least for some centuries, until they were resurrected by Mazzini, as were similar attempts in Germany, centering around King Henry I as the first German national king who, for the sake of the nation, had declined the alien Imperial Roman crown.

The watershed of this development was the sixteenth century, when Emperor Charles V fought the last rearguard action, on behalf of the universalism of the Holy Roman Empire, against the representative of the new age of national monarchy, epitomized by François I of France. Faced with great internal problems in many corners of his dominions, he gave up the struggle during his lifetime, handing over his imperial crown to Ferdinand and his Spanish possessions to his son, Philip II of Spain. Philip's ambitions were limited to being king of a Spanish national state, although there were universalist elements in his combat of the Reformation and an expansive overseas imperialism. He intervened on behalf of the Roman Catholic Church, not in the role of a universalist monarch but as King of Spain. His internal policies prepared the ground for absolutist

Left. *The Swiss Protestant Ulrich Zwingli, killed in battle in 1531 (German woodcut, 1539).*

Below. *This sixteenth-century German woodcut by Lucas Cranach shows the reformers Martin Luther and John Huss giving the sacrament, watched by their supporters among the German princes.*

rule in Spain. The separation of England from the Roman Catholic Church in the 1530s was not primarily motivated by religious causes. Papal refusal to sanction the King's attempts to gain a new wife and, he hoped, a male heir threatened the unity of the realm. Henry VIII therefore transformed the church into the Church of England. Thomas Cromwell dissolved the monasteries and requisitioned their landed property for the Crown. Due to the shortage of cash, these lands subsequently came into the hands of the nobility and gentry.

In Germany, the Reformation weakened forever the little central authority left to the Emperor, which was further diminished while the territorial princes gained strength. The continuing decline of the Holy Roman Emperor's power over the German states was confirmed constitutionally by the Peace of Westphalia in 1648. The Habsburgs withdrew to develop their crown lands.

That this was particularly disastrous for Germany is demonstrated when we look back at the Renaissance and the transformation it brought north of the Alps. One could postulate that its purpose was the rejuvenation and recovery of an allegedly golden past, a reformation of stagnant and corrupt

institutions. The guiding principle was not antiquity but the original church of the empire of the Saxons and Hohenstaufens. On the way, however, the humanists rediscovered antiquity; the German humanists in particular discovered Publius Tacitus and his work *Germania*. One must not forget that the Germans, faced by the cultural achievement of Greece and ancient Rome, felt an immense sense of inferiority *vis-à-vis* the Italians. Tacitus provided them with an instrument of compensation. The Germans, as Tacitus described them, were certainly not the equals of the Romans in culture or civilization. What Tacitus emphasized, however, were their unspoiled virtues and customs, devoid of the degeneration which his contemporary Rome displayed to him.

The significance of Tacitus to the German peoples can never be overestimated. By 1533 the complete works of Tacitus had been published in a German translation, and the picture he drew of the Germans became an indestructible part of their national consciousness, which has lasted to this day. Bravery, faithfulness and moral purity were the elements around which German national spirit crystallized. He analyzed in immense detail the structure of their tribes, their family life and kinship associations, their habits and customs, their religion, their economy, their constitutions and their military organization.

The picture of the world was changing. Medieval chroniclers had been preoccupied with genealogy and legal concerns; they sought to establish proof in the legal sense as well as provide a moral lesson. Now that was no longer sufficient. The humanist looked for something different. The individualities of the peoples and the characteristics of the nations of Europe became subjects of great interest. What divided them from one another was not only the personality of the ruler or the dynasty, but their different characteristics, their ways of life and their achievements.

Previously, there had been many attempts to establish German descent from the Trojans and the founders of Rome. Sigismund Meisterlin, one of the first to reject such false ancestors, went on to explain that the same characteristics which

Tacitus had attributed to his Germans were those which his contemporary Germans still displayed. The achievements and weaknesses of the Germanic tribes now became specifically German traits. The concept of a nation did not simply embrace contemporaries speaking the same language and sharing the same culture – the concept now established the connection of a direct character with the nation's ancestors.

Now it was a matter of some importance whether Charlemagne was a German or a Frenchman. His greatness and his achievement enriched the greatness and the achievement of the nation. That one was the son of a nation of which Charlemagne had also been a member was bound to increase self-esteem and personal honor. None were more passionate and vociferous in asserting Charlemagne's German origin than a group of historians in the Alsace. Medieval Europe had had as its examples the martyrs and saints of the Church. The humanists of the Renaissance replaced the saints with national heroes. Whereas before one had followed the example of the saints and prayed for their help, now a veritable gallery of heroes aided every German, Frenchman, Englishman and Slav to participate in the glories and virtues of his own respective past. It was a point of honor to belong to such a nation, much as formerly it had been an honor to belong to Christendom.

The concept of the nation developed by the humanists of the Renaissance exercised a double function in the development of nationalism in Europe. It gave the nation a secular unifying force, previously possessed only by medieval Christianity. Also the relationship between state and nation was fundamentally altered. A nation conscious of its language, culture and historical development was now in a position to determine its shape and future. It was a long time, however, before this theory was realized.

The territorial prince still reigned supreme and the principle of *cuius regio eius religio*, the Counter Reformation and its aftermath, sealed the divisions of central Europe for centuries. It would be a cardinal error, however, to attribute the rise of absolutism to the Renaissance, or to say that it was even one of

Left. *Henry of Navarre, wearing a white plume, leads the successful charge against the forces of the Catholic League at Ivry, 14 March 1590 (English colored engraving, nineteenth-century).*

Above. *Bombardment of a castle during the German Peasant's Rising of 1524–6 (German historical chronicle, 1619).*

Right. *The Emperor Charles V.*

Below. *The Catholic leader François de Guise defeats the Huguenots at Dreux, 1562.*

its consequences. It was the product of a combination of factors such as the disintegration of the political, social and economic structure of medieval Europe. Leaving behind territorial states, their rulers inevitably had to centralize their administration, their economy, and their military organization to establish it as a viable unit *vis-à-vis* its neighbors. Ultimately, absolutism emerged from that process.

Absolutism is a form of monarchy. Aristotle differentiated between three types of kingship of the military type: a kind of military dictatorship; the inheritable kingship of the barbarians; and legally elected dictatorship. Tyranny, in Aristotle's view, must never be confused with dictatorship since it is founded on force. Aristotle's concept of absolute rule includes the maintenance of law – the authority of the law being above that of the ruler.

Absolutism is not necessarily a personal regime as practiced by Louis XIV after the death of Cardinal Mazarin, or by Philip II of Spain, or as attempted by James I and Charles I in England. Nor does absolutism necessarily presuppose the centralization of governmental power. Such centralization is no doubt of assistance but one also finds it in states with an essentially federal structure, or in a league of states with a monarchic constitution like Spain, Austria and Prussia until the end of the *ancien régime*. In France absolutism and centralization supplemented one another. Emperor Ferdinand II made a serious attempt at establishing an absolutist regime in Germany, and was near success as long as he followed the advice and policies of Wallenstein, for some time his principal adviser and military commander. But with the latter's assassination these efforts were halted, and the Holy Roman Empire disintegrated into individual states.

It was in France that absolutism achieved its most complete and successful expression. It was a result of, or rather a reaction

to, the political and religious divisions which had driven France to the brink of national disaster during the first half of the seventeenth century. External factors such as the pressure of the Habsburgs from Germany and Spain also played a part. A central authority had therefore to be established which secured internal as well as external stability.

The result was the creation of something resembling a modern state with a highly centralized and strictly regimented administration, an active legislation and an army ready to strike at any point, at any time.

Although France serves as a good example, absolutism as a form of government cannot be dated from 1648 onward and end with the French Revolution. Trends toward absolutism are discernible in France from the days of François I (reigned 1515–47). In other countries it had also made considerable strides before the monarchy finally broke with the estates of medieval origin, eliminated their privileges and united all power within their own hands.

The system of absolute monarchic government rested on legal foundations elaborated first by Jean Bodin (1530–96) and the English philosopher Thomas Hobbes (1588–1679). They propagated the view that the rule exercised by the monarch had to be an independent unitary force and not subject to human laws. It was the will of the ruler, admittedly human, which constituted supreme law. That alone would make it possible to constrain the egotism of the individual, and to secure a just and ordered society for any length of time.

From those basic ideas grew the concept of sovereignty. It followed that a ruler could be a true sovereign power only if there was no secular control above him. Since sovereignty was indivisible, it could reside only with the monarch, who determined the law. The sovereign power was the state.

Another concept which was widely accepted at the time was the *raison d'état*, the maxim of all political action. It is the decisive criterion determining the action of the monarch. These theories and maxims must be considered against the background of bloody civil war in France and the experience of the Thirty Years' War (1618–48) in Germany. However, the ruler, while standing above the law, did not have powers above all human rights. He was supposed to respect ethical obligations, such as the natural rights of his subjects, and was expected to protect their property. Yet, he was subject to no secular controls; his power was derived from God, to whom he was ultimately accountable. Therefore the absolute monarch was theoretically constrained by his consciousness that his throne really belonged to the Lord.

However, the Renaissance had also brought a turning away from the Christian world of the Middle Ages. Advances in the natural sciences, exemplified by the achievements of Nicolas Copernicus, Galileo, Johann Kepler, Isaac Newton and Gottfried Leibniz, gave rise to a growing faith in man's ultimate ability to control nature. The great philosophers of the period endeavored to explore the possible meaning of life, with the intention of thereby advancing man's evolution. Science, so it was believed, would help to conquer the world for the benefit of mankind and its future. However, every new discovery was a product of man's power of reason; the age of rationalism was ushered in. Rationalism turned reason into the measure of all human thought and behavior. Reason was defined as the ability to understand all phenomena of life. Once that understanding existed, the whole world, not to say the universe, could be analyzed and subjected to theoretical tests in order to put it under man's systematic control.

These new discoveries of man were used by absolutist powers

Above. *The German artist Urs Graf depicts* Landsknechte *of the early sixteenth century in their characteristic slashed costume.*

Below left. *The Duke of Anjou besieges a town in the Netherlands during the long struggle for Dutch independence from Spain.*

Right. *A sixteenth-century engraving shows the Imperial army's baggage train on the march.*

in the service of the state. Successively all spheres of administration, economy and military organization were rationalized. But that was only one side of the coin; the other was the expectation that, by the power of reason, man should also be able to create a more just and equitable society. If man was the measure of all things, then he was no longer dependent on outdated spiritual and religious principles, on religious dogma, tradition and authority; in particular it was against all reason that the individual should be subject to the authority of the princely state, unfree and unequal. Therefore it was mankind's responsibility to create a new political culture based on natural human rights. Thus philosophers such as the Baron de Montesquieu and John Locke preached their gospel of the division of power, of popular sovereignty and the idea of civil liberties. Reformation had emancipated man from the established Church; the individual not only possessed liberty of conscience, it was also his duty to interpret the will of God for himself. Once the Church and its teachings had been relegated to an inferior position it was virtually inevitable that questions concerning the purpose and function of the monarchy should also be raised.

At an intellectual level there is a direct thread of continuity between the Reformation and the French Revolution, and one of the main areas in which speculative thought evolved and prospered, in spite of all repression, was France. The inner logic of the thesis of human progress directed itself against the absolutist regime. The ideas of the Enlightenment first tentatively tested the foundations of the throne, from within and without, and then they gradually eroded its position until it collapsed. However, since the standing army was perhaps the most powerful manifestation of absolutist government, political opposition was specifically directed against it, and toward devising a military system that would be a viable alternative.

The search for an alternative military system had already begun before the age of Absolutism. Spain was the first state in Europe which, as early as the sixteenth century, had a powerful standing army. Gold and other precious metals from the New World helped to finance it at first, but the costly war at sea against England, the seemingly endless struggle against the rebellious Netherlands, and in general Spain's political policies, exhausted its resources. The standing army could no longer be paid and, as it largely consisted of mercenaries, the result was frequent mutinies culminating in the sacking of Antwerp in 1576. Spain provides only the most prominent example of what could happen to an army not regularly paid; it was a feature which, in one form or another, affected the armies of all the European powers. To put an end to it one had to think of an alternative, which curiously enough developed not among one of the great powers but in the relatively small Netherlands, whose people fought against Spanish oppression. The rising was led by William I of Orange of the House of the Counts of Nassau-Dillenburg. The seven northern provinces of the Netherlands had elected him as their governor, and he reformed the military system from its very roots.

During the first half of the seventeenth century it was generally religion or the interests of some religious body that molded both warfare and the political thought of the period. Only in the wake of the devastation of the Thirty Years' War did international law and politics become sciences, developed in the works of such thinkers as Hugo Grotius (utilizing the less systematic works of Giovanni Gentile) and Hobbes (who relied heavily on Machiavelli, Bodin and Filmer). This process of secularization of political thought was paralleled by equally fundamental changes in the ultimate instrument of politics – the conduct of war. The battles fought by Gustavus Adolphus of

RUIT HORA.

HUGO GROTIUS, IC
Pencionaris van Rotterdam

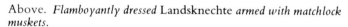

Above. *Flamboyantly dressed* Landsknechte *armed with matchlock muskets.*

Above right. *The Dutchman Hugo Grotius, 1583–1645, often considered the father of modern international law.*

Sweden were to be of profound importance to the development of land warfare; however, his skill was drawn from a tradition of innovation which goes back to the sixteenth century. Military technology, for example, had not lacked inventions from such as Leonardo da Vinci, who produced early prototypes of modern submarines, aircraft and tanks. From a more immediate and practical perspective, the main tactical problem before the introduction of the cannon was not so much how to defeat the enemy in the open field in open battle, but how to conquer his fortifications, his castle. This problem was not mastered until the late fifteenth century. Throughout the sixteenth century, artillery, followed by the musket, began to play an increasing and decisive role. Foot soldiers known as the *infanteria* (derived from the youngsters who used to accompany the army on foot), the infantry, consisting of pikemen and musketeers, began to occupy a prominent place in warfare. The combined impact of pikes and muskets reduced the effect of the cumbersome cavalry charge by heavily armed knights. Slowly, in the course of adapting themselves to a new 'technological environment,' horsemen began to rely on wheel-lock pistols and carbines, while the heavy sword was discarded in favor of the saber. Cavalrymen, still heavily armored during the early sixteenth century, attacked while discharging their firearms, until the enemy's foot troops were thought to be sufficiently worn down to make them vulnerable to a direct attack with lance or saber.

The Spanish army was the first in the history of modern Europe to develop anything resembling modern infantry tactics. The infantry was usually massed in the center of the order of battle, with the field artillery before them and the cavalry protecting the rear and the wings. Battles were fought in a parallel order, but in view of the essentially static character of the battle order, plus the presence of excessive baggage trains, it was rarely possible to follow up a victory on the battlefield by swift pursuit of the enemy. Nevertheless, in spite of their unwieldy nature, Spanish tactics were superior to the less well-trained armies which, even during the first part of the sixteenth century, consisted of mercenary and *Landsknecht* (foot soldiers armed with pikes and lances) led by professional soldiers who would keep a small selected staff of artillery, engineering and infantry experts around them in peacetime. In time of war they hired themselves out to the highest bidder and recruited their units, primarily from Germany, Switzerland and northern Italy. The individual mercenary would swear a personal oath to his leader which automatically terminated in the case of capture and was often terminated before. Since winter was a season considered ill-suited for the conduct of a campaign, mercenary forces were disbanded, to be recruited again in the following spring. Frequently these forces were little more than an armed rabble from whose ranks few men of distinction in military history emerged. The introduction of firearms, artillery, the musket and the pistol were viewed at first rather in the same light as the submarine was in World War I. However, as the cost of firearms in general was beyond the resources of the mercenary captains, overall control of the armed forces by the monarchy was indicated, as it was the one power able to raise the funds necessary for modern equipment. Hence, it can be argued that the introduction of firearms and their growing importance brought about a further concentration of power in secular hands. It raised monarchic power above that of the Church and helped transform war from a moral trial into a political instrument.

The Spanish military system, partly because of commitments in its scattered empire, especially in the Netherlands, produced the first standing army. This was seen to be plainly superior to hired bands of mercenaries and was copied by most of the European powers. However, the Spanish system was challenged

Left. *French soldiers of the sixteenth century.*

Below left. *Russian, Hungarian and Polish soldiers of the sixteenth century.*

Below. *An Italian halberd, circa 1530.*

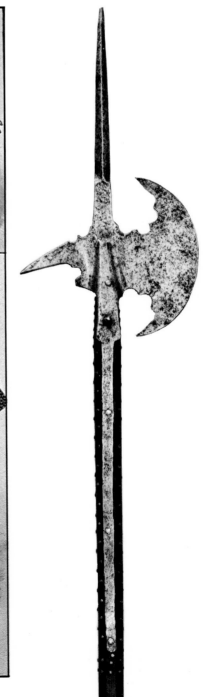

Left. *Maurice of Nassau, Prince of Orange, 1567–1625, a skillful Dutch commander who played a leading part in his country's struggle for independence from Spain.*

Below left. *Black and white half armor, made in Nuremberg circa 1648. Its quality suggests that it would have been worn by an officer.*

Below. *A ceremonial halberd carried by the Elector of Saxony's bodyguard circa 1580–1620.*

Below right. *The elaborate mother-of-pearl inlay on this sixteenth-century German crossbow suggests that it was designed for the chase rather than as a weapon of war.*

Far right. *A company of Amsterdam militia of the 1640s. The company's color is carried by its ensign, and the lavishly dressed individual on his left is probably the company commander (Dutch school, in imitation of seventeenth-century style).*

by the Dutch under Prince Maurice of Orange. His main innovation was the reforming of the rabble which so far had constituted his infantry. Realizing that the fundamental weakness of the Spanish Army lay in its relative immobility, he placed a premium on the development of mobility. Maurice of Orange would hardly have claimed to be an innovator, however; he based his system on the example provided by the Roman infantry as described by such writers of antiquity as Livy.

Superficially the novelty was uniform drill; fundamentally it was discipline. Proceeding from the premise that, in case of emergency, the United Provinces would have to mobilize its forces at very short notice, it was necessary to transform the civilians into a militarily efficient body, capable of organized and disciplined action in response to systematic official command. Infantry drill achieved just that. True, a certain amount of drill was necessary for the Spanish infantry squares, but Maurice brought mobility into his infantry by specific command to produce uniform movements. Units were subdivided into platoons and, at a mere signal given either by drums or bugle, they could dissolve and re-form, every man knowing his place in the unit. The Dutch were renowned for being able to assemble 2000 men in an hour and a quarter, whereas previously it had taken a good hour to assemble half that number.

The important point is that, besides order, Maurice's innovation rendered an extraordinary degree of mobility to each infantry unit. Even during the excitement of battle the commander had his men under firm control, always in a position to direct them wherever reinforcements were needed, or to take the initiative and attack if necessary at several different points simultaneously.

Prince Maurice and his cousin Prince William Louis of the Netherlands went so far as to build up vast formations of lead soldiers on table tops to practice what they intended to apply in the field. Their army was subjected to severe drill and field exercises which would have incited any unit of mercenaries to rebellion! The Dutch soldiers accepted this discipline, if for no other reason than that they were generously and punctually paid, which was not the case in the Spanish army. Maurice also established regular ranks within each company (about 130 strong) from captain to lieutenant downward. They were officers in the modern sense of the term rather than mercenary captains.

Well-paid, well-officered troops under Dutch command could also be ordered to build their own earthworks, a type of work which mercenaries during the Thirty Years' War had always considered below their dignity. Internal discipline was strictly enforced; Maurice had two men hanged because one had stolen a hat, the other a dagger. One man was shot for robbing a woman.

Maurice's military reforms were supported by a general wave of intellectual reform that swept through the Netherlands, expressing itself not only militarily and economically (after all, for a short time the Netherlands was a seafaring world power) but also in the sciences and arts. Holland experienced the effects of the last currents of the humanist movement. Special attention

was paid to the history of the Roman Empire and to Stoic philosophy, an ideal intellectual base for army reform. The intellectual center of this development was the University of Leyden, founded by Maurice's father; its most renowned teacher was the philologist Justus Lipsius (1547–1606), whose writings embraced Stoic philosophy, politics, military affairs and political ethics. Lipsius advocated a monarchic state in which the monarch was subject to the law and existing norms of morality, which was administered by an efficient civil service and inhabited by a law-abiding people. The military force to protect the country was to consist only of native Netherlanders. Discipline was not something to be imposed upon the soldier – it was important to educate the soldier in self-discipline. As every soldier was also a citizen of the state, his personal dignity should not be insulted while serving in the army. There was to be equality of opportunity for advancement for all soldiers. Lipsius emphasized the basic virtues stipulated by the Stoic philosopher Seneca: the will to fulfill one's duty, the will to work, the readiness to accept responsibility and asceticism. The soldier should show bravery even in seemingly hopeless situations, and should be prepared to defend his post even at the cost of his own life. The soldier's qualities should include patience and sobriety, and no act of common force should besmirch his professional honor.

This of course also implied an increased degree of responsibility for the officer, not only because of the greater demands made upon him as a leader of men, but also because of the duties which he had to fulfill toward every individual of his unit. Of

Below. *Top: South German wheel-lock pistol dated 1593. Bottom: wheel-lock pistol dated 1579. Both are high-quality weapons, inlaid with staghorn.*

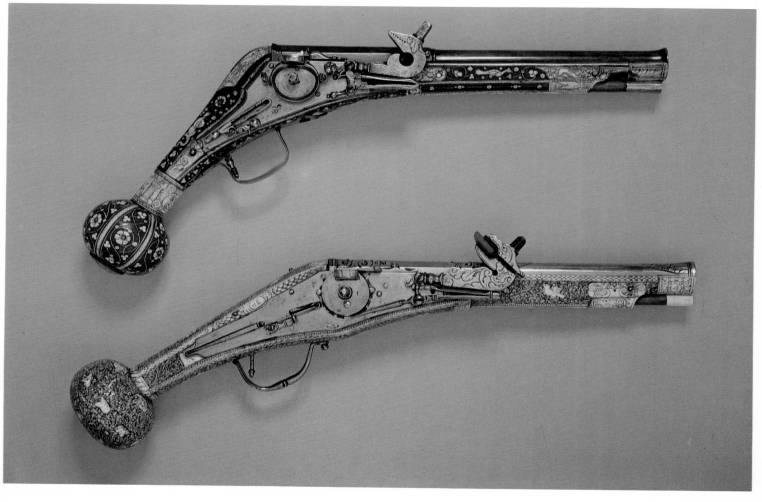

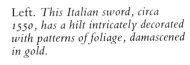

Left. *This Italian sword, circa 1550, has a hilt intricately decorated with patterns of foliage, damascened in gold.*

Far left. *Swiss half-armor circa 1600. This type of helmet, known as lobster tailed from the laminated plates covering the neck, remained popular among cavalrymen for the first half of the seventeenth century.*

Right. *A Landsknecht officer's dagger with its embossed scabbard of blackened steel (German, circa 1550).*

Far right. *A plainer Landsknecht dagger circa 1550–60.*

Below. *German officers and soldiers of the sixteenth century. Note the various types of* Landsknechte *in the lower plate.*

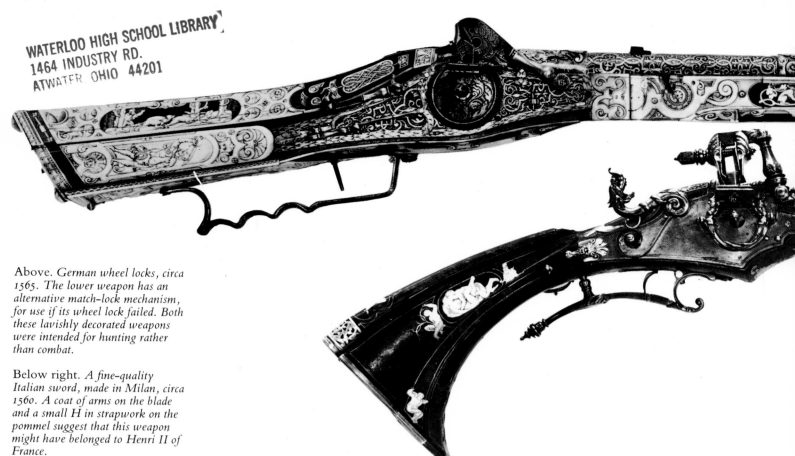

Above. *German wheel locks, circa 1565. The lower weapon has an alternative match-lock mechanism, for use if its wheel lock failed. Both these lavishly decorated weapons were intended for hunting rather than combat.*

Below right. *A fine-quality Italian sword, made in Milan, circa 1560. A coat of arms on the blade and a small H in strapwork on the pommel suggest that this weapon might have belonged to Henri II of France.*

course Lipsius' ideas could be only partially put into practice. A selective, high quality army of Dutchmen could not be fully recruited because the Estates-General and the merchants deemed it unwise, for financial reasons, to abandon completely the principle of voluntary recruitment. Nevertheless, Lipsius' ideas are reflected in the Dutch Articles of War of 1592 and, in spite of many obstacles, the Princes of Orange managed to create a highly efficient army with which they were able to defeat the Spaniards. They realized that numerical superiority could be matched by better troops, increased tactical mobility and the full exploitation of firepower.

The Dutch army attracted attention throughout Europe. Many officers of the European powers made extensive visits to study their military exercises, their drill and, above all, their discipline. In Sweden King Charles IX tried to emulate the ideas which Lipsius had preached and established a basis upon which his successor, Gustavus Adolphus, could build. Frederick William, the Great Elector of Prussia, received the main part of his education in the Netherlands, and through him Stoic philosophy, adapted for use in the administration and the building up of the army, entered Prussia to become one of the main constituents of Prussian administrative and military life until the death of Frederick the Great.

Of course, as with all reforms, Maurice's changes could not be carried out in their entirety; the habits of mercenary times, centuries old, could not be eliminated in a short span of time. The main difficulty was no longer financial, that is to say paying the soldiers punctually, but was the problem of raising the army and finding replacements. The new infantry tactics required large bodies of men and so the period of absolutism saw a gradual increase in the size of armies. By the seventeenth century the size of the French army had already reached 100,000; it continued to grow. The other great powers followed its example.

The Dutch were in a financial position which allowed them

to recruit forces from outside, but, from the point of view of quality, the recruits did not measure up to what was thought to be absolutely necessary. Also, once the immediate danger from Spain was lessened, the Dutch showed little inclination to become professional soldiers. Lipsius' proposition of opening the army and the officer corps to all men of ability failed to come about in the face of opposition from the nobility. An able adventurer therefore preferred to join the mercenaries where opportunities for personal advancement were unlimited. To respect the personal dignity of a soldier was all very well, but it made little sense when one was dealing with the dregs of society. Corporal punishment was therefore as much a feature of the Dutch army as of any other of the period, with the exception of the French, where it was introduced only shortly before the outbreak of the Revolution in the 1780s.

In other words, despite the current of reform which ran so fervently through the Dutch army, in time recourse had to be taken to more draconian measures to maintain military discipline. This applied to all standing armies which emerged during the course of the seventeenth century in Europe, and it was precisely this sort of discipline which made the military profession a rather unattractive proposition to the members of the emerging middle classes. The army was despised by those who were educated, while the decent, honorable soldier was bound to have the feeling similar to those of a prisoner.

The Enlightenment also attacked the standing army from its very inception. The wars of conquest so typical of the Age of Absolutism aroused a pacifist reaction and, consequently, the standing army was one of the major areas of attack. Philosophers and writers were in agreement that soldiers meant war and that only their removal would establish eternal peace in the world. The extremists among them branded kings and princes as the butchers of their peoples, and soldiers as useless hirelings of the state. Later, the Swiss philosopher Jean Jacques Rousseau went further and called for a militia: 'Every citizen should be a

soldier out of his sense of duty, but not as a professional vocation. Every citizen should be a soldier but only when he has to be.'

Generally it can be said that the standing army of the Age of Absolutism enjoyed a better relationship with the rural community than with the citizens of urban centers. The absolutist regimes, however, endeavored to make their standing armies represent a different social body from the rest of the population, with its own law and order; this was achieved by the introduction of the military's own judiciary, policing powers and administration.

However, we would be gaining a false perspective if we were to view the armies of that age by the shadows they cast, or to think that every soldier was no more than a maltreated recalcitrant creature. Of course, the dregs of society were well enough represented, but they made up a large proportion only in certain regiments. The problem was that an army dedicated to a high degree of discipline, requiring immediate obedience to every command on the battlefield, was dependent on human 'raw material,' a large percentage of which was of inferior caliber. One therefore had to be prepared for large-scale desertions. On the whole, however, the largest portion of recruits, and in most cases also the most valuable, came from the countryside, preferring life in the army to the work of a farm laborer; in the army one found security and one could also expect assistance in establishing a reasonably secure civilian existence if mustered out on the grounds of injury or old age.

We should not underestimate the influence of the Dutch military reform movement upon standing armies elsewhere. In some armies, such as the Prussian, religious beliefs were very strong among the officers, who imbued their men not only with bravery but also with a certain respect for the Lord and piety. If the polemics of the Enlightenment movement directed against the military had been a true reflection of the conditions in the armies at this time, one can only wonder what the source was of the courage, bravery, self-sacrifice and sheer military ability which were displayed on the battlefields of Europe and North America in the eighteenth century.

Those were the wars of the standing armies of the *ancien régime*. To understand their emergence we must turn back to the Thirty Years' War in 1618. This war was begun with tactics and strategy which still owed much to the medieval period, but which as it wore on, ushered in a new age of warfare which was to prevail in Europe until the French Revolution in 1789.

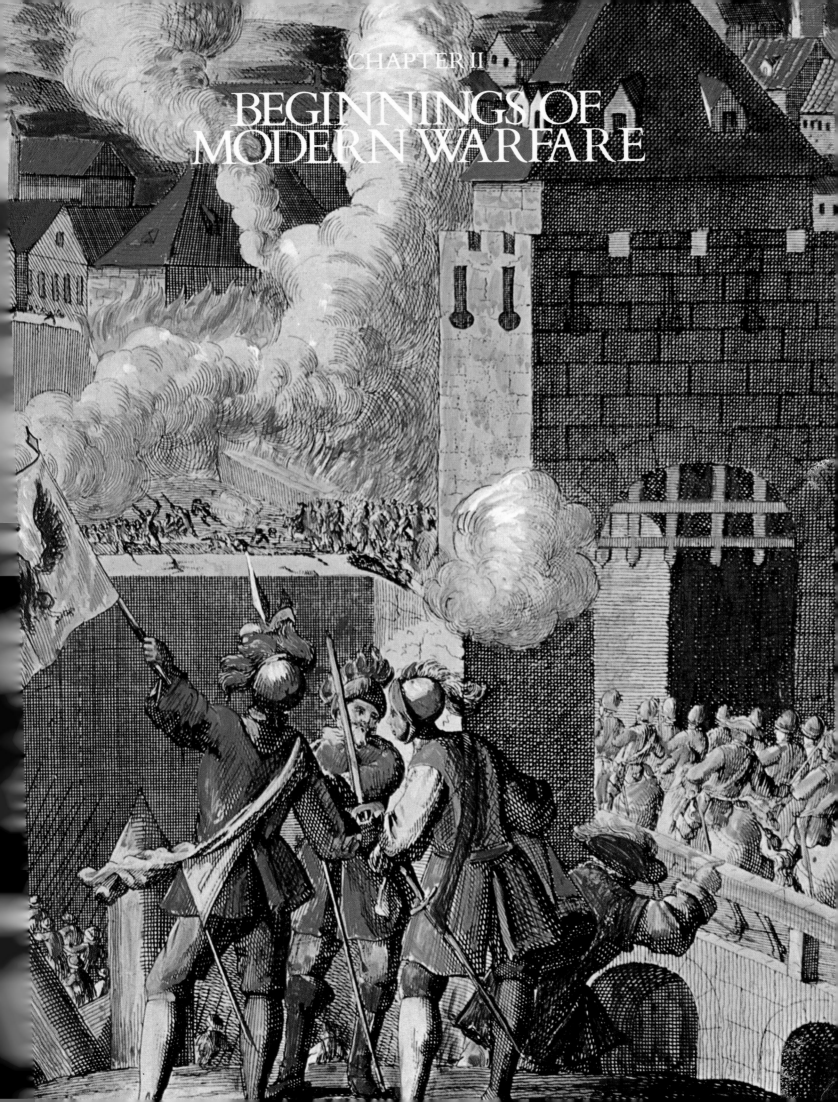

CHAPTER II

BEGINNINGS OF MODERN WARFARE

During the sixteenth century the Reformation swept across central Europe like a tidal wave. Almost the whole of Germany, including the Austrian crownlands, became Protestant or members of the rapidly developing Protestant sectarianism. It rent the German body politic asunder, the German princes deciding their religious affiliation not so much by religious criteria but political ones – namely what advantages would be gained by joining one side or the other. In vain Emperor Charles V tried to mediate, but all he managed to achieve was a compromise in the Peace of Augsburg of 1555, which established the principle of *cuius regio eius religio*: whoever ruled the state determined the religion of his subjects.

The defenestration of the imperial officials from the *Hradshin* in Prague in 1618 was not the cause of the Thirty Years' War, only the trigger. In fact, although the three officials had been thrown from a height of over 50 feet by an enraged Protestant nobility, all three of them escaped injury. The Bohemians renounced the Habsburg overlordship and in its place chose Elector Frederick of the Palatinate, a son-in-law of James I of England, as their rightful king. The issue was sealed with the defeat of the Protestants at the Battle of the White Mountain on 8 November 1620. On 20 March of the same year Archduke Ferdinand had succeeded to the throne as King and Emperor of the Holy Roman Empire of the German peoples. Ferdinand II's aim was two-fold, though first and foremost, as he was a product of Jesuit education, came the restitution of Roman Catholicism throughout the Empire as the one and only faith, and with it of course the restitution of all the lands of which the secular powers had deprived the Church for the past century. He had already carried out a Counter Reformation in his own territories. Secondly, hand in hand with achieving the victory

Previous spread. *Imperial troops sack the Protestant city of Magdeburg on 20 May 1631. Some 25,000 of the city's inhabitants perished.*

Above. *The execution of 45 Bohemian noblemen in Prague, 1621. Such scenes followed Catholic victory at the Battle of the White Mountain in 1620.*

Below. *The Defenestration of Prague, 23 May 1618. Rebel nobles hurl the Emperor's advisers through the windows of Hradcany Castle.*

Below right. *Maximilian of Bavaria, 1573–1651.*

of the Counter Reformation, following others of his time, he endeavored to concentrate power in his own hands. His opponents in this respect, however, were not simply the estates, but above all the princes of the Reich, or Empire, who, Catholic or Protestant, had managed to enrich themselves considerably in the wake of the Reformation, in terms of territory as well as effective power, with which they were loath to part. Although single-minded on the issue of the dominance of Roman Catholicism, Ferdinand II was less so in the pursuit of his second aim until the right kind of adviser stood by his side.

The defeat of the Protestants in 1620 brought the Danes and King Christian IV into play on the Protestant side. As Duke of Holstein, the King was also a prince of the Empire. In the war against the Danes and the German Protestant princes there emerged a nobleman from Bohemia, Albrecht von Wallenstein, Duke of Friedland and of Mecklenburg, a man who among the established nobility in Germany was a mere upstart. Yet he was the man who, from the first, realized the endemic weakness of the Holy Roman Empire, namely the excessive play given to the centrifugal forces inherent within it. A modern state needed centralization, and such centralization could be achieved only at the expense of the established privileges of the German princes. To bring them to heel the Habsburg dynasty required an army of superior striking power, an army permanently in being. But from where should the Emperor take such an army? The princes of the Reich, even the Catholic Maximilian I, Elector of Bavaria, were averse to the accumulation of any further power in the hands of the Emperor. And then came Wallenstein, who upset their calculations.

Wallenstein, having sound economic sense, maximized the output of his estates to such an extent as to enable him to raise,

on the Emperor's behalf, an army which was quite independent of those meager forces which the Imperial Diet of the princes at Regensburg was willing to grant. It was largely with that army that Wallenstein expelled the Danes from German territory and vanquished their German allies, concluding, in 1629 with King Christian, a peace of such moderation as to keep him out of the war until long after Wallenstein's assassination. He also frightened off the French who, under Richelieu, intervened on behalf of the Protestants. True, Wallenstein did not make Ferdinand II a present of his army; ultimately the Emperor was to pay him back. Even Wallenstein's resources were limited, however, and he introduced a war levy throughout the Austrian crownlands and the territories of the German princes of the Catholic League. The princes complained of extortion and that their lands were being bled dry, complaints which were entirely unjustified. Wallenstein, in fact, took only as much as he needed, leaving behind ample funds to maintain agricultural production – thus being able to collect the same contribution year after year. The inherent consequence of these contributions was that it made Ferdinand II increasingly independent of his liege lords. The war seemed almost at an end when, on 6 March 1629, Ferdinand II proclaimed the Edict of Restitution, according to which all previously secularized Church lands throughout the Empire would have to be returned to the Church. It was the most unfortunate document of the Thirty Years' War, for once again it consolidated the Protestant princes and also brought into play two external forces: Gustavus Adolphus in the north, from Sweden, and Cardinal Richelieu in the west, from France. To Richelieu the religious issue in central Europe was irrelevant, but the growing consolidation of Habsburg power in the Reich was a danger. Gustavus Adolphus elevated himself to the defender of Protestantism in Germany, aided financially and militarily by Roman Catholic France. Before that happened, however, the Catholic princes scored one success against Ferdinand. Since, to all intents and purposes, the war had ended, they pressed him successfully to dismiss Wallenstein, which he did on 13 August 1630.

Less than a month before Wallenstein's dismissal, Gustavus Adolphus had already landed in Peenemünde at the head of 13,000 men on 6 July 1630. His aim was to bring the entire Baltic provinces under Swedish control – an aim all the more important since Wallenstein had previously succeeded in bringing almost all German Baltic and North Sea harbors under Imperial control with the aim of fortifying them and then, with the aid of the Hanseatic League, to cut off the Swedes in the Baltic and deprive the Dutch of their lucrative trade there, and transfer this trade into Imperial hands.

If Gustavus Adolphus did nothing to stop this development, the German Empire would soon be in a position to build its own ships in its own shipyards and the Emperor would no longer be dependent on the good will of the Hanseatic League, Poland and Spain. However, without allies Sweden was not in a position to move against such a formidable enemy as the Habsburgs. Gustavus Adolphus' closest adviser, his chancellor Axel Oxenstierna, cautioned him against any kind of invasion, but in Sweden there was still Richelieu's special envoy Charnacé promising French subsidies, agreeing even to the exorbitant sums which Gustavus demanded. He also insisted that France and Sweden enter the war simultaneously. This Richelieu refused since he hoped that he could still draw the princes of the Catholic League, especially Maximilian of Bavaria, onto the French side. Gustavus Adolphus then turned to Denmark but King Christian roundly refused. It was at this point that Ferdinand's Edict of Restitution was proclaimed. Now Gustavus Adolphus had his pretext as the savior of the Reformation

in Germany and found as his first allies many of the German princes of the Protestant Union.

The Swedish army's arrival, military aspects apart, had disastrous effects upon Germany. For 18 years they marched through Pomerania, Mecklenburg, Saxony, Brandenburg, Thuringia, Franconia and Bavaria. They were in Munich, along the Rhine, on the Elbe, in Bohemia and Moravia, virtually before the gates of Vienna. The fame of their leaders, from Gustavus Adolphus to Gustav Horn, John Banér, Lennart Torstensson, Wrangel and Hans Christopher von Königsmarck, was as legendary as was the brutality and cruelty of the army, and for decades after the cry 'The Swedes are coming' was enough to silence unruly children. Hans Jakob von Grimmelhausen in his *Simplicius Simplicissimus*, published 1668, provides a very graphic picture of their actions. Gustavus Adolphus introduced the principle in this war that any country occupied by the Swedes had to be relentlessly plundered in order to deprive the enemy of any sources of supplies. He and his successors made little distinction as to whether the country occupied was Protestant or Catholic.

During the last decade of the war the population of central Europe could escape death chiefly in two ways. One was to take up residence within the walls of a heavily defended city because the Swedes were not prepared to engage in protracted sieges, the other was to disperse into the forests and moorlands and live from whatever they could find there. As the chronicler reports: 'In many parts no horse, no goat, no cat and dog has been left.' Mice, rats, cats and dogs acquired the reputation of delicacies, and instances of cannibalism were apparently common. For that reason, within the cities, guards were posted at cemeteries and at the gallows. The Swedes' conduct deteriorated particularly after the death of Gustavus Adolphus. Marshal Banér readily admitted that there was no way of stopping his troops from their excesses.

In 1630 Gustavus Adolphus was in no particular hurry. By the time of Wallenstein's dismissal he had raised his army to 40,000 men and, on 23 January 1631, an agreement with France was concluded which gave Gustavus a French subsidy of 500,000 livres and for every following year double the amount. He had to respect the neutrality of the princes of the Catholic League, which the Swedish king was ready to do providing none of them offered any resistance. By the spring of 1631 his army was fully prepared.

Gustavus Adolphus was an ardent disciple of Prince Maurice of Orange. In many respects he completed his military reforms and used them as the foundation of his own strategy. Gustavus' experience of war began when he was 17, and he was determined to learn from experience. Accepting Maurice's maxim that mobility is based on thorough drill and discipline, and discipline upon a sound administration, he insisted on high levels of efficiency during his time as a military commander. Drunkenness and coarse language were severely punished, though in an army that was to increase to 70,000 during his time, successful enforcement of discipline, such as Cromwell was to impose upon the New Model Army, must have been difficult, if not impossible.

With the exception of Wallenstein, the areas in which he exceeded all his contemporaries 'were tactics, organization and arms.' The Scotsman Munro, who fought under Gustavus at Breitenfeld and Lützen, recorded: 'A regiment such as this acts like an organism, it has one body, one movement, all ears hear the same command, eyes turn simultaneously, hands move as though they were one hand. The highest tactical unit was the brigade, arranged in linear pattern six deep, alternating with musketeer and pike units. The musketeers, to cover themselves against a cavalry charge, moved behind the pikes and reloaded their muskets while the reserve pike units would fill gaps in the line left by them.' Apart from perfecting infantry as well as cavalry tactics, Gustavus Adolphus added his own unique contribution by putting to full use the inherent potential of the artillery. He was the first great field gunner, who, in order to increase the mobility of his forces, reduced the vast range of artillery types and calibers and designed lighter types of gun carriages, and standardized his artillery into three main types. First there were siege guns weighing 60, 30 and 15 hundredweight, second the field pieces of 24, 12 and 6 pounders, and third, regimental pieces, two to a regiment, which were light 4 pounders. Gunnery drill, especially for regimental gunners, was stepped up to a pace which enabled them to fire eight rounds to every musketeer's six shots. In contrast to the Spanish system, Gustavus reduced his trains to an absolute minimum which meant that his army had to live largely off the land, although this was also supplemented by the setting up of supply depots along the army's line of advance.

During the first few months after his arrival on German soil, while Gustavus was still in the process of assembling his forces,

the German Protestant princes were still reluctant to join him; only Hesse-Kassel and the dukes of Saxony-Weimar openly did so, but gradually, through a mixture of persuasion and outright pressure, he brought the rest over on to his side.

At first the Swedes occupied Pomerania and Mecklenburg, and in April 1631 Frankfurt-an-der-Oder was stormed. In the meantime the Imperial forces, under the command of Marshal Tilly, besieged the strongly fortified Protestant city of Magdeburg. Count Johann Tilly wanted to conquer the obstinate bishopric, which the Protestants described as 'our Lord's chancellery,' for the son of the Emperor. From December 1630 Magdeburg was under fire by the siege guns of the Imperial forces; the people of Magdeburg appealed to Gustavus Adolphus for help, but the Swedish king did not react. On 20 May 1631 Tilly's cavalry, under the command of General Gottfried Heinrich Graf zu Pappenheim, went into the attack and stormed the city by way of two breeches which the siege artillery had made. As the soldiers followed, fires started to break out in all parts of the city; who laid the fires has remained a matter of conjecture to this day. For three days and nights the city was

Above left. *The Swedish King Gustavus Adolphus landing at Rugen in 1630, at the start of his invasion of northern Germany.*

Below left. *The Emperor Ferdinand II, who reigned from 1619–37.*

Above. *King Gustavus Adolphus of Sweden, 1594–1632.*

Right. *Seventeenth-century German soldiers.*

Below. *Spanish cup-hilt rapier, made in Toledo, circa 1670.*

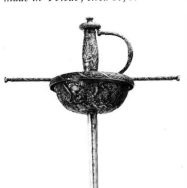

FRANCOFURTVM AD MOENVM

sacked and all that remained of what had been one of the most flourishing and richest German cities was the cathedral and some fishermen's huts along the River Elbe. Of 30,000 inhabitants, 25,000 were killed. Magdeburg was the Hiroshima of the Thirty Years' War.

Early in June of that year Gustavus Adolphus virtually forced his brother-in-law, the Elector of Brandenburg, into alliance with Sweden. Saxony followed his example.

On 17 September 1631 the first decisive battle was fought between the Imperial forces and those of Gustavus Adolphus. The Swedish-Saxon army amounted to about 39,000 men, the forces of the Catholic League, about 36,000. The Swedes were superior in cavalry by 2000 men, but, much more important, they enjoyed a great superiority in their artillery – 75 pieces against Tilly's 26. All that Tilly had to rely on was what he assumed to be the superior quality of his troops.

Tilly, coming from the direction of Leipzig, assembled his forces in 17 squares to the right of the village of Breitenfeld on top of a low ridge in front of which, at a distance of about a mile and a half, flows the rivulet Loderbach parallel with the ridge. It would be an obstacle during the attack, not a very great one, but an obstacle nevertheless. His flanks were exposed on both sides, which did not seem to matter very much considering the depth of the Spanish squares.

Gustavus Adolphus' forces approached on a wide front across the plain with the sun on their backs. At first Gustavus attempted an attack against Tilly's right wing, but had to abandon it because the crossing of the Loderbach resulted in unexpected difficulties. Gustavus' forces extended beyond Tilly's left wing and on this broad front they now crossed the Loderbach, an opportunity ideal for attack by Tilly, a man 'short in stature . . . meager and terrible in aspect; his cheeks were sunken, his nose long and pointed, his eyes fierce and dark.' Although, apart from Wallenstein, the most able Imperial general and a master of Spanish tactics, he allowed this opportunity to slip by. Fearing his exposed left wing could be outflanked and circumvented by the

Above. *The entry of Gustavus Adolphus into Frankfurt-am-Main, 1631 (contemporary engraving).*

Left. *Johan Baner, 1596–1641, the most capable of Gustavus Adolphus' generals. He commanded the right wing of Swedish horse at Breitenfeld, and distinguished himself at the passage of the Lech. The defeat of the Elector John George of Saxony at Wittstock in 1636 was his most brilliant success.*

Below right. *Gustavus Adolphus leads a cavalry charge at the Battle of Dirschau, 1626 (oil painting by Jan Marsin de Jonge, 1634).*

Below. *A contemporary view of Irish mercenaries in the service of Gustavus Adolphus, wearing plaid-like garments probably made from an early form of tartan.*

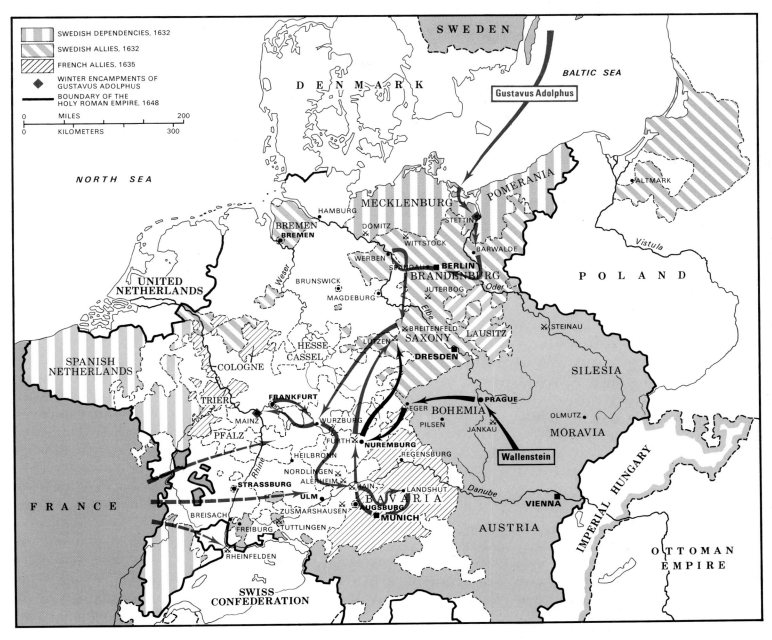

SWEDISH DEPENDENCIES, 1632

SWEDISH ALLIES, 1632

FRENCH ALLIES, 1635

◆ WINTER ENCAMPMENTS OF
GUSTAVUS ADOLPHUS

BOUNDARY OF THE
HOLY ROMAN EMPIRE, 1648

MILES 200

KILOMETERS 300

SWEDEN

BALTIC SEA

Gustavus Adolphus

DENMARK

NORTH SEA

POMERANIA

ALTMARK

HAMBURG

MECKLENBURG

STETTIN

POLAND

BREMEN
BREMEN

DOMITZ

WITTSTOCK

BARWALDE

Vistula

WERBEN

SPANDAU

BERLIN

UNITED
NETHERLANDS

BRUNSWICK

BRANDENBURG

Oder

JUTERBOG

MAGDEBURG

Elbe

BREITENFELD

LAUSITZ

SILESIA

HESSE
CASSEL

LUTZEN

SAXONY

STEINAU

SPANISH
NETHERLANDS

COLOGNE

DRESDEN

TRIER

FRANKFURT

EGER

BOHEMIA

PRAGUE

OLMUTZ

PFALZ

MAINZ

WURZBURG

PILSEN

JANKAU

MORAVIA

Rhine

FURTH

NUREMBURG

Wallenstein

HEILBRONN

REGENSBURG

NORDLINGEN
ALERHEIM

IMPERIAL HUNGARY

STRASSBURG

RAIN

LANDSHUT

Danube

FRANCE

ULM

BAVARIA

AUGSBURG

VIENNA

BREISACH

ZUSMARSHAUSEN

MUNICH

FREIBURG

TUTTLINGEN

AUSTRIA

OTTOMAN
EMPIRE

RHEINFELDEN

SWISS
CONFEDERATION

Swedes, however, he sent his ablest cavalry commander, Pappenheim, to the left to secure the position there. Immediately Pappenheim and the Swedes were fiercely embroiled in battle and Tilly was now forced to act, especially as the Swedish artillery came into action with devastating effect. Tilly therefore took four of his squares from the right wing and, with cavalry support, attacked and brought havoc among Gustavus' Saxon cavalry, who were novices in the art of war by comparison. Both these actions on the left and right wings caused a deep cleavage, which meant that the bulk of the Swedish army had no enemy in front of it. The Swedes exploited this opportunity, moved into the center and, from there, to the rear of Tilly's forces. Moreover, the Swedes had repelled Pappenheim's attacks. The Swedish cavalry and their tactical interaction with the musketeers proved superior to anything Tilly could offer. They faced the attacking Imperial cavalry with a mighty salvo by the musketeers, who then withdrew, and the momentary confusion was immediately exploited by the Swedish cavalry, who counterattacked.

The point of decision lay on the Swedes' left wing, where the Imperial square had made short work of the Saxon cavalry. Gustavus Adolphus re-formed his cavalry, and, as a prelude, exploited his superior artillery firepower of three to one and followed up this cannonade with a massive cavalry attack. The Imperial squares, not drilled effectively enough to retire systematically and weakened by the havoc caused by the Swedish artillery in their immobile squares, disintegrated and stampeded. The whole battle, from the Swedish point of view, was predominantly a cavalry action. Of Gustavus' seven infantry brigades, only three were involved in the actual fighting. Pappenheim's cavalry failed to match the combined tactics of the Swedish cavalry and infantry. His forces were so demoralized that Pappenheim could not rally them again for a new

Below. *A German soldier of the early seventeenth century in the act of loading his match lock musket.*

assault. Tilly had been wounded several times in the fracas and decided to withdraw toward Halle. His infantry, captured by the Swedes, joined Gustavus Adolphus *en masse*. Tilly had lost 11,000 men, the Saxons 3000, the Swedes 1500. With that victory, the command of the whole of northern Germany fell into the hands of Gustavus Adolphus; there were no longer any obstacles leading to western and southern Germany.

Gustavus moved to the south, entered the city of Nuremberg in the spring of 1632, and defeated Tilly again at the River Lech shortly afterward. In this battle Tilly was heavily wounded; his right leg was smashed, gangrene set in and he died a few weeks later in Altötting in Bavaria, the Black Madonna of Altötting being a traditional focus for pilgrimage. Bavaria was completely defenseless. The Elector Maximilian walled himself up in the fortress of Regensburg while Gustavus conquered Ingolstadt, Augsburg, Landshut and finally Munich. The campaign had little to do with warfare, opposition being virtually nonexistent; the Swedes could advance as they pleased and plunder along the way.

Ferdinand II found himself in a dilemma. Having dismissed Wallenstein, there was no one to replace him. Since the autumn of 1631 Ferdinand had endeavored to get Wallenstein to return, in spite of the implicit humiliation which this step meant for the Emperor, and for every Imperial general it implied a personal shortcoming because none of them had so far been able to stop Gustavus Adolphus. Wallenstein rejected Ferdinand's first approach, but Ferdinand did not give up – he even implored him to become his Supreme Field Commander. Only through the intervention of personal friends of both the Emperor and Wallenstein did the latter give in to the request. This culminated in the Göllersdorfer agreements of 12 April 1632. In these Wallenstein promised to put up a new army within a few months, to increase it to a strength of over 100,000 men, and to take over the command. In return he demanded that he exercised absolute command, in other words remained unimpeded by the obstructionist politics of the court in Vienna, and that, as far as military operations were concerned, he possessed complete freedom of decision. Ferdinand agreed and transferred absolute powers to him.

Wallenstein was the only statesman in the Imperial camp; he was also the only one who represented the cause of the Reich and not necessarily that of the dynasty. He was the only one equal in stature to Richelieu and to the Swedish Chancellor Oxenstierna. Wallenstein's basic premise was his unshakeable conviction that within the Reich there was no room for foreign powers, whether Spanish allies, the French or the Swedes. In a nutshell, he pursued a policy of purely German national interest, one which Ferdinand had unswervingly adhered to and which would not only have strengthened the Habsburg dynasty but changed the course of Germany's entire history for centuries to come.

Wallenstein began his recruitment drive and, in weeks rather than months, he had again under his banner the nucleus of his old army. He had reserved for himself the prerogative of appointing his own officers down to company level; in that way no officer's position could be bought, but was awarded according to ability. Gustavus Adolphus had not reckoned on Wallenstein's speed: hardly had the Swedish king left Munich

Above right. *Johann Tserclaes, Graf von Tilly, 1559–1632.*

Above, far right. *The sack of Magdeburg, May 1631.*

Right. *The siege of Magdeburg, 1631. This contemporary engraving shows the majestic skyline of a city soon to be ravaged by Imperial troops.*

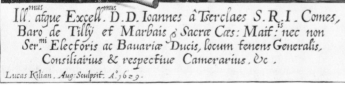

Ill.mus atque Excell.mus D.D. Ioannes àTserclaes S.R.I. Comes,
Baro de Tilly ef Marbais & Sacræ Cæs: Maitis nec non
Sermi Electoris ac Bauariæ Ducis, locum fenens Generalis,
Consiliarius & respectiue Camerarius, &c.

Lucas Kilian. Aug: Sculpsit A:ᵒ 1629.

Above. *The death of Gustavus Adolphus at the Battle of Lützen, 1632. His body, stripped by looters, was later found under a pile of the dead.*

when Wallenstein announced that his preparations were complete and that the new Imperial army under his command could take to the field. Expecting Wallenstein to turn to Saxony, Gustavus pulled his army out of Bavaria and southern Germany and marched north. But Wallenstein, instead of marching into Saxony, wanted to unite with the remaining forces of the Catholic League under Maximilian of Bavaria, cut off the Swedes and prevent them joining the Saxons. By the end of June the Bavarian and Imperial troops had joined forces. It came as a shock to Gustavus. He tried to move his forces out of Bavaria rapidly, force-marched them via Augsburg and Schwabach only to realize that Wallenstein had succeeded in cutting

Below. *The armies of Gustavus and Wallenstein meet at Lützen, 16 November 1632 (contemporary engraving).*

him off from the Saxons. There was nothing left for him but to march to Nuremberg and encamp himself behind its strong fortifications. Wallenstein moved north and established his positions southwest of Fürth between Zirndorf and the Alten Veste.

For six weeks the armies confronted one another, with Gustavus trying time and again to tempt Wallenstein to attack him at Nuremberg. Wallenstein had not the slightest intention of exposing his troops to the concentrated fire of the 500 pieces of artillery waiting to receive the Imperial troops. It was a turning point in the history of warfare. Wallenstein provided the first classic example of the strategy of attrition which was to dominate European warfare for the next century and a half.

It did not bother him that the Swedish king received reinforcements from the Rhine, Swabia and Thuringia to the extent that it trebled Gustavus' forces. Wallenstein had taken account of this in his calculations because the more troops the Swedes gathered, the more difficult would become their mobility; be-

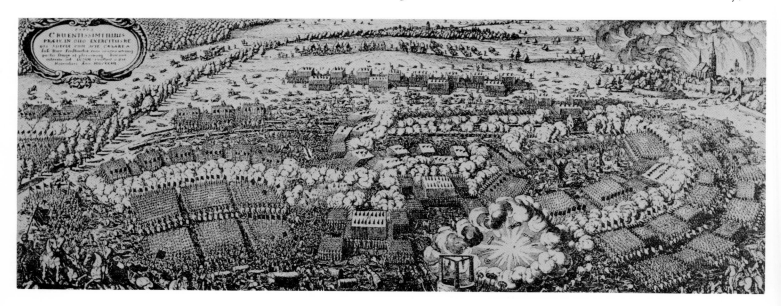

cause of the size of the trains involved, the more difficult would also become the problem of feeding and supplying an army of that size in a static position. He had maneuvered the Swedish King into a position which presented only two alternatives: to attack Wallenstein or to withdraw. His calculations proved right. At the height of his military career, surrounded by a reputation of invincibility, Gustavus attacked the Imperial positions on 1 September 1632. Wallenstein had planned his fortifications in an entirely novel way: he had not built up a continuous line, but instead established a chain of individual fortifications in an almost zigzag formation, where every corner not occupied by troops could be reached by his artillery. There were no blind spots where a breach could be made.

For four days the Swedes mounted attack after attack without achieving the slightest success. During the night of 4 September, Gustavus decided to break off the engagement. He had lost 7000 men, three time as many as the Imperial forces. According to the rules of war valid at that time, there was no victor and no vanquished, but contemporaries quickly realized that, because Gustavus had failed to conquer, because he had failed to overwhelm Wallenstein, he had also lost the battle. Wallenstein was not only a superb general and statesman, for his time he was also a sound economist. Realizing that soldiers were expensive, especially since he had put his own funds at the disposal of their upkeep, they had to be used sparingly. Under such conditions attrition paid greater dividends than the wasteful procedure of laying siege to a city or entering into an open

field battle. It was a lesson quickly learned by his successors and fellow generals throughout Europe.

On 16 November 1632 the two generals met again on the plain of Lützen, again near Leipzig. Gustavus intended to head Wallenstein off his supply base at Leipzig. The battle began during the late morning after the fog had lifted. It was the most ferocious and tough battle of the Thirty Years' War. It raged the whole day under the continuous fire of the artillery of both sides. It was fought with 'such fury, as no one has ever seen before,' as Wallenstein noted the following day. By the evening the elementary rules for open field battles had gone overboard; the battle was one mighty scene of butchery, an orgy of merciless killing. It raged on into the night and nothing was heard except the firing of guns and muskets, and the shrieks of the attackers and the attacked. Only as the night wore on did the battle gradually come to an end. Again there was no victor and no vanquished; both armies were completely exhausted. But the most important outcome of it was that the Lion of Midnight, as Gustavus Adolphus was popularly called, had been killed in battle. The war now took on a new direction.

Wallenstein's successes in 1632 were not rewarded with gratitude any more than had those before 1630. His name lay at the root of the growing power of the House of Habsburg in Germany and Europe. The German princes fully realized that

Below. Another view of Lützen. Gustavus at the head of the Swedish right wing, prepares to attack Wallenstein's weak left (contemporary engraving).

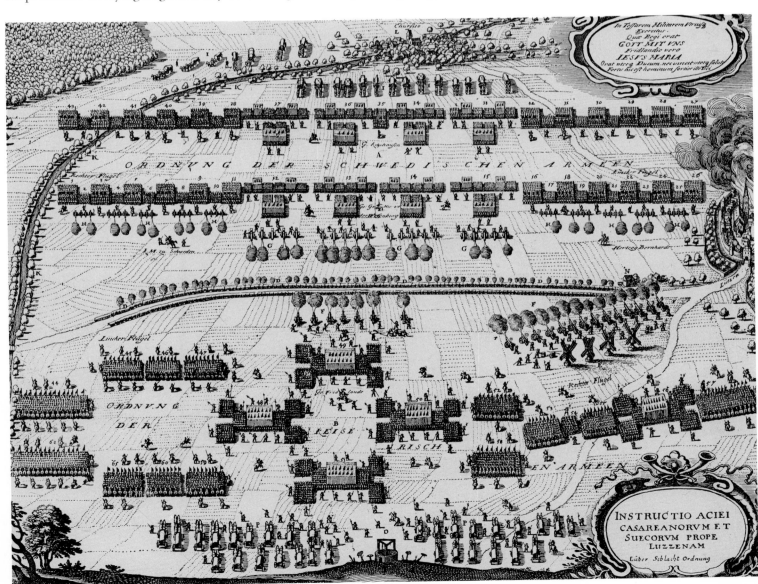

any further consolidation of the Emperor's position and any additional power he acquired was bound to have consequences detrimental to their own positions. Ferdinand's confidence in Wallenstein lasted as long as the Imperial army was and remained an indispensable instrument of Habsburg policy. The princes of the Reich, led by the Elector of Bavaria, Maximilian, sent petition after petition to Vienna directed against Wallenstein in particular and the Imperial policy in general. Wallenstein's successes threatened their own privileges, and their intractability caused Wallenstein, in a moment of anger, to remark that 'there will be no peace and quiet in the Reich until the moment when one of their heads is put before their feet. One will have to teach the Electors some manners. They must depend on the emperor and not the emperor on them.'

The crisis of confidence between Ferdinand and Wallenstein began in December 1633, when the latter explicitly ignored Ferdinand's orders and left his army in their winter quarters. Phillip IV of Spain suggested the setting up of an independent Spanish army in the Alsace and along the Rhine with the task of protecting not only the Alsace and Rhenish territories, but the whole of southern Germany including Franconia. Since the number of the Spanish troops was insufficient for this task, Wallenstein's army was to reinforce them and his position would be subordinate to the Duke of Feria. Wallenstein immediately recognized that the Spanish project would completely undermine the Emperor's position in Germany among Catholics and Protestants alike, since no forces were more hated than the Spaniards. Ferdinand's position would become dependent on Madrid. Wallenstein succeeded in making this point but, in addition to the German electors, he now had the Spaniards as his enemies at the court of Vienna. He also argued that the time was favorable for concluding peace and any additional Spanish intervention would prolong the war indefinitely.

Throughout 1633 Wallenstein tried to win over Brandenburg and Saxony to the Imperial side. What he managed to achieve was a declaration of their neutrality. He tried to negotiate with Oxenstierna, but since Sweden insisted upon gaining territory in Germany all contacts were broken off. Wallenstein acted fully within the competencies granted to him by Ferdinand in the Göllersdorfer agreements. When suddenly rumors began

to spread about Wallenstein conducting treasonable negotiations, rumors emanating from the German princes, Wallenstein reminded Ferdinand of that agreement. He defended his refusal to give up the army's winter quarters by claiming that the soldiers would otherwise perish or despair.

Wallenstein's decision, combined with his political negotiations, fed doubts in Ferdinand's mind which were strongly supported by the protests of the Electors. By the end of December 1633 Ferdinand decided not simply to dismiss him but to remove him by force. Blind to his own real interests and with a ready ear for the conspirators against Wallenstein around him, he pronounced a formal ban on Wallenstein on 24 January 1634. With that public ban, valid throughout the Reich, almost all Wallenstein's commanding officers left him. A month later, on 25 February 1634, the last Saturday of the carnival season, six dragoons led by the French captain Devereux broke into Wallenstein's residence at Eger and murdered him. The Habsburgs' bloody carnival had reached its climax. Habsburg's only statesman, a man acting for the interests of the dynasty as well as for Germany, left the scene; gone was the opportunity for the establishment of an absolutist monarchy of the House of Habsburg over a truly united Germany. In its place stepped a multitude of sovereign absolutist German princes. Had Wallenstein succeeded, there would never have been any need for a Bismarck; Cardinal Richelieu could be relieved.

The war dragged on for another 14 years, bringing more devastation over central Europe. To assess the damage of the Thirty Years' War statistically is virtually impossible as there are too many gaps in the evidence. What is relatively certain is that the German population residing in the countryside declined by 40 percent, while in the cities every third person became a victim of the war. In Bohemia the population declined from three million to 780,000. In 1618 there were 35,000 villages; at the end of the war in 1648 only one in six was inhabited, the rest having been burned down. Foreign troops brought the pestilence to Munich, and within four months 10,000 burghers had died. In Württemberg the population had already declined from 400,000 to 48,000 by 1641. In the Palatinate in the same year there was only one-fiftieth of the original population left. Magdeburg lost 90 percent of its inhabitants, Chemnitz 80

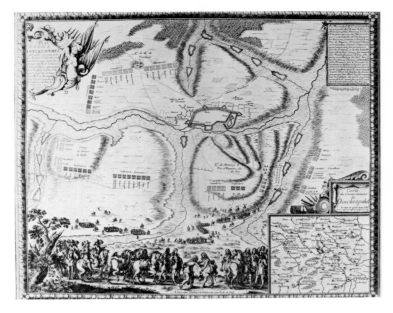

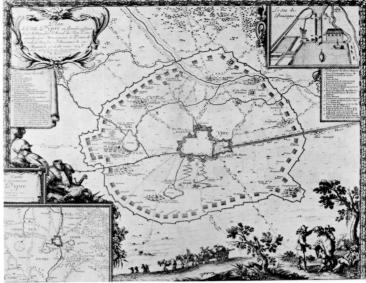

percent, Berlin and Colmar each 50 percent. The account of the Swedish army alone is debited with the complete destruction of 1500 cities, 18,000 villages and 200 castles.

The Westphalian peace confirmed Germany's fragmentation. The Habsburgs had failed in their bid to reimpose Catholicism in Germany. They were still emperors of the Holy Roman Empire, but every territorial prince now possessed the right to conduct his own foreign policy irrespective of how this policy affected the Reich as a whole. The real victor was France; although Sweden was also on the victorious side she did not possess the resources to maintain her positions in Germany longer than six decades. France gained the bishoprics of Metz, Toul and Verdun, Breisach, the entire Alsace, 10 cities and 40 villages in the Reich, and the right to traverse Germany with its troops and supplies.

What remained for the Habsburgs was precious little; the only substantial gain was the nucleus of Wallenstein's army, which became the nucleus of the standing army of the Habsburg dynasty. But it still possessed enough strength to maintain itself as a great power.

The remnants of Wallenstein's army – nine infantry and ten cavalry regiments – were the core of an army which a few decades later would repel the Turkish onslaught on Vienna, finally drive them back and storm Belgrade during the War of the Spanish Succession. Led by the genius of Prince Eugene, they played a principal part in checking once and for all the territorial ambitions of Louis XIV. This army, in fact the first standing army in Germany, was based on voluntary recruitment. The Vienna *Hofkriegsrat*, Court War Council, a kind of central organ combining general staff, military cabinet and the ministry of war, issued a directive that only Germans could be recruited to serve in German regiments, because, so the directive said, 'foreigners do not easily become accustomed to the comradeship of our people.' By 1705 the Austrian army comprised 100,000 men, and on the eve of the Seven Years' War 165,000. Ultimately it contained 12 different nationalities, all formed in their own regiments but with German as the language of command.

The work of expanding the foundations which Wallenstein had left behind was in the main that of Count Raimondo

Left. *The ambitious Czech adventurer Albrecht von Wallenstein, a freebooting Imperial general, murdered by a group of disaffected officers at Eger in February 1634.*

Far right. *Wallenstein's soothsayer surveys the body of his murdered master (nineteenth-century painting).*

Right. *A German swept-hilt rapier, circa 1660.*

Above. *French and Hessian troops under the Duc d'Enghien (soon to be Prince de Condé), besieging the Swabian town of Dinkelsbühl in 1645.*

Above right. *A contemporary engraving from the same series shows Condé's forces besieging the town of Ypres in Flanders. Ypres, whose strategic location made it the scene of numerous battles, was besieged on 13 May 1648 and fell on the 29th.*

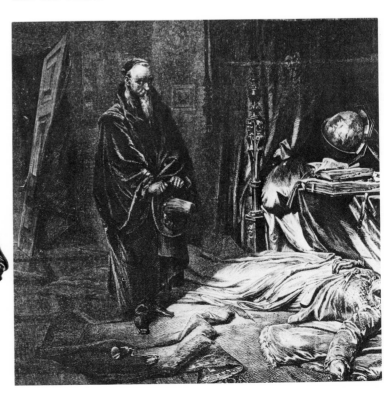

Montecuccoli (1609–81), a man who was immediately impressive for his wide-ranging, almost universal education. He was one of many in the seventeenth century who were aware of the spiritual and intellectual problems of modern life and who tried to analyze them scientifically. This general not only produced great feats on the battlefield against the Turks and the French, but was also the author of one of the major works on military theory which, more than a century later, served Scharnhorst, the Prussian reformer, very well. Thus on strategy he wrote: 'He who believes that progress can be achieved in the field without engaging in battle contradicts himself, or at least voices such a peculiar opinion as to bring ridicule upon himself. . . . Once the troops notice this, how much greater would become their fear of the bravery of the enemy! Of course one should never engage in battle without careful thought, and even less should one allow the enemy to force one into battle; all that one has to do is to recognize the right moment for battle. After all, in the final analysis it is necessary to be ready to fight and to gain control of the battlefield; whoever wins the battle wins not only the campaign but also a sizable piece of territory. Therefore, even if someone appears to be well prepared for battle, the mistakes which he may have made in maneuvering earlier on may be supportable, but however well he may have performed in other respects, if he has previously failed to grasp the lessons taught by battle he is unlikely to conclude the war with honors.' In other words, commence battle only when you possess an obvious advantage; without it, whether the battle is won or lost the long-term result is likely to be inconclusive.

In 1683 church bells rang throughout the Habsburg Empire: the Turks had launched an invasion, reaching the gates of Vienna by July 1683. The imperial court left the city in great haste for Passau. What remained behind was a defending force of 22,000 men commanded by Ernst Rüdiger Count Starhemberg. The army of the Reich rallied more quickly to the relief of Vienna than one would have expected, though some of the forces, like those of the Elector of Bavaria, Max II Emanuel, were so badly equipped and supplied that more of his soldiers died or fell sick on the march than were killed in the actual battle. For two months the Turks attacked incessantly, but, assisted by the Viennese burghers, the Reich army beat back every attack. Vienna had become the shield of Germany; the Turks were determined to take the city before enforcements could arrive:

By 7 September 1683 reinforcements had arrived; they came along the right bank of the Danube and positioned themselves at the Kahlemberg, the bald mountain outside Vienna from which, on a clear day, one can see as far as Bratislava and into the Hungarian plain, while to the south and southwest the summits

of Styria and Carinthia are clearly visible. On 12 September battle commenced. Down from the heights of the Kahlemberg marched the Habsburg and Reich regiments led by the Bavarian Elector, and, supported by a surprise attack which Starhemberg mounted from the city, victory was complete. Kara Mustafa the Vizier, commanding the Turks, received the silken cord from the Sultan: a general who lost a battle of this kind had also lost his right to live. The Grand Vizier committed suicide, his head was cut off and sent on a silver platter to the Sultan. The battle also enabled another man to make his first major mark: Eugene, Prince of Savoy (1663–1736). He was the younger son of a side branch of the House of Savoy and had first tried his luck at the court of Louis XIV. He was small of stature and quite ugly; fortune was not on his side. Therefore he turned to the Habsburgs, where his career was rapid. At the battle of the Kahlemberg he commanded the dragoon Kufstein regiment.

The victory of the Battle of the Kahlemberg was not followed up – the soldiers were too busy plundering the oriental treasures of the Turks and, above all, their wine. The campaign gathered only slowly in pace again, but two years later the Hungarian capital Ofen was captured, and a little later Max Emanuel, at the head of his Bavarians, stormed Belgrade. For the first time in 300 years the Magyar nobility bowed to the Habsburgs and accepted their overlordship, and Emperor Leopold had his son Joseph, then only nine years old, crowned King of Hungary. The Habsburg Empire's policy gained new direction, away from the Reich and into southeastern Europe and the Balkans.

The Turkish invasion had been the product of an alliance between France and the Ottoman Empire. It was repelled with the fervor of a crusade. The German princes had never been so united since the Reformation and, after the defeat of the Turks, were never to be so again until the iron hand of Bismarck forced them into unity. French policy, insofar as it included the Turks, had failed, and Louis XIV decided on a campaign of rape and pillage along the Rhine. He annexed the Reich city of Strasbourg and then moved down the Rhine conquering Speyer, Mainz and Trier. But the emperor, aided by England and the Netherlands, reacted promptly and expelled the French from the Palatinate. The French withdrawal was accompanied by a scorched earth policy to ensure that no supplies were left behind; Cologne and Bingen were burnt to the ground by the forces commanded by General Ezéchiel de Mélac; he also had the Schloss of Heidelberg burnt down, the ruins of which are a reminder of the warfare of absolutism under the auspices of Louis XIV to this day. The war over the Palatinate ended only in 1697 with the Peace of Ryswick; France held onto the Alsace and Strasbourg.

Left. *Jacques Callot's engravings often depicted the harsher side of war. Here he shows soldiers being hanged for pillaging.*

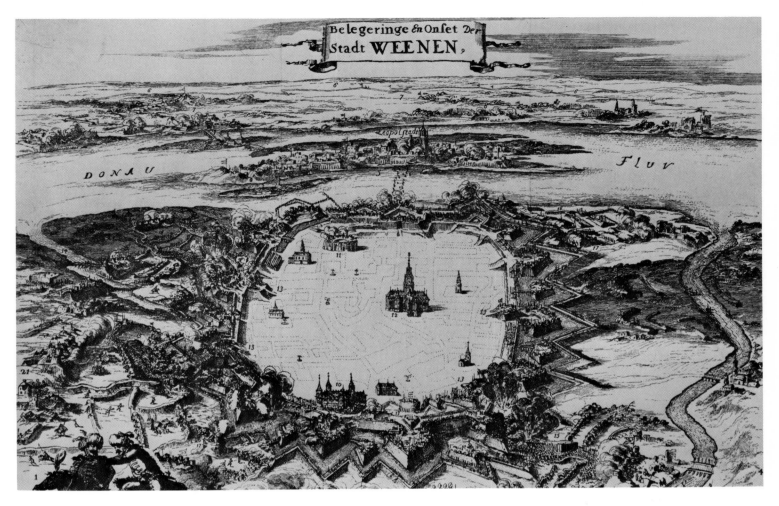

Belegeringe En Onset Der Stadt WEENEN,

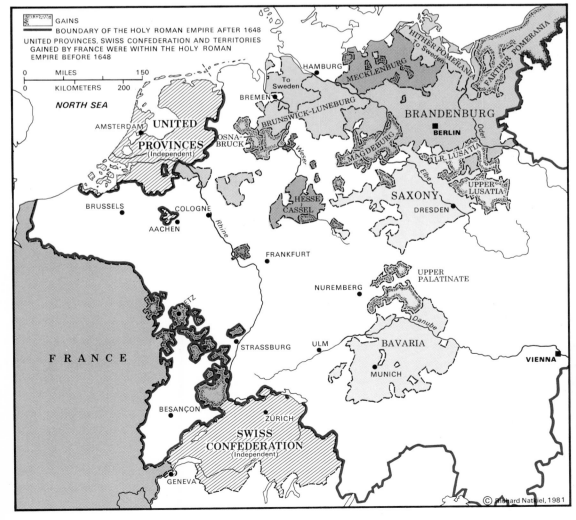

Above. C Decker's contemporary engraving shows the Turks battering at the walls of Vienna. St Stephen's cathedral can be seen in the center of the town, with a broken bridge across the Danube behind it.

Below. The Austrian Count Starhemberg, defender of Vienna against the Turks in 1683.

Above. *Graf Leopold Joseph von Daun, 1705–66. An able Austrian general, Daun was the first to defeat Frederick the Great's army, at Kolin in 1757. Though defeated at Leuthen the same year, he again defeated Frederick in 1758. Daun was a skillful strategist, who specialized in schemes which forced the Prussians to attack him in strong positions.*

In 1714 the Turks renewed their attack, and again the German princes rallied to Habsburg's side, but mostly to learn military craft from Prince Eugene. Delays ensued and only in 1716 did an actual major battle occur; Eugene defeated the Turks and then, moving toward the east, conquered within two months the entire Banat and its capital Temesvár. The Sultan had lost his last bastion in Hungary. However, Eugene wanted to achieve a durable peace as well as a military victory. Upon his initiative the Habsburgs agreed a settlement policy calling German peasants, particularly from Bavaria, Swabia and the Palatinate, to settle and cultivate the Banat, which had now been completely depopulated by the Turks. It was the last chapter of German colonization to the east.

In the spring of 1717, after thorough planning, Eugene moved down the Danube toward Belgrade, which had fallen again into Turkish hands. He crossed the River Save and established his fortification south of the city flanked by the Drave and the Danube. By the middle of July the siege began with a continuous artillery bombardment. For three weeks the Imperial forces tried to wear down the Turks: sappers laid their mines and breaches were made in the outer walls, but not enough was achieved to tempt Eugene to mount a direct assault. Moreover, Turkish relief forces were approaching from Adrianople led by the Sultan himself. After their arrival the relief army took up position behind strong earthworks and soon Eugene's forces were exposed to heavy fire. In Vienna the position was already considered hopeless for Eugene. Devoid of any illusions he decided in favor of a major surprise stroke. In the early hours of the dawn of 16 August, at three o'clock in the morning, he attacked the Sultan's forces. In spite of their ten-

acious defense, they were beaten and the Grand Vizier ordered withdrawal southward. Eugene refrained from pursuit, for it was sufficient to have thrown out the Turks and caused their withdrawal. On the following day Belgrade surrendered and the capitulation document was signed on 18 August.

Finally, on 21 July 1718, the Peace of Passarowitz put an end to the almost century-old struggle between the Ottoman Empire and the Habsburgs and this, but for a short episode between 1737 and 1739, stabilized the position of the great powers in the Balkans until well into the nineteenth century.

Prince Eugene was appointed President of the *Hofkriegsrat*, a position which gave him both military and political power. Like Wallenstein he engaged in high diplomacy, not for the sake of personal aggrandizement but to expand and stabilize the power of the Habsburg dynasty. Unlike Wallenstein, however, he considered the German Reich and its consolidation as largely irrelevant. He preferred, on the basis of a firm system of alliances, to establish a balance of power within Europe, as was also borne out by his policy toward France, and thus to contribute to a general peace.

His personality, his military genius, his sound political judgment, combined with his deep interest in philosophy and the creative arts, was ideal for the leadership of what in essence was the new Austrian army, transforming former mercenaries into God-fearing regular soldiers. He paid particular attention to the training of his officer corps, every member having to exhibit qualities of bravery and chivalry; as he put it: 'Gentlemen, you have only one justification for your life if you continuously, even in moments of the greatest danger, provide an example . . . so that no one can blemish you.'

More so than the rank and file, the Austrian officer corps represented an international body. Little wonder that the military nobility from all corners of Europe came to serve in the Imperial army. Of course, the dynastic ties with Spain and Italy provided easy access, and the fame of the great field marshal exercised its magnetic powers. As a result of the wars with France and the Ottoman Empire, national sentiments re-emerged in Germany, and the Austrian officer corps was attractive to many German officers of the Reich, among them many members of the ruling German dynasties. Last but not least, German burghers joined in numbers.

When Empress Maria Theresa succeeded to the throne in 1740, she found after the death of Prince Eugene that neglect had set in, partly due to financial mismanagement, and therefore one of her first endeavors was to put through all-embracing reforms. Obviously she faced greater difficulties than her young Prussian contemporary who succeeded to the throne in the same year; the latter's father had left behind a sound financial base. Moreover she was a woman who, by the very nature of her sex, could not enjoy such immediate rapport with her officer corps as young Frederick. However, she tried to open the officer corps to all talents, irrespective of social origins. It was always 'a sign of her particular sympathy and grace.' Soldiers who were not of noble origin and who, in the course of 10 years, performed distinguished service, were ennobled and thus taken into the officer corps. She founded the Maria Theresa Medal, which was awarded for extraordinary bravery as well as the moral courage to take independent action that deviated from actual orders given, provided the action was successful. In 1752 she also founded the Theresian Military Academy, which was a modern training institution for the officer corps as well as for future officers. The teaching program excluded anything that would turn the young man into a courtier and cavalier. Instead, they were expected to become efficient soldiers and leaders of men. Much to her regret, Austria's higher nobility was loath to send its offspring to the academy since they felt that the six-teenth- and seventeenth-century ideals of the courtly chevalier were more worthwhile than military drill combined with mathematics and the natural sciences. Thus the early products of the Military Academy, situated outside Vienna in Wiener-Neustadt, were the sons of impoverished families who had served the Habsburgs faithfully. Also, it was difficult to gain general acceptance for this new aristocracy of the sword as equals of the established nobility. They therefore served side by side with officers who had purchased their commissions. Venality in the Austrian officer corps did not disappear until after 1867.

The rank and file was subject to the same severe discipline as was customary in all armies in Europe of the time. Corporal punishment was a general rule, as was running the gauntlet for desertion. Excesses of punishment in the Austrian army took on such dimensions that Maria Theresa found herself compelled to intervene and limit the instances or the number of offenses for which corporal punishment could be decreed. That she did not entirely succeed is shown by the fact that the number of desertions in the Austrian army was considerably higher than in the Prussian army, although it can hardly be said that Prussian discipline was less severe.

Nevertheless, on the battlefield the Austrian army always gave a good, even excellent account of itself, though lack of discipline in occupied territories was always a pronounced feature. For instance, when Austrian and Reich troops, including Prussian formations, occupied Bavaria in 1704 during the War of the Spanish Succession, Austrian behavior was such as to result in a large-scale peasant rebellion throughout Franconia and Lower and Upper Bavaria, a rising which, for a moment, threatened the entire position of the Imperial forces there. In a report on this event to Emperor Joseph I in Vienna, great attention was paid to the difference in behavior found between the Austrian and Prussian troops stationed in the area; whereas the latter were always rigidly disciplined, the former became notorious for their excesses against peasants and their tendency to plunder whenever the opportunity existed.

However, it was not until 1748 that the Austrian army introduced a general training manual, compulsory for all the Austrian forces. Its author was Field Marshal Daun, who actually did little else than copy that used by the Prussian army for several decades. But Daun also insisted on thorough tactical training, a training which every year culminated in field ma-neuvers, again imitating practices followed in Potsdam since the days of Frederick William I. That Daun's reforms yielded results was shown by the improved performance of the Austrian army during the Seven Years' War. He also placed great emphasis on the instruction that no differences be made between the nationality groups.

Of course, considering the difference in the social structures between Austria and Prussia, the former being subject to the political influence of the estates and the civil service, the latter being a military state pure and simple, it was inevitable that efforts at reform took a much longer time to be implemented. To that end Austria possessed neither the inner unity nor the charismatic personality of an ubiquitous soldier king at the center whose every wish was an immediate command. In spite of the endeavors of Maria Theresa and others, it was never possible to overcome the particularism of the estates and provinces, especially when raising arms. Therefore Austria could conduct a major war only in close alliance with other great powers. On the basis of her own resources Austria would never have been capable of fighting the Seven Years' War against Prussia.

Above. *The Empress Maria Theresa of Austria, 1717–80.*

A significant role in Austria's military history at this time was the expansion and consolidation of the *Militärgrenze*, the military border which separated her from the Ottoman Empire. The early beginnings of this military border go back well into the sixteenth century, when, for the first time, François I of France entered into an alliance with the Ottoman Empire in his struggle against Emperor Charles V. The inroads made by the Turks in the seventeenth century demonstrated that the provisional measures taken then were no longer sufficient. To halt the Turkish advance and to defend the newly recruited settlers required a firm system of defense, which ultimately consisted of a protective wall intersected with strong fortification stations; garrisons secured the entire southern Slav area of the Habsburg territory over a length of 1500 km.

The border troops were partly regular soldiers complemented by special formations of militia troops recruited from the German settlers within the area. Maria Theresa aimed at a total of 47,000 troops for this purpose, though the estates were willing to grant her finance only for a third of that amount. In addition they had to be relieved annually. Nevertheless the *Militärgrenze* was more than just a fortification. By-products were the opening up of the land by a network of roads, new villages, and the irrigation of a barren plain to form an agriculturally prosperous region. Prince Eugene considered the area important and upon his initiative schools were built and compulsory elementary schooling was introduced. It was a frontier zone of military, economic and political importance. The frontiersmen were farmers and soldiers alike and, most important from the point of view of the settlers, they were all free peasants, free from any feudal or similar obligations. They enjoyed proprietary as well as possessory rights. The *Militärgrenze* fulfilled its functions for 350 years until it was swept away by the havoc of twentieth-century warfare.

CHAPTER III

THE PERIPHERY OF EUROPE
I: ENGLAND

Parliamentarian soldiers of the English Civil War, showing various types of weapons, helmets and half armor.

From a constitutional point of view the history of medieval England is largely the history of the evolution of a legal code and of an efficient administrative framework of local government, both making for an improved centralized government. This process of centralization went on continuously, though at varying pace, dominated as it was by the medieval concept of kingship, which throughout the centuries had – in spite of Magna Carta – remained unchanged. Consequently it was inevitable that the monarchy should gain more and more power, though not always uncontestedly. After there had been a breakdown in the direct exercise of power by the monarchy, as during the Wars of the Roses, it seems hardly surprising that, with the advent of the Tudor monarchy, there should not only be the reassertion of monarchical power but also a development of its ideological foundations and its propaganda. The alleged divine right of kings may well be considered an implicit foundation of Tudor rule.

Simultaneously, with the exultation of royal position, a social revolution had begun under the reign of Henry VIII which did not necessarily create but did accelerate the development of a new social class with new economic power; this development went hand in hand with what one might call – with qualifications – growth in the power of Parliament, whose sanction and support Henry VIII found necessary to obtain in his break with Rome and legal formation of the Church of England. In addition, the reigns of Henry VIII and Elizabeth I saw the rise of a propertied gentry, which had acquired considerable riches from the spoils derived from the dissolution of the monasteries and seizure of other church property. These developments, among the gentry and Parliament, represented a potential time-bomb should the king ignore this shift of economic power that had taken place in favor of an increasingly vocal and politically articulate section of the population. In a way it may be said – even at the risk of greatly oversimplifying complex issues – that the 'Reformation Parliament' and the dissolution of the monas-

teries, all shrewdly managed by Thomas Cromwell, were the first steps to the scaffold upon which Charles I was to expire.

By the time Charles I assumed the crown of England in 1625, the currents that had once forced crown and parliament into alliance had ceased to operate. On the contrary, parliament, in part representing a new class and in part reflecting reformed religious beliefs, soon began to feel the exercise of royal power as an encroachment on its political privileges. These privileges were derived in part also from a mythical source, namely the myth of the Magna Carta.

In fairness to Charles Stuart, it must be said that, from a purely economic point of view, his position was not dissimilar to that of John Lackland: dependent on static feudal revenues, he had to make ends meet in an economically inflationary environment. Moreover, while in comparison with Elizabeth I his policy and handling of parliament may be considered inept and unwise, one may also justifiably ask whether one can judge him from a purely English frame of reference. He ought to be viewed within the context of his age – as a representative of the absolutist tendencies which gained the upper hand throughout the mainland of Europe. It can be argued that, while he represented the forces of modernity, Parliament represented the forces of reaction. Can one, for instance, really accuse him of breaking promises, or of breaking an unwritten constitution? The contractual bond of a promise assumes a level of equality between the contracting partners. Against the background of the age of absolutism it is unlikely that Charles I ever accepted any level of equality with parliamentary negotiators; instead he felt that he was acting under duress. Can one accuse him of

Below left. *King Henry VIII of England, 1491–1547.*

Right. *King Charles I of England, 1600–49.*

Below. *A contemporary portrait of the Parliamentarian leader Oliver Cromwell, 1599–1658.*

Left. *The Parliamentarian leader John Hampden, who played a leading part in the events leading up to the Civil War and was mortally wounded in a skirmish at Chalgrove Field in June 1643.*

Above. *The Battle of Edgehill (engraving, nineteenth century).*

Right. *Thomas Wentworth, Earl of Strafford, 1593–1641. Initially a firm supporter of Parliament, Strafford later sided with the King and was appointed Lord Deputy of Ireland in 1633. Accused of plotting to overthrow Parliament with an Irish army, Strafford was attainted by Parliament and executed in May 1641.*

breaking the constitution, which at that stage was still in its infancy, creating precedent rather than following it? In retrospect, many of Charles's actions may be judged as politically unwise and insensitive to recent change, but many of the actions of Parliament were perhaps presumptuous.

Of that large part of Parliament which opposed Charles it is often maintained that the motivation of its actions was determined by economic interests, masked by political and religious pretexts. Some recent historians have proposed that economic considerations were important motive forces, but it is equally vital to establish what people then *felt* to be important. Taking the religious issue as one example, even superficial scrutiny of contemporary sources demonstrates that, in spite of doctrinal changes, religious sentiment still permeated the fabric of English society. Society in England and Europe was not yet secularized.

Consequently, given this circumstance together with the Protestant doctrine of free individual examination of conscience, the liberty of conscience, it was unlikely that such a principle would remain restricted to the narrow confines of theological discussion. Instead, it was immediately applied to political issues. For the Puritans – who, it ought to be emphasized, represented only one segment of the Protestant movement in England, though politically one of its most powerful and articulate segments – metaphysical freedom carried the corollary of political liberty. If God had created man to enjoy liberty, then it would be against His laws to deny him that liberty

in the exercise of his day-to-day affairs. In short, the Puritan concept of society acknowledged the existence of the all-permeating and everlasting presence of God in all spheres of life, but for the same reason rejected the assumption that the divine right of monarchs could place any restrictions on their subjects in the exercise of their full liberties. For the King and his critics the ideological factor was not a suddenly and conveniently discovered tool, but one which had been part and parcel of the fabric of British society for centuries.

It was this environment of which Oliver Cromwell was a product when he vigorously supported the 'root and branch' petition which sought to abolish episcopacy. He pushed himself into prominence with his spirited defense of John Lilburne, the radical Puritan writer, when Charles I and Archbishop Laud were set upon pursuing a policy similar to that of Emperor Ferdinand II with his Edict of Restitution. Against this background one should first investigate the developments which took place during the period 1640–60 and the career of Oliver Cromwell, particularly its military aspects.

If we compare 1660 with 1640 it can be observed firstly that the royal endeavors toward absolute monarchy had been strongly defeated and that the financial independence of the king was at an end. The struggle over this matter which had lasted from the reign of Edward I to Charles I was at long last over. The so-called 'Glorious Revolution' of 1688 was neither a revolution nor glorious but simply underlined what had been achieved between 1640 and 1660. Secondly, by 1660 the predominant influence of the House of Commons in the government of the nation was permanently established. Thirdly, in the sphere of religion the complete and definite rejection of the doctrine of the Roman Catholic Church was assured, while, on the other hand, the position of the Church of England after the Restoration was no longer quite the same as before. Fourthly, and of more immediate impact, was the permanent disappearance of the prerogative courts, and with them all danger from royal prerogative. Although an attempt was made to revive it, this attempt brought to an end the rule of the Stuart dynasty in England. Lastly, and perhaps surprisingly in view of the internal crises, in the realm of foreign policy, England's name and power was respected and feared in Europe as never before.

These developments seem vast, but to give the major share of credit for them to Oliver Cromwell is to ignore the specific nature of the Puritan revolution. The irony is that the term 'Puritan' is really a mirage of a common denominator which, as such, had no existence in reality. On the contrary, the very absence of such a common denominator on the one hand, and the monopoly of effective power in the hands of Cromwell's army on the other, successfully prevented a really revolutionary settlement from the very outset. What this settlement, if such it can be called, did was to confirm the economic and political relationship that had already existed and been recognized before the outbreak of the Civil War. In that respect one may wonder whether the Civil War was not only an act of folly, but one of futility as well.

If, for argument's sake, we now allow the description 'Puritan' to be applied to the House of Commons at a time when its endeavors and policies were fairly unanimously supported by its members, then the Puritan revolution began in 1640 and ended in 1642. Within that time span, absolute monarchy had disappeared for ever. But that, of course, was not so apparent then as it is now. At that time, the struggle with absolute monarchy was by no means over and its revival still seemed a real threat.

It could be said that legislation of 1641, approved and signed by a desperate king, was as responsible for the demise of abso-lutist royal hopes as the Civil War itself. The first act the Long Parliament passed secured its regular meeting; this was a profound development as previously it was the king's prerogative to call and dismiss parliaments at his will. A little later Parliament went a step farther in the same direction by a still more revolutionary enactment – that the existing Parliament should not be dissolved or prorogued except by its own consent. This was asking Charles to surrender even more power than the previous Bill had required, and deprived him of all his usual weapons against Parliament; however, in the excitement caused by the execution of the King's closest confidant beside Archbishop Laud, Thomas Wentworth (Earl of Strafford,) the King seems to have signed it without much consideration. The collection of such taxes as 'tonnage and poundage' or customs duties was made illegal. Also ship money, one of the most hotly disputed issues of the day, was abolished although, contrary to Whig mythology, it had been levied only on harbor towns, and was in fact used for the construction of naval craft; building the foundation of British sea power under Cromwell when commanded by Admiral Blake. Compulsory knighthood, the abuse of royal forests, and impressment for the army by royal prerogative were ended, and the royal right of purveyance limited.

Returning to parliamentary legislation between 1640 and 1642, important changes limiting arbitrary government were effected by Parliament with reference to the prerogative jurisdiction of the royal council and the special court which had grown out of it. The extraordinary jurisdiction of the king in his council, above the ordinary common law, was brought to an end; it had existed since the establishment of the Norman monarchy and, in the twelfth century, had originated the beginnings of modern common law. With it disappeared the Councils of the North and Wales and the ordinary jurisdiction of the Privy Council. Hence, from a constitutional point of view, it

Below. *The first major battle of the Civil War, fought at Edgehill on 23 October 1642. The eighteenth-century artist has shown the participants wearing the costume of his own day rather than the military dress of the seventeenth century.*

The BATTLE of EDGE-HILL

session of the Long Parliament opinion in the House was fairly unanimous over the legislative program of reform. The revolutionary changes proposed by Cromwell and his friends 'split the house asunder' and formed the parties for the Civil War. All that was required now was an understandable but nevertheless ill-considered action by Charles I to light the fuse to a very formidable powder keg.

Such then was the first act of the revolution, an act instigated and promoted by slightly more than half the membership of the House of Commons. It was the beginning of a radical revolution, no longer specifically Puritan because for a large part Puritan sentiment had found itself accommodated by the results of the first session of the Long Parliament; radicals like Cromwell and Pym precipitated the split in the Commons and helped to make the ensuing conflagration inevitable.

Cromwell's role as a politician was resoundingly negative, yet his role as an outstanding military commander seems beyond dispute. Indeed, his military ability may well explain his failure as a politician, since it is very rare to combine brilliance in the profession of arms with an ability to manipulate politics.

Before the wars, Cromwell was a gentleman farmer, descended from the nephew of Thomas Cromwell, the minister of Henry VIII. Few men realized the potential of the somewhat notorious Member for Cambridge in the Short Parliament, known as much for his political and religious radicalism as for his slovenly appearance. But it was John Hampden who remarked 'that though sloven, if we should ever come to break with the King (which God forbid), in such a case he will be one of the greatest men of England.'

Though devoid of any previous training and experience, at the outbreak of the Civil War Cromwell was commissioned as a captain in the cavalry of the Parliamentary army, commanding over 60 horsemen and noncommissioned officers. Even at this early stage Cromwell displayed a possession of those rare qualities of command and resolution which no training can impart. However, of more immediate and practical advantage was that he could gather around him a military clan such as his son plus Henry Ireton his future son-in-law, Valentine Walton his brother-in-law, John Hampden and Edward Whalley, his cousins, and Viscount Mandeville, later Earl of Manchester.

At the time of his appointment Cromwell was 43 and had a great conviction of righteousness and belief in divine sanction for his decisions, convictions which inclined him toward sectarian independency and determined his political and military career.

It seems certain that, out of the family clan under Cromwell's

may well be said that in the years 1640–41 much more was achieved than in the period of the Civil Wars and Cromwell's Protectorate, something that seems to have been overlooked entirely by Macaulay.

In devising and advocating this new legislation there exists no evidence that Cromwell played any conspicuous part. It bears out one of his main characteristics, his essential indifference to political institutions and systems, while his religious commitment is shown by the importance he attached to radical religious settlement in his advocacy of the 'root and branch' petition. He seemed to have had little success with it in a house as yet not divided against itself, though critical of the king's policies and the incompetence which had brought about the Scottish wars. The House was not inclined toward radical policies in tne ecclesiastical sphere which, in the first session of the Long Parliament, were of purely secondary importance anyway.

It was in the course of the second session that Cromwell attained real prominence when he, Pym and others helped to draw up the 'Grand Remonstrance,' which detailed their grievances and suggested reforms. This document was fathered by deep suspicion after the Irish massacres which the monarch could not be trusted to suppress. In Pym's view, taking into account the absolutist inclinations of Charles I, he could not be trusted with an army in the first place. In that remonstrance Parliament asked, among other things, that the royal ministers should be 'such as Parliament may have cause to confide in.' If we speak of Parliament here, we must bear in mind a body with a majority of 11 with 148 voting against it, while in the first

Above left. *The Battle of Edgehill: another eighteenth-century view of the action.*

Right. *Charles I addressing his army while on the march from Stafford to Wellington in September 1642. He assured his supporters that they would meet 'no enemies but traitors,' and went on state his intention of governing according to the laws of the land and maintaining the Church of England.*

Left. *Robert Devereux, Earl of Essex, commanded the Parliamentarian forces at Edgehill.*

direct influence, emerged the idea of a military association, and that because of this Parliament, on 22 October 1642 – the day before the Battle of Edgehill – approved the formation of county defense unions. From these in turn emerged the Eastern Association of Norfolk, Suffolk, Huntingdon and Lincolnshire centered on Cambridge, Oliver Cromwell's constituency. This rendered the eastern counties the most powerful bulwark of the Parliamentary army.

These counties provided England's first standing army. At the beginning of the Civil War no standing army existed except in Ireland; armies were raised when the occasion arose, as for instance against the Scots. In the Middle Ages, as a result of its strongly centralized monarchy, England had had a highly effective military establishment which virtually annihilated itself in the Wars of the Roses. By contrast, the Tudor monarchy was not based on a strong military organization but on a rather refined local policing and administrative system, seeing the growth of the Justices of the Peace.

Attempts at reviving a voluntarily recruited army were made from time to time, mainly to keep down the Irish, but Parliament's distrust of its misuse put an end to them. Indeed, the fear of a standing army such as Thomas Wentworth was developing in Ireland was one of the main issues which led him to the executioner's block. It would have seemed reasonable for England to support the Protestant cause in Germany, considering that the Elector of the Palatinate was Charles I's brother-in-law, but in Germany and the Netherlands all that was forthcoming from England were a few contingents of auxiliary troops.

What existed for the defense of the realm and the maintenance of order originated from the Middle Ages, namely that each county had to provide forces and officers proportional in size to that of the county. In other words it was a militia. Arms were stored in local arsenals and military exercises were carried out; every summer they met for a one-day exercise. They were called the Trained Bands, but it is said that they preferred to spend the day in more leisurely pursuits than organized training. Needless to say, their military value was low. Nor could they be used outside the realm. These deficiencies made themselves felt immediately when Civil War broke out.

There were English officers and auxiliary troops who had participated in the Thirty Years' War on the European mainland in the Dutch, French, Spanish and German Imperial armies. Thus, despite the absence of a standing army, on the eve of the Civil War there were numerous individuals experienced in the methods of continental warfare – particularly among the cavalry, the most important arm on the battlefield. Prince Rupert, nephew of Charles I and known as the 'Mad Cavalier,' instilled his own experience into the Cavaliers. He taught his men to charge home at the gallop, sword in hand, and only to use firearms once the enemy had been broken. Cromwell was very quick to learn from his opponent and curtailed the undisciplined charge so characteristic of the early Parliamentary cavalry.

Cromwell realized instinctively the importance of morale. While the Cavaliers fought for the 'King's Cause,' to ask men simply to fight for Parliament and against absolutist despotism

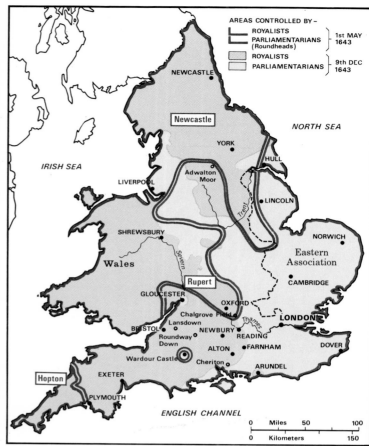

was too abstract and uninspiring. Cromwell's greatest achievement was to inspire the men under his own command with his own religious convictions and to select men of his own religious persuasion for the command of his troops. Soon the latter enjoyed a reputation for avoiding, as Baxter put it, 'those disorders, mutinous plunderings and grievances of the country which debauched men in armies are commonly guilty of.' The religious cause, the call for 'liberty of conscience,' created troops as brave, as serviceable and as eager for victory as their opponents.

This, of course, did not manifest itself in the early engagements such as Edgehill. The Earl of Essex's defeat by the Royalists put Parliament on the defensive and pointed to the need for a thorough reform of the Parliamentary army. Although Cromwell's own role at Edgehill remains obscure, its lesson was not lost upon him. The growing prominence of the Eastern Association was a direct consequence, as was the type of officer and men in it. 'You must get men of spirit,' said Cromwell to Parliament according to his own testimony to Hampden. In his Eastern Association he set out to create just that type of body. In the words of an anonymous writer of a newsletter in circulation in May 1643, 'As for Colonel (which by then he had become) Cromwell, he hath 2000 brave men, well-disciplined; no man swears but pays his twelve pence; if he is drunk, he is set in stocks, or worse; if one calls another roundhead he is cashiered: insomuch that the counties where they come leap for joy of them, and come in and join with them. How happy were it if all forces were thus disciplined.'

Though evidence of this kind must not be believed too readily, Cromwell in a series of letters during the same year pointed out, 'I beseech you to be careful what captains of horse you choose, what men be mounted: a few honest men are better than numbers. . . . I (would) rather have a plain, russet-coated captain of horse that knows what he fights for and loves what he knows, than that which you call a gentleman, and is nothing

else. . . . I have a lovely company; you would respect them. They are no Anabaptists, they are honest, sober Christians: they expect to be used as Men!'

The first really decisive battle was fought on 2 July 1644 at Marston Moor. It was brought to a successful conclusion for Parliament primarily because of Cromwell's skillful handling of his cavalry, the men of his Eastern Association whom he had trained the previous autumn and winter. It was also a battle which raised his name to national preeminence on both sides alike. Before the battle he was relatively unknown; after it Prince Rupert commented that Cromwell 'could himself evoke a more fierce and enduring spirit from the people than even that which he here magnifies. His 'Ironsides' (a name which Rupert gave to Cromwell and which was applied to his own regiment and was applied later to Cromwell's entire army) are the most fearless and successful body of troops on record, even in our annals: these fellows may have been, and I believe were, for the most part fanatics. Hypocrites never fought as they fought.' And Sir Philip Warwick added that 'they chose rather to die than fly, and custom removed fear of danger.'

But Marston Moor also demonstrated that the reforms initiated after Edgehill were still far from complete; the entire army needed the discipline and spirit of Cromwell's 'Ironsides.' This reorganization of the army between 1644 and 1645 was primarily Cromwell's work, a task completed with outstanding success. He was convinced that peace and stability could be obtained only through a crushing defeat of the enemy. The iron discipline of Swedish officers, hired especially for the purpose, molded raw levies into steady soldiers; since Parliament lacked experts in engineering and artillery, Cromwell did not hesitate to also use the services of French and German officers – though in time it proved advisable to keep them apart to prevent Franco-German feuds. What finally emerged was the 'New Model Army,' a standing force and a highly professional army – but an army in which Cromwell and his 'Ironsides' dominated.

Far left. *Prince Rupert of the Rhine, 1619–82. King Charles I's nephew Rupert served with distinction in the Dutch army before joining his uncle on the outbreak of the Civil War. He was one of the most able Royalist commanders, and was not merely the dashing cavalry leader of popular legend (engraving after van Dyck).*

Right. *A Royalist receipt of January 1644 for various armorers' tools.*

Below. *Sir Thomas Fairfax, 1612–71, besieging the Royalist capital of Oxford, 1646.*

This also meant the domination of the Independents' religious sectarianism over the Presbyterianism of Parliament – rejecting Presbyterianism as a compromise with evil.

The reputation Cromwell had established for himself is shown by the impact upon the Parliamentary army of his arrival near Naseby on 13 June 1645. Cromwell then served nominally as Lieutenant General under Thomas Fairfax. The news spread like wildfire among the army that '"Ironside" is come to head us!' The battle was fought on the following day. Though Fairfax was in overall command of the army, Cromwell's

General FAIRFAX with his FORCES before the City of OXFORD

cavalry brought victory after initial Parliamentary setbacks. Instead of committing his forces at the very beginning, he waited to see how the battle developed and then struck the decisive blow with his cavalry. Tactics of this nature were not new – both Gustavus Adolphus and Pappenheim had practiced them on the battlefields of Germany. But, unlike those leaders, Cromwell never headed the charge. He made sure that he maintained a general oversight of the battle in order to meet whatever emergencies arose.

Prince Rupert, of course, had also learned tactics on the continent but, whereas his forces scattered in the pursuit of the enemy after a successful attack (and usually allowed themselves to be diverted by plundering his baggage train,) the discipline instilled into Cromwell's soldiers allowed their commander to rally the forces again immediately, to follow up an attack or to deploy them at other vital points. At Naseby, after the initial success, Cromwell ordered three regiments to pursue the enemy horse and then used the rest of his troops to attack the enemy's exposed left flank. Having beaten them, he penetrated farther and fell upon the Royalist center, which soon collapsed. Charles I had been decisively defeated, a defeat inflicted upon him mainly through the exertions and bravery of the New Model Army. Composed as it was mainly of Independents, this meant not only the triumph of Parliament but the ascendancy of the Independents over Parliament, finally culminating in the Protectorate under Cromwell.

Naseby finally established Cromwell's military reputation among friends and foes alike. The Earl of Clarendon, a hostile witness, had to admit that 'he was one of those men whom his very enemies could not concern . . . for he could never have done half that mischief without great parts of courage, industry and judgment. He must have had a wonderful understanding in the natures and humors of men, and as great a dexterity in applying them . . . he attempted those things which no good man durst have ventured on; and achieved those in which none but a valiant and great man could have succeeded . . . yet wickedness as great as his could never have succeeded nor accomplished those designs, without the assistance of a great spirit, and admirable circumspection and sagacity, and a most magnanimous resolution.'

At Naseby the New Model Army was only one of several armies which Parliament put into the field. In the first Civil War there were no fewer than 21,000 Scots under Leslie. But after Naseby – apart from the Scots – the various separate armies, such as those of Nottinghamshire under Major General Poyntz or Wiltshire and the four western counties under Major General Massey, were absorbed into the New Model Army or disappeared altogether. Within a few years Cromwell had created one highly professional standing English army, an army in which promotion frequently depended on merit, although the principle of seniority did not disappear altogether.

Cromwell's own religious attitudes and, later, his constitutional position were not without influence upon appointments and promotions. A contemporary of Cromwell asserted that he weeded out 'godly and upright-hearted men' to consolidate his own position and replaced them with 'pitiful sottish beasts of his own alliance.' This was hardly an unprejudiced view but, when commanding his own Eastern Association, Cromwell did dismiss Presbyterian officers and later on he also dismissed officers who were opposed to his Protectorate because of their republican inclinations.

The execution of the King crowned the revolution. In six years Cromwell had become a famous and invincible cavalry commander and the creator and molder of the New Model Army. His importance as a factor in the political life of the

Above. *Edward Hyde, Earl of Clarendon, 1609–74. One of Charles I's leading advisers, Clarendon also enjoyed the confidence of Charles II and played a leading part in bringing about the Restoration (portrait by Sir Peter Lely).*

Left. *Thomas, Baron Fairfax. Sir Thomas Fairfax for most of his career, this brave and honorable Yorkshireman was the first captain general of the New Model Army.*

Right. *The Parliamentarians besiege Pontefract Castle, 1648.*

Below right. *The Battle of Naseby, 14 June 1645, was the New Model Army's first battle and a crushing defeat for the Royalists.*

country had risen correspondingly. However, regarding the execution of Charles I, it is open to question whether to attribute any preconceived designs to Cromwell; on the contrary, it seems that he was loath to encourage any such fundamental uprooting of society as would be produced by an act of regicide. The decision to take such drastic and radical action was probably a product of circumstances rather than the result of a long-term plan.

With Charles held prisoner, divisions appeared among the forces opposing him. On the one hand there was the Presbyterian Parliament, no longer radical but anxious about the potential political, social and economic consequences of its previous actions, and which was now ready to restore Charles on condition that he inaugurated Presbyterian forms of worship. On the other hand there were the Independents who controlled a large part of the army, and one feels that to a degree Oliver Cromwell himself desired a religious settlement which would include toleration of the various different forms of Protestant Puritan worship. Issues were further complicated by the fact that the Independents themselves represented a far from homogeneous body, containing a wide spectrum of attitudes ranging from the middle-class toleration of Cromwell to the religious, social and political radicalism of the Levellers. One cannot observe without a sense of irony how the revolution rebounded on Cromwell – the radical of the Long Parliament became the moderator, conciliator and appeaser of his own radicals. By his social and economic background one might have taken him for a Presbyterian, by religious inclination an Independent; in practice the former controlled the latter. Many of Cromwell's subsequent actions are perfectly explicable when one recognizes this fact, and when one also realizes that he was

not a Robespierre and Cromwell rolled into one; he was a commander who very often found himself sitting on the points of his pikes rather than commanding them. Certainly at the political level, he was a man who acted under the constant threat that, unless he represented the army's interests, 'they would go their own way without him.'

Such a situation inevitably placed Charles in a position where he believed he could play one faction against the other to his own advantage. In the ensuing negotiations between Parliament and Charles, Charles and Cromwell and Cromwell and Parliament, mutual suspicions were rife. The three bodies distrusted not only each other, but the New Model Army even distrusted Cromwell. Under these circumstances Cromwell's objective had to be to maintain the unity of the army; he was playing for time he could ill afford – a solution to the problem posed by the presence of the captive King was imperative. Charles's escape and the invasion of England by a Scottish army by agreement with the King precipitated a conclusion. The second Civil War was soon over, and Preston decided not only the Scottish issue but also that of Parliament, and by implication that of the King.

The idea of ending the farce with Charles by bringing him to trial had definitely taken root in the army, and was fostered by the Levellers throughout the country. No doubt, a noticeable shift of public sentiment in favor of the King aggravated the situation and made a solution even more pressing. The burden of the standing army rested heavily on the country and had already manifested itself in various ways. In 1648 the citizens of London, for instance, commemorated the king's accession to the throne 16 years earlier by lighting a bonfire, drinking to his health and clamoring for his return.

It is a matter for conjecture how far the months of September to December 1648 were, for Cromwell, months of inner wrestling, or whether they were months in which the army built up pressure which ultimately forced Cromwell on to the course of regicide. But the stage for the trial was set without Cromwell's initiative and direct knowledge by Colonel Pride's purge of Parliament. The dominating impression the observer gains of these months is really of a man trying to control the course of national events, trying to ride on top of a tidal wave and anxious to prevent the execution of the King so far and as long as he could, without compromising his own position with the army, but ready, if necessary, to bring him to rough justice and exact the supreme penalty. In the final analysis the security of the state was at issue and Cromwell considered himself a lawful power ordained by God 'to oppose one name of authority, for those ends, as well as another.' The decision, however, rested with Charles who, having refused Cromwell's last offer, let events take their course, believing that graves are the precondition for

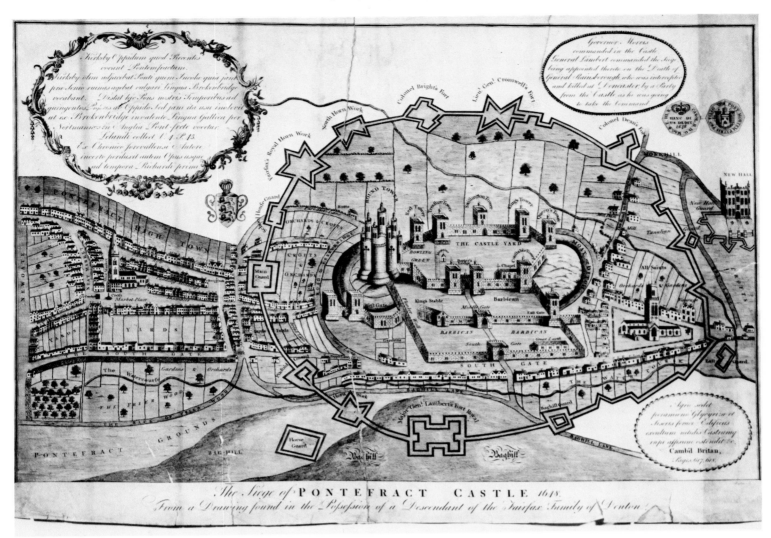

The Siege of PONTEFRACT CASTLE 1648.
From a Drawing found in the Possession of a Descendant of the Fairfax Family of Denton.

A. Seine Kön: May: an dem Block. B. Doctor Juxon. C. Colonell Tomlinson. D. Colonell Hacker. E. F. die 2. Executorn.   C R V N 1649

Far left. *Pikeman's armor of the type issued to the New Model Army.*

Center left. *Cavalry trooper's lobster-tailed helmet, breast and back plates.*

Left. *English pikeman's armor circa 1620. Although armor of this type was used during the Civil War, this suit is too elaborate for wartime manufacture.*

Right. *Steel gauntlet, circa 1650. Gauntlets of this type were worn to protect the bridle arm against sword cuts.*

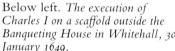

Below left. *The execution of Charles I on a scaffold outside the Banqueting House in Whitehall, 30 January 1649.*

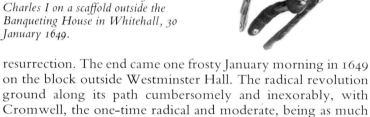

resurrection. The end came one frosty January morning in 1649 on the block outside Westminster Hall. The radical revolution ground along its path cumbersomely and inexorably, with Cromwell, the one-time radical and moderate, being as much its victim as was the aspiring absolutist King Charles I.

Nevertheless, Cromwell's political shortcomings cannot detract from his achievement of creating an army as disciplined and armed as it was effective. The pike, a prominent weapon in 1643, had been virtually replaced by 1650. When the Civil War began pikes and muskets operated together but in a rather disorderly fashion and without the tactical organization deployed on the continent. Pikes served as defense against cavalry attacks but there is also evidence that units equipped with pikes fought one another. Gradually, however, the musket won the upper hand, particularly when it could be used as a club in close combat. Another factor in favor of the musket was the greater mobility and speed of the musketeers, who wore no armor whatsoever. In the first years of the Civil War the distance infantry could cover on foot was 10 to 12 miles a day. With the discarding of armor and the introduction by Cromwell of uniforms – red coats – the average marching distance increased to 15 to 16 miles a day. The closing campaign of the first Civil War, the second Civil War and the subjugation of Ireland and Scotland bore witness to growing professionalism.

After Cromwell had taken over command from Fairfax, he was assisted by a council of officers, whose opinion, however, was also sought in matters of politics. When, in 1647, the army became increasingly dissatisfied with Parliament, the Levellers elected their councils from the rank and file to represent their grievances. Cromwell put down this potentially very dangerous development firmly and ruthlessly.

The Irish campaign in particular demonstrates Cromwell's art of generalship at its best. Politically he divided the Royalist Protestants from Ireland's Roman Catholic leaders, and he achieved an almost perfect cooperation between the army and the fleet and thus mastered his logistics problems. He deployed his troops effectively there, although the terrain was quite different from that in England.

In the subjugation of both Ireland and Scotland a series of

systematically conducted sieges contrasted strongly with early campaigns. Cromwell laid great stress on the role of artillery, which increased progressively in firepower. The sieges of Pembroke Castle, Pontefract and, later, Drogheda showed the devastating effect of Cromwell's siege trains. Both Wexford and Ross began to negotiate for surrender after the first day's cannonade.

The massive deployment of artillery and the concentration of large forces on a narrow front illustrate Cromwell's philosophy of warfare – that in order to force a decision, a decisive victory must be attained. He was not a man of slow maneuver and countermaneuver. General MacArthur's maxim in World War II might well have been Cromwell's: 'There is no substitute for victory.' A war of lengthy maneuvers was bound to deplete troops and stores; long-drawn-out sieges could involve sickness and epidemics among the siege forces. The determination to defeat the enemy completely and speedily so as to restore peace quickly largely explains the ferocity of Cromwell's attacks. He was no sentimentalist about war. Chivalry had no place in a religious conflict fought with the fervor of a crusade: it merely prolonged it. In Cromwell's eyes, war was a bloody and dirty business which must be concluded as quickly as possible by all available means. The cost in human lives of a short but decisive assault would in the long run be lower than that involved in a long, protracted siege. It would also be more economical, argued Cromwell in a letter to Parliament in 1650: 'Those towns that are to be reduced, especially one or two of them, if we should proceed by the rules of other states, would cost you more money than this army hath had since we came over. I hope, through the blessing of God, they will come cheaper to you.' However, there were exceptions. At Clonmel Cromwell's forces were bloodily repulsed and suffered about 1000 casualties.

Cromwell's power of direct command over the entire military forces increased together with the increasing professionalism of the army. During the early campaigns, councils of war had played an important part; their resolutions were not simply arrived at by a general's order, but 'after much dispute.' Councils were still held before the battles of Preston and Dunbar. However, after Fairfax had been replaced by Cromwell as Commander in Chief, the latter made sure that his influence was not only felt but that it also prevailed. He did this by first discussing the issues directly with the most important of his subordinates such as Lambert and Monk, reaching a conclusion, and then, at a full council meeting of the officers, having Lambert explain why and how a battle would have to be fought.

The eve of Dunbar saw Cromwell and Major General John Lambert 'coming to the Earl of Roxburgh's house and observing' (the enemy's) 'posture. I' (Cromwell) 'told him that it did us an opportunity and advantage to attempt upon the enemy, to which he immediately replied, that he had thought to have said the same thing to me. So that it pleased the Lord to set this apprehension upon both our hearts at the same instant. We called for Colonel Monk and showed him the thing: and coming to our quarters at night, and demonstrating our apprehensions to some of the colonels, they also cheerfully concurred.' What Cromwell does not make clear is that it was Lambert who did the 'demonstrating' and explaining to the colonels.

Of course, Cromwell, compared with his contemporaries, fought a war with limited objectives within a territory surrounded by water. That in itself ensured that he did not have to fear invasions from any side; moreover he fought with, strictly speaking, a national army imbued with the same religious and political ethos. The number of mercenaries or foreigners within

Left. *Sir George Wharton, painted by van Dyck, circa 1645. His dress, with its thick leather buff coat and back and breast plates is typical of that of mounted officers on both sides.*

Right. *Major General John Lambert, 1619–83. One of the ablest Parliamentarian generals, Lambert died in prison after the Restoration.*

Below. *Cromwell at Dunbar, 3 September 1650. Cromwell delivered the decisive blow in this brilliant victory at the head of his own regiment of cavalry.*

Le General Major Lambert, 1er Conseiller du Conl de My-lord Protecteur d'Angleterre &c.   B. Moncornet

his troops was small and limited to certain arms like artillery and the engineers. In addition, he fought civil wars, even when these extended to Scotland and Ireland. Civil war is the only form of war in which one knows exactly whom one kills, and this knowledge imparts a brutality and cruelty which completely excludes the slightest element of chivalry. The opponent is not only the enemy but an antagonistic principle which has to be exterminated. This very much applied to Cromwell's wars and their ferociousness, brutality and cruelty were unparalleled in British history up to that time.

In his New Model Army Cromwell had established a rough proportion of one horseman to every two footmen. Among the cavalry the horseman with spear and the heavily armed cuirassier gradually disappeared, making way for the harquebusier armed with carbine, pistol and saber. The dragoons, of which the New Model Army contained one regiment, were simply mounted infantry, whose name derived from the name of the short-barrelled musket they carried. Originating in France and

Germany during the Thirty Years' War, they fulfilled the task of vanguards and reconnaissance units in Cromwell's army. Unlike the rest of the New Model cavalry, dragoons did not wear buff coats but red ones like the infantry, and hats instead of helmets. Tactics of infantry and cavalry alike were not new but adapted from those of the continental armies.

While Cromwell's relationship with his army was excellent at all times, that with Parliament was anything but good. By 1660, 'the predominant influence of the House of Commons in the government of the nation was permanently established.' This had little to do with Cromwell personally. Although Parliament had appointed him Lord General, he sometimes appeared to have been as great an enemy of that institution as had been Charles I and Archbishop Laud: the Long Parliament was first purged by his army, and then violently expelled by him; his own Parliament, the 'Parliament of Saints,' nominated largely under the influence of the army, was carried away in hysteria and in the end committed suicide; and of the Parliaments of the Protectorate, elected on the basis of a new franchise and operating within limits determined by Cromwell, the first was purged within a week and then dissolved, with the second lasting just a week longer than its predecessor. Such a record would hardly suggest a striving toward 'the permanent establishment of the House of Commons in the government of the nation.'

To conclude, however, that Cromwell was an uncompromising enemy of parliamentary institutions would be to distort the actual record – he was indifferent toward any form of government, indifferent to a degree of ignorance. All that mattered to him was that parliament fulfilled that function which he considered of overriding importance: to guarantee the security and liberty of conscience, Papists excluded of course. Unfortunately Cromwell's concern for religious liberty was not matched by one for effective practical politics, leading in the end

Above. *A contemporary broadsheet pays tribute to the achievements of Cromwell in Ireland.*

Below. *The Battle of the Boyne, 1 July 1690. William of Orange secures his grip on the English throne by defeating the deposed James II.*

to a parliament incapable of any positive action. This incapacity was not due to its composition but because of Cromwell's utter inability, shared by his predecessors Charles I and James I, to control parliament by the methods which had been employed by Elizabeth I. James's failure to follow her example had led to the winning of the initiative by the Commons, while the failure of Charles involved him in a predicament that ultimately proved fatal. With Cromwell it put him in a position which almost inevitably branded him as an enemy.

The methods by which Elizabeth so effectively controlled her parliaments were electoral maneuvering, patronage and the development of a nucleus of experienced privy councillors and royally controlled Speaker of the House, in Parliament itself. In the last years of her reign these methods were challenged both by the development of a Puritan parliamentary machine independent of the Privy Council and also by the Earl of Essex's plan to pack the House but, fortunately for Elizabeth, both challenges were weathered by the political acumen of the two Cecils. The indifference of James I to any shrewd approach in handling the Commons allowed them to turn tables upon him and his son. John Pym, a successor of the Cecils but working against Charles I, controlled patronage, the Speaker and the front bench. With his death in 1643 such control ceased and Parliament dissolved into fragmented interest groups, finally purged by Colonel Pride.

Whatever there may be said against the Rump Parliament, it nevertheless provided the most systematic government of the interregnum; 'it governed efficiently, preserved the revolution, made and financed victorious wars and carried out a policy of aggressive mercantile imperialism,' the basis of Britain's future world power. Its managers were a small group of determined and single-minded men such as Sir Arthur Hesselridge and Thomas Scott, stout republicans all. In their eyes, republics alone were the political systems capable of producing a commercial empire. On the other hand, their policy of mercantile aggression, as exemplified in the Navigation Acts, was diametrically opposed to the sentiments of the Independents whom Cromwell represented; it was the policy of an 'oligarchy' and therefore detested by that body which had really made the revolution – the army.

In the absence of a firm extension of the hand of the executive in the Commons, it was inevitable that policymaking would be surrendered to that group which was sufficiently organized to wield political power. For the Independents the only alternative was either to organize themselves equally as well, or to remove their rivals by force. Their sentiment being largely that of the army, the result was expedient, swift and clear-cut – the Rump was ejected by force.

What followed was the Barebones Parliament, dominated not by an oligarchy but nominated on the basis of lists drawn up by the Independent sects; the oligarchy was replaced by an equally well-organized small body of radicals which stood in place of the broken Levellers: Anabaptists and Fifth Monarchy men, supported and controlled by Cromwell's alter ego, Major General Harrison. It does nothing to recommend the political acumen of Cromwell as a parliamentarian that, in contrast to

Above. *General George Monck, Duke of Albemarle, 1608–70. Captured while in the King's service, Monck joined the Parliamentarian army and fought in Ireland during the Second Civil War. A leading architect of the Restoration, Monck served on Charles II's council and earned popular acclaim by remaining in London during the Plague of 1665.*

Left. *This vigorous contemporary engraving shows William's troops fighting their way across the Boyne.*

the extreme wing of his own army, he himself had failed to recognize the root of the trouble of the Rump's failure and therefore took no action, despite the fact that the Parliament was one of his own choosing. Having urged them to make good laws, he withdrew, refused to sit on committees to which he had been elected, and expected Parliament to manage itself. Hence Harrison and his men took control to the extent that, within six months, the moderate sections within it 'surrendered back to the Lord General the powers which, through lack of direction, they had proved incapable of wielding.'

In response, Cromwell, far from having a plan of his own, four days after the dissolution, accepted a new constitution devised by Major General Lambert and his party of more moderate senior army officers, another piece of evidence of the total absence of any grand design on Cromwell's part.

This constitution invested Cromwell as the Lord Protector and altered the franchise, not by changing the social base of representation, but by cutting down borough representation and greatly increasing county representation. This really meant a shift from the boroughs, where patrons and parliamentary managers had built up their forces in Parliament, to the county gentry. The latter were seemingly independent of patronage and, being freely elected from within the fold of the Puritan Independents, they would naturally agree with aims and methods of Cromwell's rule. Individual patronage would be replaced by government patronage. But, having taken the first step, Cromwell failed to take the second: no direct and effective management of the House was attempted, with the result that into the power vacuum created stepped Hesselridge, Scott, Bradshaw and others who had managed to get themselves elected into the House from which they had been purged in 1653. Needless to say, in the end they were ejected, as they had been before. What followed was a policy of political makeshift and improvisation – the second Protectorate, but no consistent policy.

Paradoxically Cromwell and his army were one another's greatest liability. For Cromwell the army was the base of his power and, in the absence of a political counterforce, his military force was the only pillar of support and reliance. Consequently he was not always his own free agent when making political decision. With the army Cromwell stood – without it he would fall.

Cromwell's singular failure to put any tangible institution with clearly defined powers and limitations in place of the monarchy, which he had helped to depose, made him a liability to the army because, in essence, he also failed to devise an acceptable constitutional framework within which a standing army would have its proper place. This placed the army in a position outside what had hitherto been considered as constitutional in England. Consequently, by 1658, and even more so two years later, the majority of Englishmen who desired nothing more than a return to constitutional legality regarded Cromwell's army as a glaring extra-constitutional institution to be done away with. Cromwell's failure as a politician ensured the unpopularity of any standing army in Britain for the next 150 or so years.

Cromwell was brilliant as a military leader of men and brilliant in his generalship – but it was a brilliance which relied on the successful adaptation of techniques and tactics already in practice elsewhere. As his campaigns in Ireland and Scotland showed, he was also as bold a strategist as he was a tactician. Yet to evaluate his position in relation to his European military contemporaries is virtually impossible, since he never had to face men of the caliber of Gustavus Adolphus, Wallenstein, or Tilly – the master generals of the Thirty Years' War.

CHAPTER IV

ARMY AND ABSOLUTISM
IN FRANCE

Under the guiding hands of Cardinals Richelieu and Mazarin, during the second half of the seventeenth century, the French monarchy had established its reign firmly throughout France. The religious wars had come to an end, the nobility had been subordinated to the crown and the opposing estates had been reduced to a state of political impotency. France was a unitary state and had an absolute monarchy epitomized and personified in Louis XIV, who, after the death of Mazarin, exclaimed: 'Now gentlemen it is time that I shall rule. You shall support me with your advice if I ask you for it.'

Louis XIV ruled with absolute authority. Believing that the King possessed this authority by divine right, it was taken for granted that his training and insight was therefore superior to that possessed by any other man. He concentrated all power in his own hands, refusing to share any part of it with anyone, even with members of his own family; even his private life was used to enhance the public display of his majestic divinity, representing the personification of the French state.

The French people accepted this absolutism; its right to dominate the life of millions was not doubted. After the extensive period of internal civil strife in the sixteenth century, the desire for peace, order and effective authority was paramount. One not only kissed the hand of the king, one respected him almost like a deity. For a long time no objection was raised, even though Louis XIV's personal regime meant the continuation of the unequal distribution of social burdens and privileges. It was accepted that it did not exclude acts of personal arbitrary action; that the subject was virtually nothing other than the tool of the whim of the monarch; that Louis' policy involved France in a whole chain of wars of aggression which sapped the lifeblood of France, as well as straining France financially and economically beyond its resources. On the contrary, it may be suggested that the French basked in the glory of the Sun King.

Under his rule France experienced the strongest concentration of power she had so far possessed, power which attracted the whole of Europe but also limited him in the field of foreign policy. The hegemonic ambitions of Louis XIV, in spite of great territorial gains, could not be realized simply because Britain and the Habsburgs blocked any further French expansion. All the more intensive, however, was France's intellectual and artistic predominance. Since 1648 France was considered the motherland of civilization. The influence of the French language, philosophy, literature, poetry and theater was tantamount to a world conquest. The culture of the Versailles court and its luxurious lifestyle found admiration and imitation throughout Europe. The machinery of state, built and refined by Richelieu and Mazarin, was so efficient that it continued to work successfully for a long time, even after Louis XIV's reign.

France was the richest and most populated country in Europe. It would have remained the wealthiest if its policy of war, its expensive buildings and the squandering lifestyle of the Age of the Baroque had not overtaxed the physical and economic resources of the nation. The political purpose of its economic strength was not based on any idea of individual happiness but on the intention to serve the glory of the state, to enrich its fame and power. While its power shone in its fullest glory, however, the seeds of decay and downfall were already present.

This strong, secure state was the result of a highly centralized administration and the exercise of strict discipline in all spheres of life. The king ruled with the assistance of a cabinet comprising only three able ministers for finance, military affairs and foreign policy. Because they were experts in their respective fields, they could influence royal decisions, but the final decision was made and the last word spoken by the king. The bureaucracy was divided into various *ressorts* representing the executive

branches of the state administration. The decisions of the cabinet were handed on for execution to *intendants* who, with full executive powers, ruled the provinces and cities, responsible only to the king. They could be dismissed and replaced at any time. The higher nobility was deliberately drawn into the court at Versailles; their tasks were limited to local administration and the carrying out of the lower judicial functions. Ancient privileges and special regional rights were, with a few exceptions, removed. The *parlements*, the local courts of appeal in Paris and other cities, were completely deprived of their powers. An army of royal civil servants ran the bureaucracy and ensured the execution of royal edicts.

This development was paralleled by a thorough change in the military forces, which the sovereign now required in the form of a standing army. This in turn required a considerable amount of money derived from general taxation. To obtain the necessary revenue required a strict centralization of the financial administration. The power of the estates to dictate the granting of money supplies had been broken. The old concept that general welfare was guaranteed only when the requirements of the sovereign did not reduce the property and welfare of the individual was abandoned. The subjects had to carry the burden if the state was to maintain its stability. Direct and indirect taxation increased significantly, and, as long as general prosperity existed, the state's revenue increased correspondingly. The Minister of Finance, Jean-Baptiste Colbert, directed the nation's finances with great care and circumspection. He was anxious to exhaust all possible sources of revenue, but was reluctant to increase taxation. However, as time went on, he found it difficult, if not impossible, to balance the budget of the state with the expenditure required for the hegemonic policies of Louis XIV. His aim was to establish economic self-sufficiency with a favorable balance of trade; this was to be achieved by ventures in foreign policy which, at the expense of other countries, would increase the power of France. He was the inventor of mercantilism, according to which national wealth rested on the monetary resources of the state, resources achieved by the export of goods and services. The unitary state was also a common market, which did away with local and regional tolls but expanded the network of roads and waterways, supported trade and commerce as well as overseas trade. Manufacturing industries were subsidized. To ensure that surplus production was exported abroad in order to increase the royal revenue, Colbert protected infant French industry by tariffs and prohibited the export of raw materials. The attempt to expand France's economic power through overseas expansion, however, aroused the enmity of Holland and Britain.

The social structure, at first glance, remained the same as in the Middle Ages. Nobility, clergy, burghers and peasants seemingly appeared as a body of subjects subordinated to the crown, though living side by side in great social inequality. The king held all the power, the feudal estates all the rights.

The nobility, being the First Estate or class, was reduced or deprived of its political functions but it still possessed its property, was exempt from taxation, and enjoyed the exercise of patrimonial jurisdiction, pensions and other sinecures. By these

Previous Spread. *The second siege of Besançon, May 1674.*

Left. *Louis de Bourbon, Prince de Condé, 1621–86.*

Right. *Cardinal Mazarin, 1602–61.*

Below. *French warships repulse the Duke of Buckingham's ships in their attempt to relieve the Huguenot stronghold of La Rochelle, 1627.*

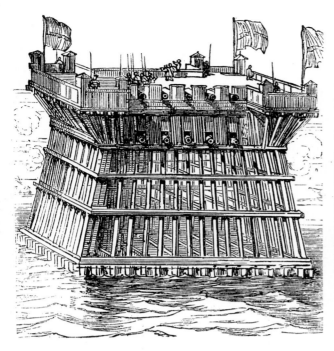

privileges Louis XIV tied the nobility to his crown. He particularly favored it by granting it commissions in the army. To
the privileged nobility also belonged the upper ranks of the
clergy.

The Second Estate was formed by the *haute bourgeoisie*, some
members of which Louis elevated to the nobility of service.
Since the deficit in the royal household continuously got larger,
Colbert vastly increased the number of purchasable offices
and thus introduced venality in office holding; this resulted
in a spread of the privileges and the monopolization of many
sources of income, be they in trade or commerce, in the hands
of a few families. Merchants, bankers and manufacturers thus
began to form independent circles in the cultural life of France.

Most of the population belonged to the Third Estate, deprived of any political rights and privileges and carrying the full
burden of taxation; they performed feudal services on the estates
of the nobility. The Fourth Estate, the peasants, were in a parti-

cularly depressed state since agriculture was held back in favor
of emerging industry by prohibitions of exports and the holding down of prices for agricultural produce, to allow cheap
bread for urban workers in lieu of raising their wages. On the
day of the storming of the Bastille, 80,000 workers were in
Paris; an urban proletariat was emerging.

The social structure of the absolutist state also influenced the
structure of the army, the central pillar of French absolutism.
Upon it rested the prestige of France. Although the country had
possessed a powerful army under Cardinal Richelieu during the
first half of the seventeenth century, it was not a unified institution or the backbone of absolutism; it was the private
property of the colonels and captains who, empowered by the
king, recruited their soldiers.

To achieve his political aims, however, Louis XIV required a
strictly disciplined, well-trained and reliable army. This was all
the more necessary after such victorious generals as Condé and
Turenne joined the nobility's uprising known as the Fronde, in
the middle of the war against Spain. The army had therefore to
be dedicated solely to the king. By 1640 the French army
amounted to 100,000 men. Changes were made when Louis
XIV began to control things himself; under his Minister of War,
Le Tellier (1603–85) and his successor, his son the Marquis de
Louvois (1641–91), a thorough reform was carried out and the
army more fully integrated into the state. The external form
was maintained, such as the division into regiments and companies as military, economic and administrative units; so was the
structure of command. The internal structure, however, needed
changing. The most important measure introduced was the
transfer of supreme command to the king. The mercenary
elements were eliminated – every soldier was now the soldier of
the king, a factor underlined by the swearing of a personal oath
of allegiance. Some of the former colonels retained their posts,
but their troops became the property of the sovereign; the
colonels were now servants of the state. Gradually their rights of
jurisdiction over their troops were eliminated as was their right
to appoint their own officers. The granting of a commission was
now the right of the king, as was any promotion. Auditors were
introduced who, in the name of the king, exercised jurisdiction
and monitored the behavior of each unit. Strict military discipline was introduced, although corporal punishment was not
applied.

As in any other army of the time, the main problem was to pay soldiers promptly and punctually. This function was taken over by the state as well. Increased revenue had to be raised, and one consequence, among others, was the emergence of a modern bureaucracy which dominated administration. The *intendants*, subject to the Minister for War, had full powers of military administration, including the responsibility for supplies when the army was on the march. It was up to them to pay the soldiers punctually and to prevent any misappropriation of funds. This implicit distrust of the officers was fully justified – there were numerous instances when officers had to be reprimanded or threatened with severe penalties for financial irresponsibility. The soldier was supplied with everything he needed. Throughout the country arsenals and depots were established for the supply of equipment, and a medical corps was formed.

The standing army maintained the principle of voluntary recruitment. However, since the Crown did not want to deplete the number of peasants and workers, as many foreigners as possible were recruited. Swiss, Italian, German, Hungarian, Scots and Irish soldiers formed their own regiments. In times of peace the army was not dissolved but the nucleus of each

Above left. During Richelieu's siege of La Rochelle a fortified mole was constructed to seal the city off from the sea.

Below left. Geometrical fortifications developed by Vauban.

Right. King Frederick William I of Prussia, 1688–1740.

Below. King Louis XIV of France watches the progress of a siege.

Far left. *Vicomte de Turenne,*
1611–75.

Left. *Claude Louis Hector, Duc de*
Villars, 1653–1734.

Below left. *The family of Jean-*
Baptiste Colbert, Louis XIV's
financial expert.

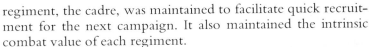

Right. *John Churchill, Duke of*
Marlborough, 1650–1722.

Far right. *Prince Eugene of Savoy,*
1663–1736.

regiment, the cadre, was maintained to facilitate quick recruitment for the next campaign. It also maintained the intrinsic
combat value of each regiment.

Louis' expansionist aims, however, were out of proportion
to the numbers of voluntary recruits he could obtain and, very
much against his original intention, forcible recruitment had to
be resorted to in rural districts, sometimes by drawing lots.
Also, in November 1688, the Minister for War reintroduced
militia regiments, which had had their origin in medieval France
and had since almost disappeared. They were to serve in garrisons and fortresses. By 1670 France's standing army amounted
to 138,000 men, a century later 290,000, and, by the beginning
of the French revolution in 1789, 173,000.

An entirely new innovation was the building of a line of
fortresses reaching from Dunkirk to the Pyrenees to protect the
country against foreign invasion. Even during the Thirty Years'
War, Spanish troops had managed to penetrate as far as Paris.
This new work was essentially the product of Sébastien le
Prestre de Vauban (1633–1707), 'the King's Engineer.' He built
90 fortresses, all based on precise mathematical calculations,
containing depots and arsenals. Their purpose was not primarily
to provide an unbroken line of defense, but rather a secure base
for any offensive operation.

The French art of building fortifications at the end of the
eighteenth century developed with the rising age of technology.
The trained engineer and mathematician replaced the traditional artisan architect. The universal soldier of the time, the
most educated individual in the army, was the engineer, who
not only built fortresses but specialized in improving and inventing new arms.

Before military garrisons were built, the bulk of the soldiers
were still quartered with civilians, whose relations with one
another were strictly laid down in a special manual devised for
this purpose. New uniforms, unified leadership, common training and common arms and equipment were the foundations of
the army's discipline, with the primary purpose of maximum
efficiency.

In time the old colonels had been replaced and the officer
corps had become the domain of the nobility; it was another
way of subordinating a potentially rebellious nobility to the state.
The French nobility soon considered the commission as its
exclusive privilege and closed itself off from other social strata.
The extent of Louis' warfare, however, severely decimated it;
three sons and one grandson of Colbert were killed in action in
the years between 1688 and 1702. There were no longer enough
noblemen to make the number of officers required. This in turn
introduced venality in the holding of commissions – the sale of
officer patents. The positions of supreme command from the

colonels upward remained a preserve of the nobility, however,
while the sons of the second estate became the subalterns.
Soldiers of the king's bodyguard who had particularly distinguished themselves were promoted to *officiers du fortune*, but
the highest rank they could obtain was that of captain.

For a long time the army of Louis XIV was regarded as the
best when considering performance and organization. Marshal
Turenne (1611–75) was seemingly invincible until he met
Prince Eugene and the Duke of Marlborough during the Wars
of the Spanish Succession. At the beginning of these wars, the
French army was allied with the Elector of Bavaria, Max Emanuel, a general of great ability, and it was intended to unite the
armies operating in Italy and Germany and then to make a
thrust toward Vienna. Max Emanuel was not only a good
general, he was also very ambitious and the refusal of the
Emperor to elevate him from an elector to a king, as he had done
in the case of the Elector of Brandenburg in 1701, led him to
seek his royal fortune in alliance with the French king.

In 1704, however, the Imperial forces gained the upper hand
when the Duke of Marlborough marched southward toward
the Danube against the will of the government in London. In
the true tradition of the strategy of attrition, engagements were
avoided at first, and maneuver was met by countermaneuver.
But when the allied forces defeated a Bavarian contingent and
they were able to cross the Danube, the possibility of a decisive
battle was envisaged. The supreme command was divided,
however, one part of the allies being commanded by Marlborough and Prince Ludwig von Baden, the other by Prince
Eugene. French and Bavarian troops then managed to gain
a seemingly unassailable position. Max Emanuel played for
time, hoping that the longer he held out the stronger the

possibility became that Marlborough would have to withdraw and return home on orders from London. However, Eugene and Marlborough decided to attack the Bavarians at Blindheim (Blenheim) near Augsburg on 13 August 1704. The allies enjoyed a slight numerical superiority, but it was not that which secured their victory but their superior generalship. Although the allied French and Bavarian troops were taken by surprise, Eugene's attack on the enemy's left flank was temporarily halted by the French. But while they held one another in check, Marlborough succeeded in breaking through the middle between Blindheim and Ober-Glauheim, scattering the center of the enemy's forces and then attacking the flanks and the rear. The French and Bavarians at Blindheim had to capitulate. The myth of French invincibility had been broken, Louis XIV's territorial ambitions had been checked once and for all, and his hegemonic policy had been broken. Nevertheless his army organization served as a model for many of his contemporaries.

In fact, his rule had inaugurated a military revolution. For the first time a new type of soldier, the professional soldier in the service of a dynasty, the *miles perpetuus*, made his appearance, replacing the mercenary and the *Landsknecht*. True, the beginnings of this development were already visible in Wallenstein's

Left. *The Duke of Marlborough discusses plans for the siege of Bouchain with his chief engineer, Colonel Armstrong.*

Below. *The Battle of Blenheim, 13 August 1704.*

Right. *This tapestry, completed in 1715, is one of a series commemorating Marlborough's victories in the War of Spanish Succession.*

Top and above. *Silver medal commemorating the victories of Marlborough and Eugene.*

Left. *A holster cover used by Marlborough.*

Below left. *Another part of the Duke's holster covers.*

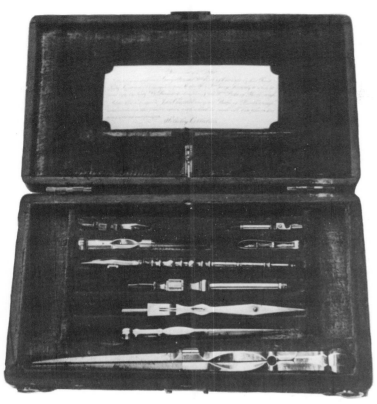

Above. *A case of mathmatical instruments used by Marlborough.*

Below. *Plan of the Battle of Blenheim. The most remarkable of Marlborough's victories was this defeat of the French forces of Marshal Tallard in 1704.*

army, but their full results were cut short by his assassination. He had left a nucleus with which the Habsburgs could continue, but Louis XIV's army subsequently became the model to be followed.

In contrast to his historical predecessor, the soldier was now dependent upon the existence of the state for which he served. Also, in contrast to the former mercenary, he was subjected to the severest discipline and acquired an extensive and thorough basic training before being thrown into combat. He was a small cog within a highly complicated war machine, the product of new tactics and arms technology. He was part of a firmly disciplined body of men, not of a band of warriors who strolled toward the enemy, the battle dissolving quickly into individual engagements. A strictly disciplined body of men also had to apply its weapons systematically. Therefore every part had to react promptly to a central command and with great precision to maintain the order of battle. Within the framework of this structure every soldier fulfilled a precise function. And in order to fulfill the purpose of combat he had to transform the orders of his commanders into immediate action. The professional ethos also produced solidarity between comrades and superiors and led to a community of a unique sociological type.

The mercenaries had deteriorated into brutal bands, a pest to friend and foe alike. Only with the greatest of effort could they be kept within the bounds of discipline. Originating with the rise of the cash nexus, they were always dependent on the solvency of their masters; they were military entrepreneurs. But, despite their articles of war, there was never any real possibility of the establishment of a military tradition, let alone the tradition of a particular military group. They were not tied

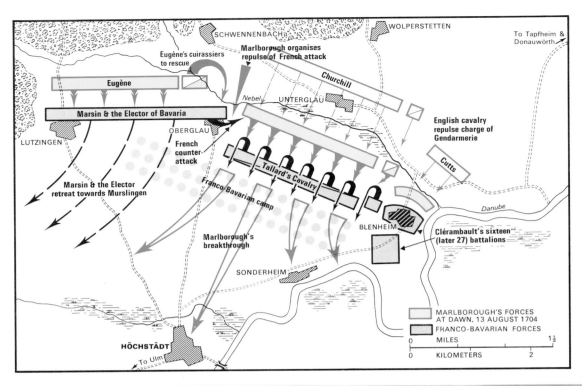

Above. *A grenadier lighting his grenade.*

Below. *The Battle of Ramillies, 23 May 1706, a telling defeat for the French under Marshal Villeroy at the hands of Marlborough.*

to any state, their officers rarely shared a common social background and, more often than not, they degenerated into an undisciplined band. They were dependent on their own supplies, and were therefore accompanied by an immense train which was even more difficult to keep in proper order than the mercenaries themselves. The lack of any medical corps often caused a substantial depletion of their numbers through illness and disease. Even the strictest of mercenary captains regretted condemning many of the men they sent to the gallows simply because they were the ones who had had the bad luck to be caught plundering. The new infantry tactics and the introduction of firearms had furthered their existence because what counted was the number of mercenaries one could put in the field. Therefore every prince hiring them was intent upon putting the largest possible number in the field, irrespective of whether or not he could pay for it. Consequently, pay remained in arrears and, since every man has to live, they plundered wherever they could; they also mutinied, with all the associated consequences. The original intention of selecting mercenaries carefully according to character and ability could never be put into practice. These were the shortcomings which made any reforms such as Emperor Maximilian I attempted abortive.

It was the achievement of the absolutist monarchy as exemplified by Louis XIV which put an end to these basic evils step by step. With the integration of all the military forces into his absolutist unitary state, he transformed the disadvantages of keeping a standing military force into an asset of the highest military efficiency. According to his example, other sovereigns throughout Europe created military legislation which promoted military discipline from its very foundations. This legislation, often called 'Articles of War,' had little in common with similar articles existing among the mercenaries. It provided an absolute yardstick for soldierly ethos and behavior, and contained, next to a catalog of soldierly duties, judicial and disciplinary measures which secured internal order. In great detail it told the soldier what and what not to do while in garrison or on a campaign, and informed him of the punishment to expect for any contravention. The articles of war also determined the relationship between subordinates and superiors. At the beginning of this list of duties was a paragraph stressing that an obedient, brave and decent soldier was also a true Christian, who would therefore regularly attend church services. The heaviest penalties were meted out to rebels, mutineers, deserters, thieves, plunderers, marauders and rapists as well as excessive drinkers. Considering the recent historical background there was every reason to list every conceivable offense. Once the recruit had thoroughly familiarized himself with these articles, he was taken under oath, and thereafter they were read to him time and gain to ensure that they were never forgotten.

Like the mercenary armies before it, the new standing army divided itself into three main groups: infantry, cavalry and artillery. The branch which at first provided the greatest difficulties for Louis XIV was the cavalry, because the French nobility was loath to part with its medieval traditions – it was reluctant not to fight with heavy armor and, although light cavalry had come to the fore, they preferred German mercenaries to fulfill this function. But in time they, too, came to accept it. The basic formation was the regiment: it was the largest closed body of troops and consisted of infantry companies and cavalry squadrons respectively. This form of organization was the most suitable for administrative reasons. Each regiment had its own contingent of troops responsible for recruitment and supplies. But, while the regiment was primarily an administrative unit, the battalion was the primary tactical unit in combat. On the battlefield several battalions could be combined into a brigade under one commander. Larger formations did not yet exist, as the principle of mixed arms was still unknown. Therefore in peacetime one served only in the regiment and the company.

In the course of the eighteenth century the artillery gained its own importance and recognition as a separate branch, equal in status with infantry and cavalry. It took some time to overcome the traditional prejudices of the infantry and cavalry against this purely *technical* weapon, and for a long time it was reserved for the lower orders of society. In peacetime, like the other two branches, it was divided into regiments and companies; in time of war it was formed into batteries.

The mercenaries and the *Landsknecht* already had their own engineering units. With the development of modern fortress war, these technical auxiliaries were now required even more and from them ultimately emerged the modern engineer, another separate branch of the army.

The structure of the army in peacetime actually meant that generals had no practical work to do since, above the regiment, there were no positions of command. They were therefore entrusted with other posts such as that of governor or other offices of state. During the war they led army contingents of varying size, either within the existing order of battle or as

Guerard inue

GRENADIERS.

Chaque Regiment d'Infanterie a une compagnie de Grenadiers qui n'ont ni pique ni dra:
peau, ils sont armé de fusil depeé et bayonnette, et d'une grenadiere pendant en bandou:
liere, le Roy Crea en ... une compagnie de 100. Grenadiers à cheval tous gens choisis et
en fit M.' de Riotot Capitaine ils marchent à la tete de la maison du Roy Sans y être
compris, la recruë'sen fait des troupes de l'armée, et celle des Grenadiers a pied de leurs Reg.

Les Cavaliers sont app.
ils sont armé de mous:
cela sappelle vedette ..
de rang dans l'armée r
pour armes le fuzil le

independently operating formations. The military supreme command was in the hands of a field marshal with a wide spectrum of duties. For the duration of a campaign he was surrounded by a body of military advisers, a very select group to which the term general staff was applied, but it was not the general staff within the modern meaning of the term.

The standing army also required continuous drill in peacetime, and training manuals were written and issued with which all training had to conform. Less than a century before, training was left in the hands of the individual bodies of mercenaries.

Army uniforms were rather colorful and corresponded, insofar as a military uniform allowed, with the fashion of the day. But first and foremost they fulfilled a military function. The first basic uniform was introduced in the armies of Gustavus Adolphus, followed by Cromwell's red coats and those of the French army designed in Paris. At first French uniforms were rather elaborate but, within a relatively short time, functional needs predominated. The French army wore white coats with facings of different colors. The Bavarian Elector Max Emanuel dressed his troops in light blue, the Russians used dark green and the Austrians, white. Prussian troops wore dark blue, since Frederick William I was determined to use as much as he could of Prussia's own resources; Prussia produced its own cloth and the only dye which they could manufacture and which would stand all weathers was dark blue. Indeed, during the reign of Frederick William I and his son Frederick, Prussian military fashions pushed French influences into the background.

Of course, colorful uniforms also served as a demonstration of power by the individual princes, particularly on the parade ground. But they served also a more practical purpose: in battle vision was often obscured by dust and smoke and the color of the uniform allowed the commander to estimate the number of troops confronting him.

Departments of the military bureaucracy directed the entire economic administration of the army. Their staffs, too, had to be well trained and efficient because on them in turn depended the efficiency of the entire army. Regimental and company chiefs were no longer military entrepreneurs in the old sense, but nevertheless one of their major tasks was to dedicate themselves to the adequate supply of their troops. This applied particularly at the company level. The prince, the chief and owner of the army, had delegated responsibility for this to company commanders, who received money and supplies for their troops, plus additional funds for the recruitment of new soldiers. The recruitment fund was a particular source of complaint since it helped the company commander to increase his own income. Wherever he could impress or recruit soldiers cheaply the surplus went into his own pocket; the same applied to supplies. In addition certain weapons, and other equipment such as horses, were often the personal property of the company commander, particularly in the French army; to take over a company required personal wealth and property.

Every general and colonel had his own lifeguard, which was usually the first company of the regiment. He was their 'chief.' But, as already indicated, in peacetime generals and colonels did very little practical military work – they left the task of working with the troops to a deputy or lieutenant colonel; the lifeguard, life company or *Leibkompanie*, if not commanded by the chief

VALIERS ET DRAGONS.
t pourquoy l'on dit une compagnie est composée de 35 maîtres
stolets et de sabre quand ils sont en faction hors du camp
combattent a pied et a cheval selon les occasions et nontpoint
t ou sur les aisles suivant les ordres du General ils ont
let d'un coté une hache pelle ou pioche de lautre

Far left. French horse and foot grenadiers, circa 1710.

Left. French cavalrymen and dragoons of the early eighteenth century. At this period dragoons were trained to fight on horse or foot.

himself, was commanded by lieutenant captains or staff captains, while all other companies were commanded by premier lieutenants, which is roughly equivalent to today's first lieutenant.

In France the influence of the Estates had been removed, so they no longer put any obstacles in the way of the standing army. Things were not as easy elsewhere, however, as the Great Elector of Prussia was to experience. But wherever there was a struggle between a ruler and his estates about maintaining a standing army, it was usually decided in favor of the former.

The French army, like any other at this time, was a state army, but it was not yet in the true sense of the word a national army. It was largely made up from more or less voluntary recruits and contained more foreigners than natives; they were sometimes supplemented by citizens but only in cases of dire emergency. The duty for every subject to perform military service, however, did not exist, and for very good reasons: society and state or monarch did not represent an entity, they existed side by side, the people were excluded from political life and enjoyed no political rights worth speaking of, and their interests were not necessarily, in reality, identical with those of the state. Populations, in the cabinet politics of the Age of the Baroque, were traded like chattels and they consequently may have had little interest in the defense of their country. Armies of that age were not defensive forces but primarily used for conquest, highly qualified and well equipped; this required thorough training in logistics, tactics and control of weapons, and took time to achieve. For this purpose the popular levy was virtually useless.

Nevertheless the medieval laws concerning popular levies were never revoked. Machiavelli was one of the first modern theoreticians of war who advised the prince to base his power not on doubtful mercenaries but upon a patriotic citizens' army according to the Roman example. The implications of this demand, however, were not fully recognized by him insofar as they concerned military discipline and the rigors of military training. There were occasions when princes took recourse to the medieval levy, and attempted to transform it into a kind of national service; Brandenburg-Prussia and Bavaria are outstanding examples. Elector Max Emanuel of Bavaria tried to do this but, his ambitions being far in excess of the country's resources, he failed. Others, like Count Wilhelm von Schaumburg-Lippe, attempted to raise an army exclusively from their own subjects. Considering the small size of his state he became the object of ridicule by his contemporaries and his army always suffered heavily in battle. In the sovereign absolutist state where the subjects were pressed into military service, it was on orders of the sovereign and the idea of national service could consequently strike no deep roots.

Ideological principle was involved in the question of national service. But the profession of arms served specific needs and functions, and it was in the interests of a civilized state strictly to separate the military and civilian populations. Mercantilist principles set natural boundaries to the size of armies. In practice this meant that the productive sectors of the nation, who also did so much for raising its material and cultural riches, had to be exempted from any kind of military service; this applied to all burghers of the towns. Only the lowest layer of society, the daily-wage laborer for instance, could be made available. The net result was that every soldier recruited abroad deprived the enemy of a soldier and retained for the state a working individual. Those exempted had their military service transmuted into money payments in the form of taxation – thereby increasing the royal chest and its military striking power.

The operation of recruitment lay in the hands of the regi-

Right. *A French bronze cannon, circa 1670.*

Below. *Uniforms of French infantry of the sixteenth, seventeenth and eighteenth centuries.*

ments and companies. Recruitment was carried out within one's own boundaries as well as elsewhere. The French army found a rich recruitment ground in the devastated regions to the east of its frontiers; German cities were also profitable areas. Prohibitions and limitations on recruitment existed only in the Habsburg crownlands and in Silesia; permission was given on the basis of contracts, ensuring that the recruitment commander paid a certain sum to the sovereign or the city fathers.

What has been said so far about standing armies does not

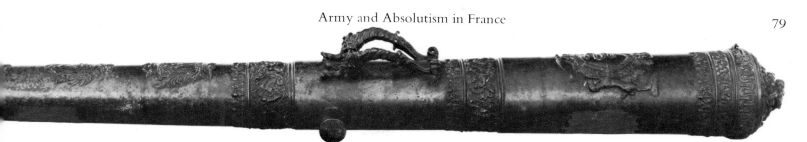

mean that they eliminated all the evils of the mercenary armies. The profession of arms had been considerably improved, though problems still remained. The main difficulty was no longer the financial support of the forces, but raising and replacing them. Armies throughout Europe were getting bigger all the time. The numerical factor played an increasingly important role in existing infantry tactics, which were steadily advancing along with the improvement in firearms.

The large size of an army which had to be paid at all times,

during peace or war, resulted in a reduction of pay for the individual soldier. He was paid roughly three talers per month as compared to the 10–18 guilders in the Thirty Years' War. The times had passed when one joined the army simply because of the profit motive. Nor did the soldier possess the automatic right to gain booty at will: plundering, requisitioning and marauding were offenses which were strictly punished. As a result recruits were less forthcoming.

Furthermore, continuous drill in barren garrisons was

unattractive to many. Nor was there much opportunity for promotion, in contrast to the armies of the mercenaries and *Landsknecht* in which every member had the marshal's, or rather the colonel's, baton in his knapsack. The highest a soldier could rise was to non-commissioned officer. With a few exceptions, in reality the officer corps of the absolutist army remained a closed community.

Stricter discipline did not encourage recruits. Offenses against military discipline were severely punished, and this process was now subject to proper military jurisdiction. Every punishment was meant to constitute an example to the rest. To be beaten by the corporal's stick was still the mildest form of punishment, yet it was considered to be deeply dishonoring. A more severe punishment was riding on a wooden horse or donkey, or being tied to a pole with the feet standing on sharpened poles. Equally severe was being tied hand to feet for several days. Fortification work, particularly pulling a heavily loaded cart to which one was tied with iron rings, was as feared as was running the gauntlet, a punishment introduced particularly for deserters. Because desertion was so frequent it was uneconomic to punish it by death; the deserter was therefore subjected to a kind of punishment which would incapacitate him for only a few days. According to the seriousness of the offense, he had to run the gauntlet several times, the maximum being 36. In a case such as this, however, the punishment was spread over several days, as a soldier could not be expected to run the gauntlet more than 10 times on any one occasion; nevertheless, fatalities did occur. Mutiny was punished by death through shooting, and other forms of capital offenses were punished by the standard punishments also in use for certain breaches of civil law, like death on the gallows, the sword or the wheel.

As volunteers were increasingly hard to come by, recruiting teams took recourse to guile and force, even though the impressed soldier, rebelling at first against his fate, was all the more likely to bring upon himself the wide range of punishment. Forcible recruitment resulted in increased desertion, resulting in even more forcible recruitment; a vicious circle. Desertion proved to be an insoluble problem in the armies of the absolutist age.

Nor did the treatment meted out to the common soldier do much to elevate the standing of the professional army in the eyes of the burghers. They despised it as an institution, while the soldier himself felt like a prisoner in an establishment from which escape was difficult and associated with serious risks. Soldiers could no longer maltreat civilians, at least not in their own country – they maltreated themselves. For this reason the emerging Enlightenment considered the standing army as the greatest evil of the age.

In the higher echelons changes had different implications. It is true that Prince Maurice of Orange had established a socially homogeneous officer corps; but with the integration of the nobility in the absolute state, however, commissions gradually became their exclusive preserve. They became even more of a caste, ranging above the bourgeoisie. United by the same social origin and a personal oath to the king, and with claims to special privileges, the officer's code of honor developed; the officer corps lived a life characterized very often, particularly in France, by rather unmilitary and cavalier habits, aggravated by the venality of office holding. In action, however, they led at the front and not from behind; in the middle of battle they had to be an example to their men. Within the officer corps, the artillery officers were an exception insofar as they lived a separate existence. Technicians and mathematicians, in most cases, they did not share the same social origins and were consequently not considered equals by the rest. This changed only with the changing role of artillery toward the end of the eighteenth century.

On the whole, however, the officer corps of Europe formed an international caste of warriors; on every battlefield where European armies encountered one another, it also became a rendezvous for the European nobility. In Canada at Fontenoy, the officers first complimented one another and then each asked the other to fire the first volley. Their exclusiveness, however, often degenerated into sheer arrogance, particularly toward civilians. To ensure perpetual social homogeneity, Louis XIV established cadet institutes in which the male offspring of the military nobility were educated, ultimately to become officers, an example followed by the Great Elector in 1653, who established a Knight's Academy, but more systematically by his grandson Frederick William I, who established regular cadet institutes.

All this was accompanied by a revolution in tactics. Medieval knighthood did not primarily owe its decline to the invention of firearms, but to the superiority of effective bodies of infantry. In the days of the mercenary and the *Landsknecht*, the main emphasis lay in the superior numbers and mobility of their infantry squares. As already indicated, the rediscovery of the military writers of antiquity supplied Maurice of Orange with new tactical theories. The main organizational unit was the regiment, subdivided into 10 companies, each company about 150 men strong. Its arms consisted of pikes and muskets on support forks, the pikes being about eight yards long. Each company comprised 75 pikemen and 75 soldiers armed with firearms – harquebusiers and muskets. At first the pikemen formed the center of the battle order, flanked on both sides by firearms. It was a broad front divided into three parts, but it was not identical with the company structure, containing between 600 and 750 men and called a half-regiment. Though still large

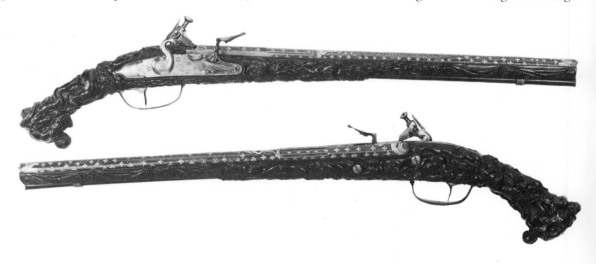

French flint-lock pistols, presented to Louis XIV by the city of Lille. The stocks, of dark walnut, are carved with Hercules skinning a lion.

formations, they were more maneuverable than the large Spanish squares. A Dutch half-regiment covered a front of about 80 yards. To ensure that any breakthrough by the enemy could be held up within a distance of about 150 yards, a formation of the same strength was arranged in the same order, 10 men deep. It was a return to the Roman example. Initially, artillery was used very sparingly: about 10 guns to 10,000 infantry.

The cavalry was subdivided into companies of 100 men arranged to protect the rear and flanks. Gustavus Adolphus developed the reforms of Maurice of Orange, closing up even further the ranks of his infantry which he called brigades, numerically as strong as the half-regiment but integrated with cavalry and artillery. The infantry brigade was now only six men deep, and the introduction of lighter muskets, which did away with the cumbersome forks and used paper cartridges which improved the speed of loading, allowed the infantry to advance six deep, fire and retire behind the pikemen for reloading. Gustavus' main arm was his cavalry, organized in squadrons of 200 to 300 horsemen; its impact had to be so overpowering as to throw the enemy. He placed equal emphasis on his artillery. Toward the end of the seventeenth century, the new French infantry line, the *ordre mince*, made its appearance; it was the first appearance of linear tactics in modern warfare – a result of greater troop maneuverability and progress in arms technology.

The firepower of the infantry increased after the demise of the old musket and harquebusiers. After the Thirty Years' War they were replaced by flintlock muskets of English origin. The combination of paper cartridges, bullet and gunpowder facilitated the loading process. The new musket however, was still vulnerable to the weather and was to remain so until the middle of the nineteenth century. Whereas with the old musket the rate of fire was one round in three minutes, this now increased to five rounds in two minutes. The loading process took about 24 seconds. The new musket weighed nine pounds, about three pounds less than the old one, but its effective range was not much beyond 250 yards; the most effective range was between 80 and 170 yards. Since these muskets were muzzle loaders, it was practically useless to fire in a prone position; to reload, however, the infantryman now required less room and could thus operate closer to his neighbors, which helped to tighten up the formation. The formation could now fire also in a kneeling position while the second line fired above it, the third line being engaged in reloading. Vauban's invention of the bayonet with socket and short horizontal arm was also of decisive importance. The rifle now fulfilled the dual function of firearm and pike; the pikemen had become obsolescent and by the end of the seventeenth century, had disappeared altogether, though the theory was perpetuated – until his defeat at Kolin, Frederick the Great believed that a massed bayonet attack was to be preferred to an aimed volley of muskets.

Nonetheless, it was believed that victory could be achieved only by superior firepower. The introduction of the iron ramrod by Prince Leopold of Anhalt-Dessau, *der alte Dessauer*, improved reloading speed. By thinning out the linear formation to three lines, one hoped to avoid providing the artillery with an all too easy target; moreover, by extending the order of battle in width, there was the possibility of outflanking the enemy.

The thin line was the characteristic of the new infantry tactics, stretching miles across the battlefield. On the whole it was a very fragile formation which had always to avoid losing touch with neighboring companies. To ensure that, the formation had to march at an equal pace, at equal step; running into the attack was impossible. Changes of direction, turning off to the left or the right, was virtually impossible since it would have dis-

organized the entire line. Attack and withdrawal were carried out as one. Natural obstacles, such as villages and woods, were whenever possible avoided.

The tactical basic unit was now the battalion, while the regiment remained intact for organizational purposes, such as administration and logistics. Every battalion was one formation within the line of battle. It comprised approximately 700 men. Attached to each battalion were two light pieces of artillery to strengthen the resistance against the enemy's cavalry attack. The object was to decimate the enemy through continuous fire before the assault was attempted. The battalion was subdivided into divisions and these in turn into platoons. The most effective arrangement consisted in dividing the battalion into four divisions and eight platoons. Each battalion comprised five companies but, in the application of linear tactics, the lines of division very often cut through a platoon. In the center of the battalion was the flag group. Surrounded by NCOs and a platoon of musketeers, the flag group, like the banners of the knights of the Middle Ages, served as a point of orientation during the confusion of battle. Beside the infantryman the grenadier made his appearance, originating in France in 1625, equipped with musket and grenade. In the course of the eighteenth century they became the elite formations. Behind the first battalion came the second within a distance of 200 to 300 yards; they not only supported the front line but had to repel attacks on the flanks. If the numbers permitted, a third battalion followed the second, the entire formation being an elongated square.

The purpose of the cavalry was to protect the flanks until the battle had developed to a stage where they could be used in attack. It was divided into heavy and light cavalry, heavy cavalry, like the dragoons, being infantrymen on horse. They were arranged in squadrons two deep. The basic unit was again the regiment consisting of five squadrons, each squadron having 150 horses and men. Light cavalry was actually a Hungarian invention, first adopted by the Austrian hussars and subsequently becoming an integral part of all European armies. A feature of cavalry attacks was that they were not mounted with the firing of pistols, but with the saber; only in close combat was recourse taken to firearms.

The artillery included light artillery – three and six pounders – used with the battalion front. Their range was about 1000 yards, but they were really effective only at half that distance. Ammunition consisted of cannon balls or bullets and rusty fragments in a linen sack or tin container. Grapeshot was very effective against cavalry, providing the gun crew was well drilled and disciplined. The heavy artillery consisted of 12 and 24 pounders, seven- and eight-pounder howitzers and 10- to 50-pounder mortars. The range of the 12 pounder was about 1200 yards.

Their tactical deployment was related to the position of the line. Reference has already been made to how the light artillery was arranged. Heavy artillery was at first posted in front of the line, but had mainly a defensive rather than an offensive function, except in the case of sieges.

The battle picture was roughly as follows: both lines advanced toward one another at about 15 yards per minute, the cavalry accompanying the infantry at the same pace. Once in firing range, infantry fire began until one side or the other decided that the opportunity to attack with cavalry had come; close combat then followed until one side was thrown back and retreated. One of the drawbacks of linear tactics was the great care that had to be taken to avoid one formation losing touch with another; this weakness was solved, partially, by Frederick the Great.

The crushing victory of Frederick William, the 'Great Elector' of Prussia
over the Swedes at Fehrbellin in 1675.

CHAPTER V

THE RISE OF PRUSSIA

The defeat of the Teutonic Order by the forces of Poland and Lithuania on 15 July 1410 was not the end, but the beginning, of the Prussian state. Several more engagements followed until the combined pressure exerted by military defeat, internal dissension and the German settlers in Prussia compelled the Order to submit. By the Peace of Thorun in 1466, Prussia became a vassal state of Poland; eastward expansion of Germany and Europe had come to an end. A century later during the Reformation, when the last Grand Master decided to secularize the land of the Order, the *Deutschritterorden* in Prussia also came to an end. What remained was the name of the country and the one-headed, black imperial eagle which Emperor Frederick II had given to Hermann von Salza and the black cross upon a white background. The most important remnant, however, was the nucleus of a future Prussian state.

When Frederick William, later known as the Great Elector, of Brandenburg, came to the throne in 1640 he was 20 years old. Some of his territories were still held by the Swedes, such as West and East Pomerania with most of the harbors on the River Oder. His inheritance consisted of five very different and separate territories: Brandenburg – 'the Holy Roman Empire's sandbox,' the Duchy of Cleves, the counties of Mark and Ravensburg, and Prussia. As Duke of Prussia Frederick William was the vassal of the King of Poland. In other words, his possessions were strewn across the north of Germany, touching the northwestern and northeastern extremities of the Reich.

Brandenburg was totally ravaged, and had a population of only a million and a half. Fewer than 10 farmers were found in some villages between the River Spree and the Oder, and they lived hand to mouth. This German territorial state had either to grow strong again or else perish.

With the appearance of Frederick William, the military element stepped to the fore for the first time in the history of Brandenburg. On his mother's side he was descended from the House of Orange and he had spent part of his youth in the Dutch Netherlands, where he paid great attention to the organization of the standing army; this knowledge was transferred to Brandenburg together with French modern arms technology. He was also, however, deeply influenced by Dutch Calvinist thought, which differed from German Lutheranism in that it promoted all state activities for the purpose of its expansion and prosperity.

The Calvinist striving for success in all spheres of life had been one of the driving forces of the Dutch Protestants in their struggle for liberation from the Spaniards. Experience of such a religiously motivated policy of state was vital for Frederick William, as well as its corollary of being personally accountable to God. In accordance with Calvinist creed, he saw himself as a chosen tool of the Lord whose task it was to consolidate his political position, to expand it and thus help his people who were on the verge of starvation.

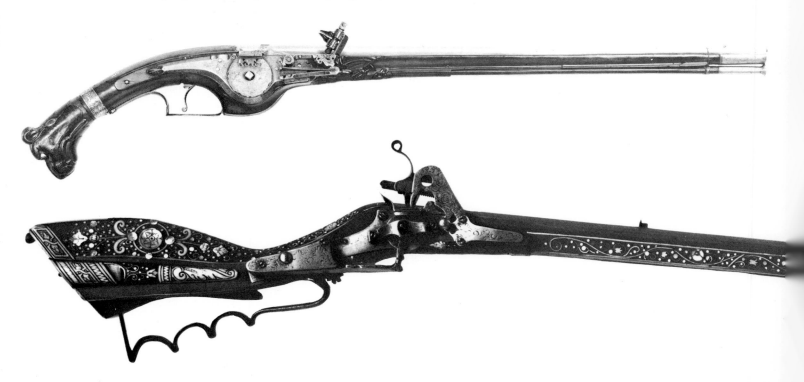

It was not enough to have inherited territory. What the Hohenzollern prince lacked was the effective strength to maintain it – his territorial possessions existed only at the mercy of his stronger neighbors. This in turn had allowed the Estates in each territory to assert their own power and pursue their own interests without considering the impact on the Hohenzollern territories as a whole. His greatest territorial asset was Prussia, which had been spared most of the ravages of war; here the Estates used their position to play off the Hohenzollerns against the Poles. Yet, from an economic point of view, Prussia was more important to Frederick William than was Brandenburg. As Duke of Prussia he possessed immense domains with considerable economic resources and a great number of subjects. This was a direct consequence of the settlement policy of the Teutonic Order, which had concentrated the largest part of the land in its own hands, a large percentage of the population having been reduced to the state of serfdom in the course of the preceding century. The primary economic importance of this population was that it could be taxed without first having to ask the representative assembly of the Estates, and this made Prussia the Hohenzollern's most important single source of revenue.

Another important source of revenue was Königsberg. It exported not only Prussian but also Lithuanian produce, major commodities being wheat, hemp and furs. The Teutonic Order had already attempted to acquire a share of the resulting revenue by introducing an export toll. Then, during the course of the Thirty Years' War, the Swedes occupied Pillau at the exit of the *Frisches Haff* until 1635, although, after that date, the toll revenues reverted back to the Duke of Prussia. Since the Duke of Prussia was still a vassal of the King of Poland at the time, however, the latter demanded his share as well. This his predecessor had to concede, and Frederick William was compelled to accept the situation upon his accession. The revenue of that part of Jülich-Cleves held by the Hohenzollerns was also in Dutch hands.

The political position of the Hohenzollerns in Brandenburg was, relatively speaking, still stable. After all, they represented the resident ruling house. Brandenburg relied on extensive sheep farming and wool production, although this had seriously declined because of the war. Other major sources of revenue were the river tolls levied on the Oder and the Elbe; as the mouths of these rivers were in the possession of other states, however, control of trade lay outside the power of the Hohenzollerns. Stettin, for example, always managed to maintain its predominance over Frankfurt-an-der-Oder.

Thus the legacy left to Frederick William was not an enviable one. In the early years of his rule he relied heavily on the advice of his mother. Upon her initiative several memoranda were drawn up to analyze Brandenburg's problems, but they failed to supply practical solutions. They emphasized the impossibility of continuing the war against the Swedes, but at the same time stressed the need for loyalty toward the Habsburgs and the Holy Roman Empire. How these two policies could be reconciled remained unanswered. But one point was made to which Frederick William paid great attention: the need for an effective standing army, without which the House of Hohenzollern would not be in a position to pursue active politics at all but would simply remain the political objective of others. A policy of general appeasement toward the Estates was recommended.

At first Frederick William tried to pursue a course of establishing cordial relationships with the Estates. He attempted to involve them in discussions about the relationship of Brandenburg with the Holy Roman Emperor, the problem of Pomerania

Above left. *The Great Elector, Frederick William of Prussia, 1620–88.*

Left. *A German wheel-lock pistol, made in Nuremberg, circa 1630.*

Below. *A German wheel-lock rifle of about 1600.*

Right. *The Swedish King, Charles X, 1622–60 overlord of Frederick William and Brandenburg – Prussia until the treaty of Labrau in 1656.*

CAROLVS GVSTAVVS King of Swethens, Goths, & Vandalls, greate prince of Finland, Duke of Esthonia, & Carelia Lord of Ingria & Crowned Añ: Dom̃: 1654. P S excudit

Deutsche Soldaten.

Deutsche Soldaten.

and the question of disarmament. From his experience in the Dutch Netherlands and his observations of the politics of the Estates-General, he expected constructive assistance. But he was to be disappointed. The Estates showed little interest in questions of grand politics; all that mattered to them was the preservation and extension of their own material privileges. This was a lesson Frederick William remembered when formulating his future policy. During the process of joint consultation, it was agreed to investigate the complaints raised about the Brandenburg troops and to reduce the army.

The combat value of the existing army was highly doubtful. Most of the officers and men represented the dregs of society, swept to the surface by the Thirty Years' War. A precondition of forming a new army was the dissolution of the old one. On the other hand, it was imperative to come to an arrangement with the Swedes as soon as possible, and negotiations without the backing of an army would be futile. His endeavors met with limited success, and in 1641 a two-year armistice was agreed between Brandenburg and Sweden. While it relieved Brandenburg from making war, the armistice left the Swedes in the positions which they held in Brandenburg. In other words, the armistice highlighted Brandenburg's political and military impotence. Sweden sacrificed nothing at all, which may have been the reason why Frederick William never exchanged the document of ratification, managing time and again to raise another point in need of further clarification until the general settlement of the Peace of Westphalia in 1648.

As for his predecessors, Frederick William's relationship with Poland was of primary importance. The Stuhmdorf armistice with the Swedes had given the Poles cause for alarm, for they feared that they would now be exposed to military pressure from the Swedes. Frederick William assured the Poles that he would not put Prussia's harbors at the disposal of the Swedes. In

Above left. A German ensign and musketeer of the first half of the seventeenth century.

Above. A fifer and infantry officer of the same period.

general, however, he tried to keep King Vladislav IV of Poland in the dark about his arrangements with the Swedes, so that he could use them as a lever with which to obtain a formal investiture of the ducal crown or the *de facto* assumption of power in Prussia through his deputy. But Vladislav, contrary to Frederick William's plan, insisted that he also appear at the investiture, which finally took place on 7 October 1641. Little less than a month later, on 1 November, Frederick William entered Königsberg and attended the Prussian Diet. The Diet granted him, among other things, the introduction of an excise tax which was to become one of the most important forms of taxation throughout Brandenburg-Prussia. It represented a form of indirect taxation by taxing consumption. As the administration of taxation in Prussia lay in the hands of the nobility, however, this ensured that they did not suffer too much.

The nobility has generally become known as the 'junkers,' yet it is a misleading term because its present-day connotation does not go back farther than the revolution of 1848, when among liberals it became a term of abuse directed against the Prussian nobility. In fact a *Junker* was originally the son of a noble house; in the Middle Ages he often served his military apprenticeship as the esquire to a knight. In more modern armies there was also the *Fahnenjunker*, or ensign, the rank held prior to receiving a full commission.

Moreover, the term as generally used tends to obscure the fact that in Prussia, as elsewhere, the nobility consisted of what, for the sake of convenience, one might describe as the higher and lower nobility. In East Prussia there were the *Grafenfamilien*, the families of the earls and counts, the knights bound to them by feudal obligations, and in the sixteenth and seventeenth centuries that class from which the higher nobility drew country administrators such as the *Landräte*. The greater number of lower nobility during the same period, however, ensured that they ultimately dominated the provincial Diet and to all intents and purposes entered into a lasting alliance with the higher nobility. With the development and extension of demesne farming and the decline of the manorial system came also a substantial increase in the economic power of the Prussian nobility east of the River Elbe. It acquired and usurped privileges which were, in view of Frederick William's need for the assistance of the nobility, confirmed by him in 1653 and remained fundamentally unchanged until the Prussian Reform Movement of the early nineteenth century.

The build-up of the army dates from the spring of 1644, after Frederick William had achieved a degree of internal as well as external stability. The strength of the army varied according to need and circumstance, and only after 1660 was it possible to transform it into a regular standing army. Nevertheless Frederick William and his councillors were clear in their minds about the need for a small, efficient army in Brandenburg-Prussia. Only two objections were raised: the money an army would cost, and the suspicion it would arouse among the Swedes.

Against those objections, however, stood the considerations

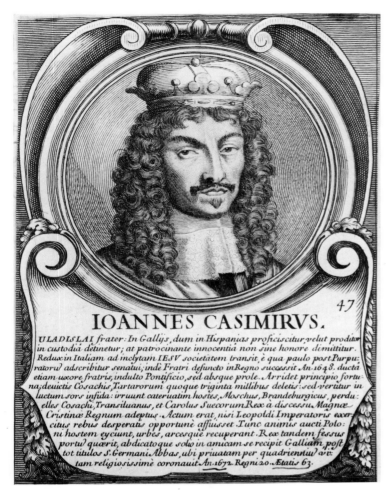

Above left. *King John Casimir, who succeeded his brother Vladislav on the throne of Poland.*

Below left. *King Vladislav IV of Poland, 1595–1648.*

Below. *A more martial portrait of Vladislav.*

in favor of an army, succinctly put in a memorandum submitted in 1644 by Curt Bertram von Phul, a member of the Brandenburg nobility who had served in the Swedish army. Phul argued in favor of an army because its existence would increase the diplomatic prestige of Brandenburg-Prussia; he also made the point that a disciplined standing army would be of considerable economic benefit, as it had proved in the United Netherlands and in Sweden, where the army was one of the driving forces of the infant manufacturing industries and also, by its very needs, stimulated commerce. Though basically sound, the expectations inherent in these ideas were not realized until the eighteenth century.

Frederick William proceeded cautiously with his recruitment program, entrusting it to a close confidant, Johann von Norprath. It was to be conducted in the region of the lower Rhine, in other words away from the close proximity of the Swedes who might become suspicious. The garrison fortresses in Brandenburg and Prussia were also slowly increased. But the core of the new army was built up in Cleves, where, because of the war between Spain and the Netherlands, the Estates-General decided to pull out their forces, thus leaving it to Frederick William. By 1646 approximately 3000 men were garrisoned on the lower Rhine, recruited mainly from Dutchmen and Prussians.

One major problem remained, the endemic problem for most armies at the time, namely how to pay the army. The main contribution came from the Duchy of Prussia, though, because of the Swedes, payments were made secretively and the Estates were circumvented. Councillors and members of the Prussian

Diet, as well as representatives of town and countryside, were approached individually and persuaded to give their support. But there was still a substantial gap between Prussia's contributions and the amount needed. Loans were raised in the cities, but we still do not know all the sources from which the army was financed in its early years.

Major difficulties were encountered in Cleves, for the Estates there were vehement in their opposition to army recruitment and the consequential levying of contributions. The need for an army, its purpose and function in the general context of the policy of Brandenburg-Prussia were explained to them in great detail. It was to no avail – they were willing to grant supplies only if Frederick William would pull the troops out of Cleves. Although Frederick William was willing to concede the point and transfer the troops to the county of Mark, he could only do so once the respective garrisons there had been evacuated by the Imperial troops. Therefore, because of the unreasonableness of the Cleves Estates, Frederick William had little choice other than to raise taxation without consent. This was possible in the countryside but met strong opposition in the cities, where, because of their refusal to cooperate, no administration existed to assess and collect the taxes. Frederick William also encountered the opposition of Austria and the Dutch, who opposed this kind of taxation on political principle. For the time being Frederick William and the Estates could reach no common ground; both sides got themselves involved in an extensive pamphleteering war about the rights and wrongs of taxation without consultation – arguments which, across the North Sea

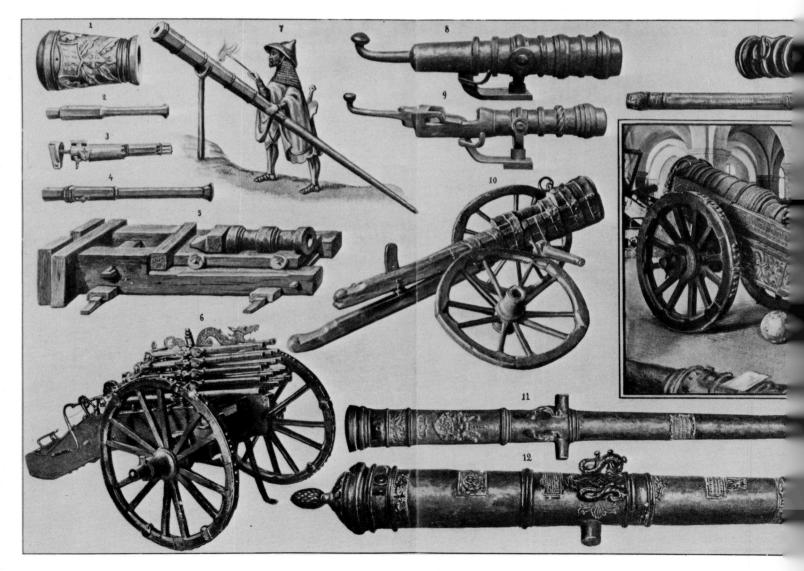

in England, John Pym and John Hampden, among others, had put forward a short time before.

Meanwhile Sweden was turning its attention away from Germany and toward Denmark. Frederick William tried to mediate, but his attempt was ignored. However, the changing military situation compelled the Swedes to give up their occupation of the fortresses of Frankfurt-an-der-Oder and Crossen, which they could have defended only with great difficulty against Imperial troops; Brandenburg-Prussia had to promise that it would not allow these fortresses to be occupied by the Austrians. Obviously this was an embarrassing demand because it was by no means certain that Brandenburg-Prussia had the necessary strength to prevent them, nor whether such forces were strong enough to obstruct the transit of Imperial troops. Apart from that, Brandenburg-Prussia was still, at least formally, the ally of the Habsburgs. After lengthy and protracted negotiations, in which, by force of necessity, the representatives of Brandenburg-Prussia were not always the most honest of men, a treaty was agreed upon and the fortresses evacuated by the Swedes in July 1644. The first soldiers of the new army of Brandenburg-Prussia entered virtually upon the heels of the Swedes.

The Swedes also seemed ready to discuss the question of Pomerania, which Frederick William wanted returned, but, because of his connections with the Empire, Brandenburg-Prussia could not overindulge in such negotiations. The impotence of the state when faced by a major power, however, was demonstrated during the course of the same year when, in order to support the Danes, Imperial troops traversed Brandenburg with impunity, leaving Frederick William in a position he could do very little about.

It was that impotence which caused Frederick William to look for support from any major power ready to give it. During the discussions leading to the Peace of Westphalia feelers were stretched out in all directions. France seemed sympathetic but was not yet ready. Yet, the rise of Brandenburg-Prussia during the seventeenth and eighteenth centuries was facilitated by the Peace of Westphalia in 1648, which brought it important territorial acquisitions. Although, for the time being, Sweden exercised control at the mouths of the Oder and Elbe, Brandenburg-Prussia's position along these rivers ensured it an important role, since they carried by far the greatest part of German exports. In addition, her territorial holdings along the River Weser and the lower Rhine placed her in a key position between Germany's north and south, between the northwest, particularly Hamburg, and the territories southeast of Brandenburg, those of the upper Oder and their neighboring territories. A policy of opening up and expanding the existing network of communications, roads and canals, which continued for over a century, consolidated that position. It allowed the export of Prussian grain into the densely populated regions of northwestern Europe, and this trade contributed to Brandenburg-Prussia recovering relatively quickly from the

Cannon of the fifteenth, sixteenth and seventeenth centuries. This plate depicts an assortment of weapons, including some early breech loaders (left center), and multibarrelled weapons for use at close range.

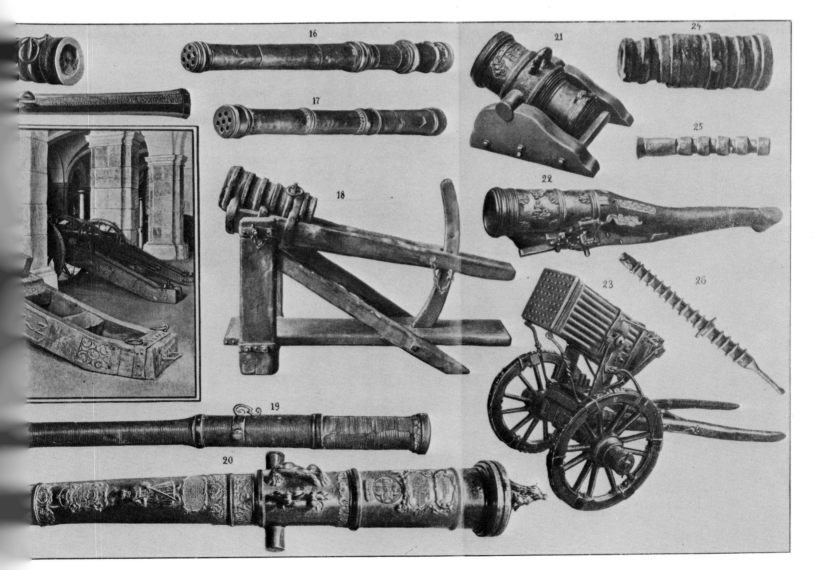

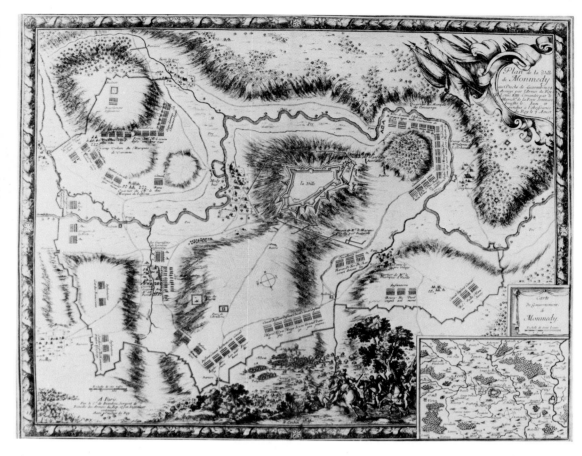

devastation of the Thirty Years' War. The territories of Cleves, Mark and Ravensberg provided additional economic resources; while Ravensberg produced cotton, Mark possessed a sizable iron-and-steel industry and Cleves, cloth and silk manufacture.

In 1655 war broke out between Sweden and Poland, which posed a serious problem for Frederick William as the vassal of the Polish crown. He had to rally to the support of King John Casimir but, by that time, Poland was already showing serious internal weaknesses of the kind that, little more than a century later, led to its destruction. The Swedes advanced victoriously, casting an eager eye upon Prussia, which would have been useful to them as an important operational base against Poland. Frederick William endeavored to mediate but was met by outright rejection from the Swedes. Confronted by the choice of supporting Poland or eventually being destroyed himself, he abandoned his liege lord. The victorious Swedes chased John Casimir out of his country, from where he sought refuge in Upper Silesia, and Frederick William was forced to accept Swedish overlordship. On 17 January 1656 the Treaty of Königsberg was concluded, in which he accepted Prussia from the hand of Sweden's Charles X. He also opened the Prussian harbors of Memel and Pillau to the Swedes and shared with them the revenue from the harbor dues. Apart from that, he had to promise to support the Swedes with 1500 men of his own army.

Hardly had the treaty been concluded when the fortunes of war turned against the Swedes. At the head of a popular movement, John Casimir returned to Poland and expelled the Swedes. This, of course, further increased Brandenburg-Prussia's value as Sweden's ally and, on 25 June 1656 by the Treaty of Marienburg, the former was promised part of the Polish spoils, should Poland be defeated. The alliance culminated in the three-day Battle of Warsaw in which the army of Brandenburg-Prussia received its baptism of fire. For the first time it proved highly superior to its opponents. It was hardly in Frederick William's interest, however, to have a Swedish overlord. When Austria

and Russia seemed to rally to the side of the Poles, the Swedes were even more on the defensive. Now the moment seemed opportune for Frederick William: he was in a strong enough position to demand that Charles X agree to the revocation of the bonds of vassalage and recognize Frederick William as Duke and sovereign of Prussia in his own right. This was agreed upon at the Treaty of Labiau on 20 November 1656. Negotiating in all directions, Frederick William would have been quite prepared to support John Casimir, only the Polish monarch overestimated the strength of his own position and rejected demands identical to those accepted by Charles X. However, the court of Vienna indicated to Frederick William that he would receive its fullest support if he refrained from helping the Swedes. The Swedes, now also under attack from the Danes, were in a dangerous position and demanded that Frederick William take on the Poles by himself.

At this point an election proved decisive. Emperor Ferdinand III had died on 2 April 1657, and it therefore proved important to win over the Elector of Brandenburg-Prussia to the Habsburg side for the ensuing election. The Elector's main condition was the recognition by Poland of his sovereignty over Prussia, a condition to which John Casimir agreed only under the severest of pressure from the court of Vienna. By the Treaty of Wehlau of 19 September 1657, Prussia once again became sovereign; the former territory of the Teutonic Order became a German state again.

The Swedes, quite rightly, felt betrayed, but Frederick William could not, in view of the general vulnerability of his territories, afford to pursue a policy other than one that actively furthered the interests of his state. Adherence to rigid loyalties would have been praised by none of the surrounding major powers; his situation demanded flexibility, involving changes in alliances according to the needs of Brandenburg-Prussia. The Elector of Brandenburg-Prussia's vote decided the election in favor of the Habsburg Leopold I against the other candidate, who was none other than Louis XIV of France.

Far left. *The siege of Montmédy in Luxembourg. The citadel capitulated to the French on 7 August 1657.*

Left. *Early seventeenth-century incendiary devices.*

Above. *The Emperor Ferdinand III, whose death in 1657 led to Prussian independence from Poland.*

Right. *The army of Louis XIV in Spain, 1645.*

In August 1658 the Swedes renewed the war, this time against Denmark. Frederick William's army had now increased to 30,000 men and precisely at this moment he decided to attack the Swedes, expelling them from Schleswig and Holstein. Sweden's major ally France had her hands tied in the war with Spain and could give no support. Only after the Peace of the Pyrenees had been concluded in 1659 was Mazarin in a position to be of assistance. He objected to Prussia holding Eastern Pomerania and assembled an army 40,000 strong, enough of a threat to persuade the Poles and the Empire to cease supporting Frederick William. Poland had liberated its territory. The new emperor, in spite of Frederick William's decisive vote, was not interested in continuing the war since Spain had made its peace with France. Brandenburg-Prussia was on its own.

France now acted as mediator, but a settlement was arrived at only after the death of Charles X. At the Peace of Oliva, near Danzig, on 3 May 1660, Frederick William was in an isolated position and had once again to cede Eastern Pomerania to the Swedes. The only major concession he obtained was the confirmation of Prussia's sovereignty. He was a disappointed man whose ambitions seemed to have come to little.

For almost 20 years now he had governed by listening to his closest advisers. Oliva represents a watershed in his style of government, because, from then on, he accepted no counsel other than his own and became one of the main representatives of princely absolutism in Europe. His position was strengthened by a sense of mission to establish Brandenburg-Prussia as a major power within the Holy Roman Empire, a sense of mission strengthened by his stern Calvinism. As the Elector, elected by divinity, he took it upon himself to turn his state into a formidable power, come what may, and if necessary against the will of his Estates. In 1653 the Brandenburg Diet had met for the last time. The Prussian Diet proved recalcitrant, trying to play off the Poles against the Elector. Open conflict broke out until, in 1662, Frederick William landed with 2000 men in Königsberg. The Prussian Diet was brought to heel. When one of his

Prussian noblemen conspired with the Poles and escaped to Poland, he had him abducted and Colonel Christian Ludwig von Kalckstein was decapitated in the city of Memel. In 1673 and 1674 Prussia paid the first taxes not granted by the Estates, and, without its consent, troops were garrisoned in Königsberg. Brandenburg submitted in the end, but, as in Prussia, at the price of confirming the privileges of the nobility, notably exemption from taxation.

The Rhenish provinces proved more difficult. After the Peace of Oliva, however, Frederick William largely stripped them of their privileges and brought them into conformity with the rest of his territories. His major instrument of enforcing centralization was the establishment of a uniform financial administration, closely connected with the administration of the army. The army of Brandenburg-Prussia developed along similar lines to the French army, and the policies of Louvois were closely emulated by the Elector.

An army that in peacetime was kept in its garrisons, with apparently little purpose other than drill, was something which most of the Elector's subjects could not understand. At best it was a useless luxury which heavily increased taxation. For every cow, pig or sheep slaughtered, a fee had to be paid which went into the army coffers. After many previous abortive attempts to explain his reasons to the Estates, the Elector did not see any need to try again.

One innovation finding general approval was the introduction of severe discipline in the army. Parsons and chaplains in their pulpits and officers before their men had to announce that any act of plundering would be punished by hanging. Any officer who physically attacked a civilian would be stripped of his rank for a year and would have to carry a musket as a common soldier. Every unit had its own Bible and a religious service was to be held every morning and evening.

Some of the new measures did not survive the Elector's reign. For instance, he proscribed the beating of soldiers by their officers and NCOs and abolished the system of running the

gauntlet. Even deserters did not automatically go to the gallows. Every court martial sentence had to be confirmed by the
Elector personally. All recruitment had be carried out in the
name of the Elector himself. Artisans and peasants were exempt
from recruitment. In other words, he tried to professionalize the
army and give it the same degree of respectability which other
professions and trades enjoyed.

Frederick William created the regiments and appointed
colonels, though throughout his reign the general practice continued that the regimental officers were appointed by their
colonels and not by the Elector. He recognized that there was a
need for reform and equally recognized that an officer corps of
some homogeneity could not be created overnight but would
be the product of decades of growth. As a result, he was quick to
see the advantages of Louis XIV's creation of a cadet corps for
the training of officers. Such officers were therefore essentially
products of a common mold shaped by the French absolutist
monarchy. The Elector adapted this idea by creating the *Rit-
terakademie*, which his grandson was to transform into regular
cadet institutes. The officers of Brandenburg-Prussia were no
longer to be soldiers of fortune who came and went as they
pleased, but a group of military leaders whose fate was closely
associated with the fate of the country which they served.

This, in the long run, made the army an ideal instrument for
integrating the nobility into the Hohenzollern state, but, in the
short run, it was precisely this nobility who provided some of
the main opposition to the standing army. Reasonably enough,
Frederick William did not trust his officers drawn from the
nobility to the same extent as did his successors. In the composition of his officer corps the attempt is clearly discernible to
balance officers of native Brandenburg-Prussian origin with
those of perhaps doubtful social origins. His most redoubtable
general, Field Marshal von Derfflinger, was an Austrian, the son
of a peasant according to one source, of a tailor according to
another. He had made his fortune as a *condottiere* in the Thirty
Years' War before he joined the service of Brandenburg-Prussia.
The Elector made a point of keeping counsel with his senior
officers when on campaign; these meetings were forerunners of
the consultations of a general staff.

It took time to infuse the officers with a sense of personal
loyalty toward the dynasty, an *esprit de corps*, and it equally took
time to organize them into men capable of operating within a
centralized framework of command. Problems of insubordi-
nation were endemic. The bulk of the army came from recruitment on the 'open market' and the size of the army was dependent on whether there was war or peace. The Elector did

Above. *Field Marshal von Derfflinger, 1606–95, who rose from humble origins to eminence in the Great Elector's army.*

Left. *The Great Elector crossing the ice of the* Kurisches Haff.

the Netherlands, England and Sweden. But Frederick William went a step farther – in return for an annual subsidy of 40,000 thalers, he promised Louis his active support after the death of the king of Spain. It would have amounted to a secret alliance against the Netherlands, against whom, in spite of admiring them in principle, he had serious practical grievances. Because of debts he owed them, they still occupied parts of his Rhenish territories, and they took sides, so he believed, with the unruly Estates there. There was another side to this question: which would be preferable, an uncomfortable and occasionally uncouth Dutch Netherlands as a neighbor, or a strong France whose ambition to acquire the left bank of the Rhine was clear to everyone?

The issue was debated by the Elector's family, by his councillors and by his generals. It divided all, but gradually a majority in favor of an alliance with the Netherlands emerged. It was concluded on 6 May 1672, the Netherlands bearing half the cost of the recruitment of an army of 20,000 and their pay. The talks subsequently turned on Frederick William, however, when England and France opened hostilities against the Netherlands, but the Netherlands remained isolated save for their alliance with Brandenburg-Prussia. Also, the Netherlands did not pay the subsidies they had promised.

The Emperor refrained from interfering and, although Frederick William had not yet declared war upon France, this did not stop the armies of Louis XIV from occupying his Rhenish possessions. The quick collapse of the Netherlands enabled Frederick William to extricate himself from the affair with as little damage as possible. He undertook to give no further aid to the Dutch while the French returned most of the territories which they had occupied; all were to be returned after the conclusion of peace with the Dutch. Louis XIV also undertook that, in the course of a negotiated settlement with the Dutch, he would press them to pay the arrears of subsidies due to Brandenburg-Prussia. At the same time he granted a subsidy of his own. In the wake of this settlement, France embarked upon a series of annexations of territories of the Holy Roman Empire, for example the Reich cities in Alsace, which mobilized public opinion in Germany against France. In the pamphlet literature of the time, Francophobia, caused by a fear of French predominance, was closely allied with the ridicule of Brandenburg-Prussia, and the Elector in particular because of his inconsistency and untrustworthiness.

Vienna now attempted to form a Great Coalition against Louis XIV. Austria allied with Spain, Denmark and the Netherlands, an alliance joined ultimately by Brandenburg-Prussia; Spain and the Netherlands paid his subsidies. The campaign brought no laurels for his troops, however; they suffered serious reverses and outright defeat at the hands of Turenne. The Imperial commanders and Brandenburg-Prussian generals blamed each other for the adverse outcome. While the mutual recriminations reverberated through Central Europe and the Elector's forces were moving into their winter quarters in Franconia, alarming news arrived: on Christmas Day 1674, the Swedes had invaded Brandenburg and were ravaging the territory. Sweden had joined France. Frederick William was now standing on his own again – no Imperial troops rallied to his support and the problem that faced him was to cross the whole of central Germany in the spring of 1675 as rapidly as possible to meet the Swedes. His army was not simply an army on the march, but a migration – apart from supply and baggage trains, there were the dependants of the soldiers as well. For every 7000 soldiers there were approximately 2000 to 3000 dependants.

The achievement of getting the army to Brandenburg in time was mainly that of Derfflinger. In order to give greater

once entertain the idea of introducing, at least in Prussia, conscription or some kind of national service, but quickly abandoned this idea because, as yet, he did not trust his subjects enough, least of all those in the duchy of Prussia. In peacetime the army averaged approximately 7000 men, in time of war about 15,000 up to a maximum of 30,000.

In spite of his introduction of a uniform system of taxation and its efficient collection, the revenue was not enough to keep a force of that strength under arms. This made the Elector dependent on subsidies paid by the great powers – the Dutch Netherlands, Austria, Spain and France – subsidies which necessitated a considerable degree of dependence on the foreign policy of others and frequently changing sides, always according to the advantages offered by one side or the other.

When, in 1667, Louis XIV attempted to bring the Spanish Netherlands under his control, Frederick William's reaction was determined by another problem. In Poland John Casimir had abdicated and the French advocated the Prince de Condé as his successor, which was hardly promising for the security of Prussia. Louis XIV was prepared to drop the candidacy of Condé, however, providing Prussia maintained neutrality in the war over the Spanish Netherlands. Frederick William agreed, and Brandenburg refused to join the alliance between mobility, he divided it into small contingents spread over a distance of 130 kilometers, maintaining continuous contact between them by the use of cavalry units. Within two weeks the army was back in Brandenburg. Derfflinger, by that time already 70 years old, surprised the Swedes at Rathenow and they pulled their troops out of the fortress there; the Swedes were far superior in numbers, but simply did not know it. Derfflinger ordered their pursuit while the rest of the army caught up with them at Fehrbellin. In the early morning of 28 June 1675, the Elector issued his last orders and Derfflinger attacked the Swedish encampment with his dragoons and infantry. He was very weak in artillery; only 13 pieces were available to him, while the Swedes had 38 guns of which, fortunately for Brandenburg-Prussia, only seven managed to fire. The battle was a great victory for Brandenburg-Prussia; it cost the Swedes 2000 men, while Derfflinger's casualties totalled 500 killed and wounded. Fehrbellin, taken by itself, was a minor battle, but it established the fame and reputation of the Prussian army.

To ensure that the Swedes would be chased out of Brandenburg entirely, Derfflinger took a selected force of soldiers and cavalry, covered over 300 miles in 10 days on horseback – one has to bear in mind that the cavalry horses of the Prussian army of that period had all the graces and characteristics of carthorses! – and inflicted another defeat at Tilsit. Frederick William realized immediately that, if he could maintain his success against the Swedes, it would cost them the whole of Pomerania. He allied himself with Denmark, and both the Danes and the Dutch fleet exerted pressure upon the Swedes. The campaign now became drawn out, both main antagonists reverting to the strategy of attrition to save men and resources. But it was systematically and thoroughly conducted, lasting through 1675 and 1676 and into 1677. Frederick William's main objective was the capture of Stettin in order to control the mouth of the River Oder. From July to December 1677 it was besieged and bombarded from sea and from land. Toward the end of December, the walls of the city were breached and the final assault was about to be launched when it capitulated. The garrison was

offered honorable conditions which it accepted, and the city's privileges were fully confirmed by the Elector, who since Fehrbellin was referred to as the 'Great Elector'; on 6 January he entered the city and was paid homage. With Stettin, Greifswald and Stralsund were also captured – Pomerania was in Prussian hands.

If Frederick William believed that the other powers would agree to his conquests, he was seriously mistaken. The Netherlands and Spain had already made their separate peace with France, and in Vienna it was said that it would not be in the interest of the Emperor to allow the emergence of a new *Vandalking* on the shores of the Baltic. In the meantime, the French had encouraged their Swedish allies to undertake a new diversion against Brandenburg-Prussia, culminating in the winter campaign of 1678–79, which was far more demanding than the battle of Fehrbellin. It was a campaign of attrition in which the Swedes sustained heavy losses both of men and equipment. The culmination was Frederick William's crossing the ice of the *Kurisches Haff* with horses and sledges and successfuly expelling the Swedes once and for all, or so he believed. It was an immense personal effort on his part – almost 60 years of age, his body was ravaged by pain and gout. But the gains which he had expected were not forthcoming. At the Peace of Nymwegen on 5 February 1679 the Emperor made peace with France and Sweden. The Great Elector had only one ally left: Denmark. He no longer possessed the strength to maintain his position in the north and northeast as well as in the west. Peace with France and Sweden became imperative. In the Peace of St Germain of 29 June 1679 he had to return Pomerania to the Swedes; all he gained were minor frontier corrections. The territorial *status quo ante* had been reestablished.

Frederick William believed himself betrayed by Emperor and Reich, conveniently forgetting the vacillations of his own alliance politics. His policy and attitude were also influenced by the Silesian question, or rather the Emperor's attitude toward it. In 1675 the last of the Silesian Piasts, Duke George William of Liegnitz, died. By a treaty dating back to 1537, parts of Silesia

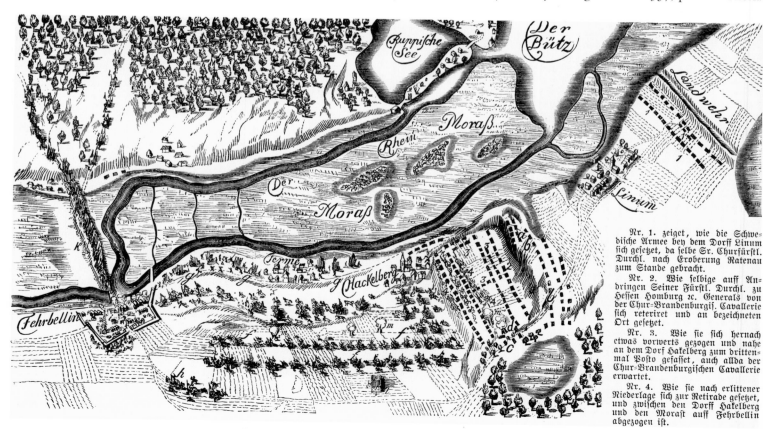

Nr. 1. zeiget, wie die Schwe= dische Armee bey dem Dorff Linum sich gesetzet, da selbe Sr. Churfürstl. Durchl. nach Eroberung Ratenau zum Stande gebracht.

Nr. 2. Wie selbige auff An= dringen Seiner Fürstl. Durchl. zu Hessen Homburg ꝛc. Generals von der Chur-Brandenburgis. Cavallerie sich retiriret und an bezeichneten Ort gesetzet.

Nr. 3. Wie sie sich hernach etwas vorwerts gezogen und nahe an dem Dorf Hakelberg zum dritten= mal Posto gefasset, auch allda die Chur-Brandenburgischen Cavallerie erwartet.

Nr. 4. Wie sie nach erlittener Niederlage sich zur Retirade gesetzet, und zwischen den Dorff Hakelberg und den Morast auff Fehrbellin abgezogen ist.

Right. *The Great Elector presides over the destruction of the Swedish army at Fehrbellin in June 1675. Although scarcely a major battle, Fehrbellin established the Prussian army as a force to be reckoned with.*

Below left. *A plan of the Battle of Fehrbellin, clearly showing the marsh which hampered the Swedish retreat.*

were to become Hohenzollern possessions, but Vienna would not hear of it and simply annexed it as part of the crown lands of Bohemia. Even the demand for compensation was rejected. As a result of the Emperor's treatment, Frederick William again turned toward France. Having been deprived of Pomerania by France's power, he now accepted the inevitability of the country's rise and, by joining it, hoped to regain what he had lost.

Complex secret negotiations ensued. At the same time Louis XIV continued to be engaged in a policy of annexation toward German territories which he chose to call *réunions*. But Louis and Frederick William wanted an alliance with one another for different purposes: Louis in order to back his policy of *réunions*, Frederick William, who also wanted to draw Denmark into the alliance, in order to direct it against the Swedes. The alliance was concluded, but without Denmark, and ultimately benefited France and not Brandenburg-Prussia. Louis XIV's 'Rape of Strasbourg' in 1681 tarred Frederick William with the same brush, probably even worse, for his support of France was taken as a betrayal of the Reich. Still, Frederick William continued to entertain hopes that France would support him against the Swedes. Only in 1683, when Sweden, instead of renewing its treaties with France, accepted subsidies from the Emperor and the Netherlands, was France interested in keeping Sweden in check with the aid of Brandenburg-Prussia and Denmark. On 30 April 1683 two alliance treaties were concluded, one between France and Brandenburg, the other between France, Brandenburg and Denmark. Sweden was to be expelled completely from Germany. In point of fact the treaties were not fully fledged alliances at all, but preliminary provisional agreements; Frederick William made the mistake of not realizing this. The treaties were never ratified. Furthermore, additional aid for France arrived on the political scene of Europe which was less expensive, while being a much greater threat to the Emperor: the Turks. Realizing how low his value had sunk *vis-à-vis* France, Frederick William now offered his aid to Vienna in return for subsidies and territorial compensation. Thoroughly disillusioned and distrustful of Frederick William by now, the Emperor rejected the offer, insisting that, as a Prince of the Empire, it was the Elector's duty to come to the assistance of the Reich now that it was threatened by the armed might of the heathens. The relief of Vienna from Turkish siege took place with the help of the king of Poland – John Sobieski – and the Elector Max Emanuel of Bavaria; except for a very small contingent, Brandenburg-Prussian troops had no part in it.

In the meantime the Emperor was once again deeply involved in negotiations aimed at a settlement with France, or at least an armistice. Louis was prepared to conclude it, providing he could hold the gains he had made by his policy of *réunions*; in this he was successful. His alliance with Brandenburg-Prussia had served its purpose, but it was not a Brandenburg, let alone a German, one.

At the time of his death in 1688, the Great Elector had succeeded in transforming his state into a formidable power, but not yet, as he had hoped, into a major one. All his foreign policy objectives had been frustrated. Even belatedly turning his back on France did not change anything. Nor was he able to transform Brandenburg-Prussia into a commercial power of any significance. His ambitions still lacked the solid base of power, political and economic, with which to sustain and expand them. Hence it is not because of his achievements that he is to be remembered as an impressive monarch of the Baroque, but because of his vision and because he laid the foundations upon which others could build and transform at least part of his ambitions into concrete reality. What he left behind were the beginnings of the Prussian state, the Prussian army, its bureaucracy and, perhaps among its subjects, an emerging awareness of Prussian statehood.

When the Great Elector died he left an army 30,000 strong. Taxation and subsidies from other powers alone were no longer sufficient to maintain this army; the need to finance the army was one factor responsible for his expanding trade and commerce. One of the main aspects of his domestic policy had been to attract immigrants to Prussia and in this context, during the last years of his life, the revocation of the Edict of Nantes in 1685 had played into his hands because it attracted some 20,000 French and Walloon Huguenot immigrants. Possessing more highly developed commercial and industrial skills than the majority of the native population, and having also a rather better education, the Huguenot immigrants represented an asset. Their contribution to the commercial, industrial and intellectual development of Brandenburg-Prussia can never be overestimated.

In terms of institutions, he left behind the General War Commissary, the Secret Court Chamber and the Secret Council that represented the nucleus of the bureaucratic machinery which was to develop over the next century and imposed a centralized administration. Naturally, even this nucleus changed in course of time. The Secret Council declined into insignificance while the Secret Court Chamber, assuming the administration and control of all electoral domains, gained immensely until, in 1713, it was transformed into the General Finance Directory.

Of the three aims of the Great Elector's foreign policy – the achievement of sovereignty in Prussia, the acquisition of *Vorpommern* and a general rounding off of his territories to give his state greater coherence – only the first had been achieved. Of this he was very much aware, indeed after the Peace of St Germain he had a memorial medal struck bearing a line of Virgil: *Exoriare aliquis nostris ex ossibus ultor* (May from my bones an avenger arise.) He did.

The political subordination of the Estates established the Prussian absolutist regime, a regime which, in spite of the concessions that had been made to the nobility and in the light of the political and economic circumstances, could hardly afford to degenerate into a dictatorship of the nobility, let alone the dictatorship of one prince in the interest of one group. The very fragility of Brandenburg-Prussia demanded the integration of more than just one interest group into the state. Brandenburg-Prussia was in the process of emerging as a European power, but its fundamental vulnerability remained, resulting from its geographical position, scattered dynastic possessions and poverty of natural resources. Within the confines of the Germanic body politic, this emergence of the new state was of revolutionary long-term significance. But it was also revolutionary at its very source. In terms of colonial territory of the Holy Roman Empire of the German Nation, Prussia represented the northeastern marches. As Britain's American colonies were later to demonstrate, colonial existence tends toward benevolent neglect on behalf of the central power, and it tends to weaken the ties of tradition and encourage creative independence.

Like England, the Prussian state rested upon a single radical act of secularization of land, carried out in Brandenburg-Prussia by its adoption of Protestantism. With a single stroke Duke

Above. *The Great Elector's son Frederick I, styled King in Prussia rather than King of Prussia.*

Above right. *The international jurist Samuel Pufendorf, 1632 – 94, whose* Life and Deeds of Frederick William *was a major advance in the writing of contemporary history.*

Left. *The Treaty of Nymwegan, 1678, ended Louis' Dutch war on terms which gave the French room for subsequent expansion.*

Right. *An enthusiastic if confusing view of Prince Eugene's victory over the French at Luzzara in northern Italy, August 1702.*

Albrecht had cut the ties with the past, and his excommuni-
cation inevitably elevated Protestantism into a constituent principle of state. The subsequent influence of Calvinist thought
simply underlined this fact.

A further revolutionary feature which can be attributed exclusively to the Great Elector was its character as a military state,
extending its territory and maintaining its presence on the
battlefields of Europe for almost two centuries.

Prussia as a state was a work of art, a Renaissance state in the
true sense of Jakob Burckhardt's term: 'With immense effort
Brandenburg-Prussia raised herself from the debris of Germany.' Prussia would hardly have survived in the interest of
only one group exclusively or predominantly. During the reign
of the Great Elector a major constituent principle of this new
state became visible, namely a kind of *étatisme*, an ideology of
the state community which subjected dynasty, aristocracy and
subjects alike, and which represented a revolutionary break
away from the still-prevalent feudal dynastic conceptions of, for
example, the Habsburgs.

Given that condition of natural weakness, compensated for
only by highly artificial devices, it had to be the object of the
dynasty, of the state, to regulate society in such a manner which,
on the one hand, would prevent periodic discontent from
becoming a source of internal unrest and revolution, while, on
the other, making it unnecessary to maintain law and order by
force. It was an essential point of policy to prevent dissatisfaction from arising in the first place and to absorb political, social
and economic conflicts within the existing institutional framework. This was the distinguishing feature which characterized
absolutist monarchy in Brandenburg-Prussia, in contrast to
France and other absolutist countries. Again, the first signs of
this policy are discernible during the reign of the Great Elector,

as are the beginnings of an institutional framework capable of initiating and carrying out reform from above and thus preventing revolution from below. Prussia's governmental apparatus was to be the very embodiment of the ideology of the state community.

By 1688, when the Great Elector died, the general European situation had changed in a way that favored the rise of the Hohenzollern state rather more than had been the case during his lifetime. Sweden, whose external ambitions were in inverse proportion to its actual resources, lost its predominance over the Baltic, while Russia emerged as a great power. This did not immediately lead to Brandenburg-Prussia acquiring the position she desired in the Baltic region, but Sweden's decline nevertheless removed a major threat. Poland, in the throes of dissolution under its future Saxon rulers, removed for the time being another threat from the frontiers of the Hohenzollern state.

Most important was the Anglo-French conflict, global in character but focused in Europe, over the question of the Spanish succession, in which Britain supported the House of Habsburg in the interest of a balance of power and thus effectively contained the French interests in the hegemony of Europe. The Peace of Utrecht reestablished a balance of power in Europe between Britain, France and Austria with the additional power of Brandenburg-Prussia.

The Great Elector's successor, Elector Frederick III, was born of a very different mold from his father – he loved the splendor of the Baroque and introduced it into his court and country irrespective of the expense, with the result that his country ran seriously into debt. But, nevertheless, by supporting the Habsburg cause in the War of the Spanish Succession with an army, which under Prince Leopold von Anhalt-Dessau was constantly improved, he gained the Habsburg's agreement to royal dignity. He became Frederick I, King *in* Prussia. Prussian troops had proved decisive at Blenheim in 1704, their contribution had been vital at Turin in 1708, and they earned themselves the reputation of being the most steadfast soldiers on the battlefields of Europe during the last great battle of the War of the Spanish Succession, at Malplaquet. Prussia's Crown Prince Frederick William, a participant, was horrified by the slaughter. The total casualties amounted to 42,000 men. Upon his return to Berlin, and assisted by the *Alte Dessauer*, he initiated further improvements in Prussia's army. While the king squandered the country's resources, his son drilled his troops. When King Frederick I died in 1713, the influence of Versailles upon the royal court in Berlin disappeared abruptly; the influence of Sparta was to come.

Right. *The Battle of Ramillies, 23 May 1706. Allied troops engaged in the congenial tasks of pursuit and plunder.*

Below left. *Marlborough and Eugene enter the French position at the costly victory of Malplaquet.*

Below. *A letter written in French by Marlborough announcing his victory at the Battle of Oudenarde in 1708.*

12 July 1708

Duke of Marlborough
from Warcester informed Battle of Oudenarde

Monseigneur.

Comme Monsieur le Comte de Hompesch a l'honneur de faire part à Vostre Altesse Electorale de l'heureux succès que le Bon Dieu nous a donné hier sur les Ennemis, j'ay esté bien aise de me servir de la même occasion pour Luy en faire mes tres humbles félicitations, espirant qu'avant que la Campagne finisse, il s'en rencontrera quelque

It is virtually impossible to describe the origins of the standing army in Russia without taking account of Russia's early historical background; comparisons with central and western Europe simply do not apply.

About 500 AD the Slavs, as a result of vast migrations, became divided into the following groups: Eastern Slavs comprising the Russians, Ukrainians and White Russians; the Southern Slavs such as the Slovenes, Croats, Serbs, Bulgarians and Macedonians; and Western Slavs such as the Poles, Czechs, Slovaks, Kashubs and Sorbs. Tacitus pays great tribute to their steadfastness as fighters on foot. In the present context, the Eastern Slavs are of most importance; they lived by tilling the soil and occupied the area of present-day Russia. Their military organization was very similar to that of the early Germans.

In 862 the Swedish Varängian prince, Duke Rúrik, founded the Russian Empire in Novgorod and introduced military institutions according to the Germanic pattern. Thus early feudalism made its way into Russia. Every prince of the House of Varäg gathered around him his own military following, so that the core of the early Russian army was made up of these various groups. Slavs joined in increasing numbers and any large military group gradually became known by the Slav term *Druzhina*.

Above the *Druzhinas* stood the personal *Druzhina* of the grand duke, who exercised unlimited power; he was supreme commander of the army and supreme judge. The members of his *Druzhina* naturally enjoyed the highest reputation, supplied his immediate aids and deputies and acted as his executive. They were called the 'princely men' and were divided into five ranks. On top were the *Boyars*; they represented the council of the grand duke, the *Duma*. Simultaneously, they were his governors and army commanders, the *Vojevody*. Below them were the *Metshniki*, the warriors. They were followed by the *Griny*, the bodyguards of the grand duke and the guards of his palaces. The fourth class consisted of *Otroki*, who performed all kinds of services at the court and as messengers to the other army commanders. The last were the *Tiúny*, the judges. The last three ranks were selected from the sons of the *Boyars* and other men of princely origin and renown.

All the other princes, as well as the *Boyars*, also had their own *Druzhinas*. In composition they were like the grand duke's *Druzhina*, but did not enjoy the same rank. The understanding of this is fundamental to understanding Russian conditions and later developments in the army. In its basic constituents, this type of order was maintained until the days of Peter the Great, some features continuing right up to the Russian Revolution of

Previous spread. *The battle for the crossing of the Dvina, 1701. This painting, in the Royal Palace at Drottingholm, Sweden, shows an incident at the start of the Great Northern War, which began so well for Charles XII of Sweden but was to end in his defeat and death.*

Above. *The coronation of Ivan Danilovich Kalita, Grand Duke of Moscow, who was to lay the foundations of the Muscovite state (Russian miniature, fourteenth century).*

Above right. *Alexander Nevsky, 1220–63, who also defeated the German Knights of the Order of the Sword on Lake Peipus.*

Left. *The Russian hero Alexander Nevsky battles the Swedes on the Neva, 1240 (engraving, nineteenth century).*

1917. Since in the early phase of its history the cash nexus was unknown, the members of each *Druzhina* were rewarded with land. In contrast to what was customary in Europe in the Middle Ages, the members of the *Druzhina* of the grand duke, the *Boyars* and the 'princely men,' were always present at the court of the grand duke and divided their land among their own *Druzhinas*, who, for that reason, owed them allegiance in time of war. The dependence of the *Druzhinas* on the grand duke was much greater than that of the vassals on the princes of medieval Europe. Gradually the House of Varäg became Slavic, at the latest under Iaroslav I in the tenth century, at a time when the entire country was called by the name of *Rus*, and Slav customs became predominant.

In 988 Vladimir I (978–1015) had himself baptized according to Greek Orthodox rites and then married a Byzantine princess, Anna, the sister of Emperor Basil II; this was Russia's first contact with the West. He turned Kiev into the center of the Empire and the seat of the Greek Orthodox metropolitan. Thus, stage by stage, the early feudal-patriarchal relationship of the prince to the grand duke was replaced by a Byzantine absolutist relationship, in which the princes were firmly subordinated to the grand duke. By the end of the twelfth century the grand ducal *Druzhina* assumed the name *Dvor*, which roughly means court; with the exception of the *Boyars*, all serving in it were called the *Dvorians*. It was virtually impossible for a knighthood to emerge according to the European pattern with such a socio-economic basis.

The strong forces of centralization which mark the history of Russia, and which very often degenerated into despotism, were favored by this development as much as by the old Slav custom that, in the village community, the *Mir*, or the *Vetshe*, resolutions in the town assembly could only be passed unanimously. The consequences were hardly encouraging – dissenting factions were shouted down and, if they persisted, the majority shut them up for good. Elements of the current 'Peoples' Democracy' were already present. However, for the army, which could function only according to the principle of command and obedience to it, this custom did not apply. Difficulties over discipline and squabbling among the army leaders, marked features of European warfare, were virtually unknown in Russia, nor did they have mutineering bodies of mercenaries.

The Kiev *Rus* represented an Empire of urban centers which began its decline with the rise of Moscow. In 1147 Yuri Dolgoruki, Prince of Suzdal, founded a military settlement along the banks of the Moscova, which, from a tribal center, ultimately grew into a full-sized town and became the center of the Great Russians. The rise of Moscow implied a turning away of the Eastern Slavs from Europe; positioned as it was in the middle of a vast area of uninhabited land, it was devoid of strategically defensible frontiers. This in turn resulted in the establishment of a military state, a state which in time expanded in all directions. When this shift of power had been completed, so had the division of the Eastern from the Western Slavs, the latter concentrating around Vilna, the former around Moscow. The decline of the Byzantine Empire further reduced contact between them, especially after the sack of Constantinople by the Crusaders in 1204.

The less influence the Grand Duke Vladimir Monomakh (1113–25) had, the greater became the political and military importance of the princes of the other cities, or their deputies residing there. The land around the cities was sparsely populated, so that one can speak of the old *Rus* as a purely urban culture. The prince residing in the city was supreme commander of the armed forces, supreme judge, and the leading merchant as well. Around him were the residences of the *Boyar* nobility which had emerged from the *Druzhinas*.

The *Druzhinas* of a prince could amount to about 3000 men, and the rise into the *Boyar* nobility was only possible via the *Druzhina*. This nobility lived on booty and payments of money, but it also received landed possessions. They were not fiefs in the European sense of the word, however; land, though abundant,

Above. *Kievan cavalry under Svyatoslav I, father of St Vladimir, rout a party of Bulgars in about 971 (Sclavonian manuscript, tenth century).*

Right. *The envoys of Ivan III, who styled himself 'Ruler of all Russia,' are received at the court of the Emperor Maximilian.*

Far right. *Ivan IV, known as 'the Terrible,' although a better translation might be 'the Stern,' was given to fits of cruelty. He murdered his own son in an outburst of rage.*

Below. *Grand Duke of Muscovy Ivan III, whose many achievements included the final rejection of Mongol authority in 1480.*

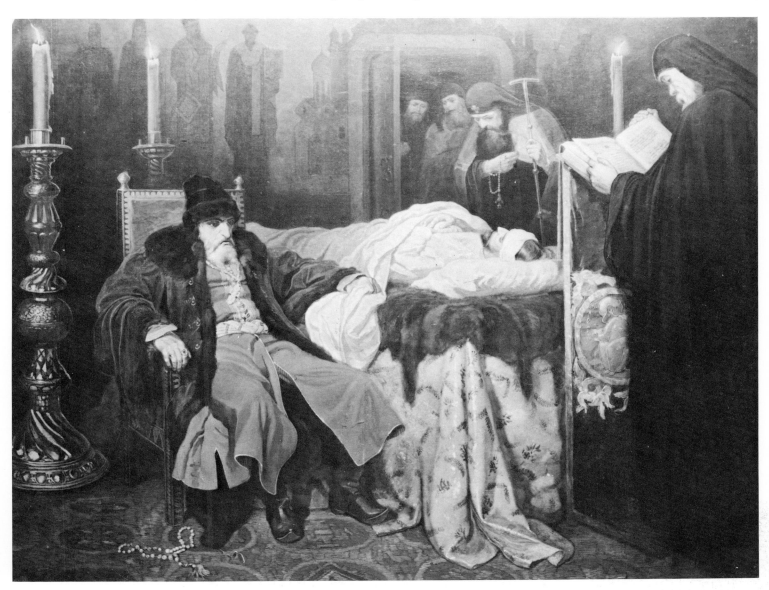

was not made arable and therefore its possession did not imply increased economic power as was the case in Europe. Moreover, the nobility was not tied to its landed property but to the court of the prince, who changed his residence frequently. The members of the *Druzhina* were not obliged to follow their prince when he changed his residence, but most of them did so because of the value of the booty taken on the way and the pay, often in the form of slaves. The riches of the individual were measured by the number of slaves in his possession, and this custom prevailed well into the eighteenth century. Of course, male slaves had the greatest value.

The mass of the population was composed of freemen, the half-free and slaves. Many of the princes and *Boyars* reduced the freemen and the half-free to slaves, especially those residing on their landed property. The freemen lived partly in the cities and partly on the land, where they toiled on their own soil or in the service of a *Boyar*. They had to pay their dues to the state, that is to say to the prince or grand duke, and at no time ever possessed the liberty of the freemen in Europe. The German saying that *Stadtluft macht frei*, that 'city air makes free,' did not apply in Russia. One of their military duties in time of war was to supply the contingents of infantry.

In the case of battle, most of the *Druzhinas* followed their prince, supported by a large number of freemen. It seems a reasonable assumption to make that the army of each prince was about as strong as the army of the Holy Roman Emperor, who generally managed to rally about 10,000 men around him. Since

every man also carried his supplies, the baggage trains must have been considerable, as must have been the devastation of the areas through which armies of that size moved. *Boyars* and freemen showed great bravery in battle; nevertheless, both leadership and organization were faulty or else they would not have given way so easily to the assaults of the Tartars and Mongolians.

The arrival of the Mongols represented another incisive event in Russian history. Under Batu, the grandson of Genghis Khan, they overwhelmed the Russian armies in three major battles: the Battle of Klakan in 1224 and the battles of the Oka and Sit, both in 1238. With the exception of Novgorod, every town of importance was sacked and burned down. Even after the vast empire established by Genghis Khan crumbled away, the Golden Horde led by Batu remained on the steppes of the lower Volga in the vicinity of present-day Volgograd, formerly Stalingrad. For more than a century the Mongols dominated Russia, another factor which encouraged separation and alienation from Western influences.

The Battle of Lake Peipus, in which Alexander Nevsky defeated the German Sword Order based in Latvia and Estonia, gives us some indication of how a battle was fought and with what numbers. Nevsky disposed his forces in the shape of wedges, a rather outdated arrangement at that time. The Knights of the Sword Order managed to break through the infantry, but the downward slope of the lake edge prevented this success from being pursued. Instead, the Germans were attacked on the flanks by the cavalry led by Nevsky, and they were defeated resoundingly. German as well as Russian chroniclers highly exaggerated the numbers involved; Russian books even to this day speak of 10,000 to 12,000 German knights slain on the battlefield. Considering that even the Emperor could never muster a force as large as this, the figures must be highly exaggerated. A more correct assessment is about 400 German knights killed and 50 taken prisoner. All in all, it seems fair to say that no more than about 2000 German knights participated in the battle. German accounts about the sheer unlimited numbers of their opponents have to be treated with equal scepticism. Recent Soviet research speaks of 15,000 to 17,000 men, a strength corresponding approximately with what would be a realistic figure at the time. The Battle of Lake Peipus also demonstrates that only a part of the grand ducal *Druzhina* was a match for the German knights in terms of equipment and military ability.

In order to supplement the army earlier on, the *Druzhinas* of the *Boyars*, freemen and Varängian mercenaries had been hired in addition to the grand ducal *Druzhina*; they were replaced in time by Petshenegen, Chazar, Traker, Polovtser, Ugrier and other mercenaries.

The subjugation by the Mongols also transformed the Russian army insofar as, like the Mongolian army, it became an army organized around the cooking pot. It was divided into units of 10, 10 of these units comprised the 'hundred,' and 10 of these, the 'thousand.' Each unit had its commander, who was subordinate to the next higher commander. The leader of the army was the *Vojevode*. The tactical unit comprised several 'hundreds' called the *Polk*; it was not the equivalent of the European regiment. Also as a result of Mongolian influence, the cavalry now became the predominant arm. They fought as light cavalry armed with bow and arrow and heavy cavalry armed with swords and lances. Attacks were carried out at a very fast pace in order to sweep the enemy from the battlefield at the first attempt. If the first attack failed, a second one was mounted, and so on until the enemy was exhausted or the Russian-Mongolian army had to withdraw.

Although the fighters on foot were tactically well structured, attack by cavalry in the open field was something to be avoided. Therefore the infantry in the main fulfilled a defensive role. Mobility was impeded by the large trains accompanying the forces when on the move. In contrast to European practice, however, this was not because of the additional womenfolk but because of the transport of all sorts of Mongolian luxuries, such as elaborate tents for the leaders, a habit which characterized the Russian army until the end of the nineteenth century.

Once the Mongols had subdued the Russians, they established the beginnings of an efficient bureaucracy, and the Russian princes became the tax gatherers. This enabled the latter to line their own pockets and increase their power, so much so that Grand Duke Ivan Kalita ('Money Bags') could afford to annex Moscow and establish a position above his fellow-princes. Ivan I, as he was called, endeavored to unify Russia again. At first he paid heavy tribute to the Mongolians and Tartars for his position. He simplified the structure of the army administration, and it is under him that Moscow became the capital of Russia. As the Tartars showed signs of decline, Ivan and his successors set out to exploit every weakness; only the coming of Prince Timur, however, put an end to Tartar and Mongolian supremacy. Between 1390 and 1394 he overran the Golden Horde and established the supremacy of the grand dukes of Muscovy, at the same time reestablishing contact with the Byzantine Empire until its fall in 1453.

By the time of the reign of Ivan III, Grand Duke of Muscovy (ruled 1462–1505), called 'the Great,' the Mongolian threat had been eliminated and, by his marriage to Sophia Paleologus, niece of Emperor Constantine XI of the Byzantine Empire, the last emperor of Constantinople, Moscow became the center of the Greek Orthodox Church; it laid claims to be the 'Third Rome' and its rulers, the rightful heirs of the Caesars. Consequently, Ivan III elevated himself to the position of Czar and devoted his reign to expanding the rule of Russia, in the course of which he also expanded his own personal domains. He invited foreigners from the West to his court, among them Italians, and it was Pietro Antonio Sulari who built the Kremlin for him.

After the establishment of a Russian Empire under Ivan the Great, he increased the number of ranks and classes among the court and the civilian and military administration. Those belonging to it by birth and by the nature of their service stood above the people and formed the nobility in the European sense of the term. The various classes of civil servants were much the same as the former *Druzhinas*. There were sharp differentiations between the various ranks, however. Those serving in or near Moscow were higher in rank than those serving, for instance, in Smolensk, and a hierarchy developed. This structure was ultimately reflected within the Russian army as well.

Having learned their lesson about the importance of cavalry, due emphasis was placed on its development. It consisted of the Moscow cavalry, of so-called city Cossacks and baptized Tartar horsemen. Infantry was made up of the *Strelzi* and city Cossacks on foot. The fifteenth century also saw the developppmmment of artillery in Russia with cannoneers, fortress artillery consisting mainly of artisans recruited from among the metal foundry workers. The first guns were produced by foreigners from the West. The czar was supreme commander of the army but often delegated this role to a member of his court, the *Vojevode*, who occupied a position equivalent to that of a field marshal in western Europe. Around him was a formidable staff made up of the commanders of the main branches of the armed forces, such as the cavalry, infantry and artillery, as well as engineers, composed mainly of foreigners, artisans, judges, doctors and priests.

Since the days of Ivan the Great, the army had consisted of five *Polks*, each of which had now reached the size of a corps. They were subdivided into the great *Polk*, which contained the masses, two *Polks* for the right and left wings, the vanguard *Polk* and the rearguard *Polk*, which also served as reserve. For the early fifteenth century this was a highly modern structure. Whenever the czar himself was with the army, a sixth *Polk* was created for him, the *Gosudarev-Polk*, 'The Ruler's Corps.' Each *Polk* had two commanders, originating mainly from the *Boyars*, sometimes from the *Okolnitshije*. One of the commanders led while the other was his assistant and deputy. For the leadership of the *Polk* itself, at first eight, and later three, subcommanders existed, all subordinate to the *Polk* commander. The supreme commander of the great *Polk* was also the supreme commander of all the other *Polks*; in the line of command he was followed by his deputy, then the commanders of the *Polks* protecting the wings, and so on.

An integral part of each *Polk* was the *Guliai Gorod*, the wagon castle. This consisted of large, thick boards mounted on wagons or sledges and provided with slits from which weapons could be fired. If, for example, the initial attack of one's own cavalry had failed, it withdrew behind or into the wagon castle while the infantry opened fire from the castle with their muskets. The commanders of the second rank, according to the function and significance assigned to their *Polk*, commanded more or less numerous troops. It was quite possible that a *Golova*, a rank equivalent with that of colonel and who, in the Moscow cavalry, commanded a *Sotnia*, that is to say a hundred, in the next operation commanded an entire *Polk*. Conversely the leader of a

Left. *A procession of Russian boyars (nobles).*

Below. *A Boyar* wedding. *This nineteenth-century painting gives a good idea of the splendor of boyar dress.*

The first Cossack formations emerged when the old *Rus* was threatened from the west and east alike; the Latvians and Mongols had subjected large parts of the country, much in the same way as the Russian upper class suppressed their own people. To evade or escape these conditions, many Russians took to the vast open spaces, particularly those lying between the Poles, Tartars and Mongols, such as the Prijpet marshes; others moved into the Don region. There they lived without any rule other than that which they established themselves. These were the origins of the Cossacks, a body in no way comparable with the medieval knights. They defended their Orthodox faith tenaciously against other Christians and heathens alike. As Russia again consolidated under Ivan the Great, the Cossacks became the guardians and defenders of the Russian eastern and southeastern frontier; at the same time, they spread the Greek Orthodox gospel. It took great efforts by a succession of czars, however, to convert them into a systematic instrument of military defense for the Empire.

The Cossacks had their own military structure. Their leader was not appointed but elected. He was their *Ataman* or *Hetman* and occupied the position of army commander. The most renowned and well-known Cossacks were the Don Cossacks and, in the course of the further southwestern expansion of the Empire, the Kuban and the Terek Cossacks. The Don Cossacks were the great army of the River Don and their first mention is found in 1551 in a letter of the Sultan, who complained of their continuous attacks against the Tartars and the city of Asov. In

Above. *Czar Alexei Mikhailovich, whose reign witnessed the growth of serious social and religious problems. (portrait painted 1657).*

Right. *Dmitri Donskoi, whose victory over the Mongols at Kulikovo on the Don in 1390 was a turning point in Russian history.*

Far right. *Alexei Mikhailovich and his* boyars *feast while on a hunting expedition (watercolor, nineteenth century).*

hundred in another *Polk* was allowed to command only a unit of 10 in the Moscow cavalry. Whatever the rank held within the army, service in Moscow was valued highest, socially as well as financially. Until 1884, officers of the Russian Guards up to the rank of colonel stood two ranks above the equivalent rank in other units. A captain of the guard was equivalent to a lieutenant colonel of a regiment of the line. After 1884 the difference was reduced to one rank.

This disparity was a cause for dissatisfaction within the Russian army, complicated further by the *Polk* commander being not only elected from the highest classes of rank, but also having to be a man of noble descent. Every appointment in the higher ranks was preceded by a close scrutiny of the candidate's descent. Hence the rank occupied was not only determined by the officer's own position, but also by that occupied by his ancestors. It was called the right of *Miestnishestvo*, and was the cause of widespread internal arguments about position and rank. Only in 1682 was this problem solved by the simple destruction of the records containing the rank order.

Three new and separate formations joined the czar's army, the Cossacks, the Tartars and the *Streliza*.

1570 Ivan IV, 'the Terrible,' was the first czar officially to acknowledge the Cossack army and establish a contractual relationship with them. Still, the Cossacks were not a people who easily bowed to central power, and force of arms had to be used against them on occasions to enforce their obedience.

The official recognition of the Cossack army had significant consequences. A Cossack leader, Jermak Timofiev, separated from his troops in battle, made his way to Perm in Siberia where his future hosts, the merchant family Stroganov, lived. The Stroganovs had been permitted by the czar to make use of as much of Siberia as their resources permitted. In 1581 Timofiev, heading 540 Cossacks and 300 members of the House of Stroganov, set off to cross and conquer western Siberia to the banks of the River Irtysh. By 1584 he had conquered the Khanate of Sibir. To secure his lines of communications, he established along his route simple fortresses or fortifications. In 1610 the Cossacks reached the River Yenisey, by 1640 western Siberia was penetrated to the River Lena, and by 1689 they were as far as the banks of the Amur. This little-known episode can only be compared with the achievements of Cortes and Pizarro in the conquest of Central and South America; it established the fame of the Cossacks once and for all in Russia.

The urban Cossacks should not be confused with the Cossacks described above; they originated as permanent urban soldiers from protective levies established in the towns by the Tartars.

The second formation were the Tartars. In the Russian army it was mainly Tartar princes and noblemen who adopted the Greek Orthodox faith. They supplied their own units of light cavalry.

The third group were the *Strelzi*. Ivan the Great founded them as the first standing unit of the Russian army. Their most important task was to protect the czar and his court, to suppress internal revolts and to defend the frontier until the entire army could be assembled. They were called the *Strelzi*, or 'musketeers' because they carried firearms, the importance of which had been quickly recognized in Russia. They were recruited from freemen and promised to serve permanently. They were a caste of their own, often married, and the occupation became inheritable from the father to the son; newcomers from the outside needed a large number of sponsors from among the ranks. Peasants, serfs and vagrants were not admitted. They considered themselves as an elite force, and their function as soldiers to defend the country specifically against threats from within really makes them forerunners, in many ways, of Hitler's SS, envisaged for much the same function.

In their garrisons, insofar as these existed at that early stage, they divided themselves into units called *Prikaze*, each of about 500 men. Moscow also had a cavalry and 11 infantry *Prikaze* of 500 men each. In 1682, when the rivalries between the *Strelzi* and the *Boyars* culminated in the great *Streliza* rising, Moscow alone contained 30 *Strelzi* regiments, totalling 20,135 men. The point was taken and Peter the Great dissolved them.

Beside the Moscow *Strelzi*, all larger cities had their own city

Above. *Czar Mikhail Fyodorovich.*

Below. *Dinner in the Hall of Facets after the coronation of Mikhail Fyodorovich Romanov. For the first part of Mikhail's reign, from 1613–33, his father Philaret, head of the Orthodox Church in Russia, was the real ruler.*

Strelzi, cities such as Archangel, Astrakhan, Kazan, Novgorod, Pleskow and Smolensk.

By the end of the sixteenth century, the *Strelzi* numbered approximately 12,000 men, the same number of *Landsknecht* commanded by Frundsberg at the Battle of Bicocca. At their peak they numbered 50,000 cavalry and 45,000 infantry. Ironically, they also supplied the fire brigades in the cities. Their privileges were considerable: they lived in their own part of each town and were the only section of the Russian army that received its pay in cash. The annual expenditure on them is estimated at 100,000 rubles. They also enjoyed the privilege of trading without having to pay any tax or contribution. In cases of litigation, the state paid for their legal expenses.

Clothing and armaments were also supplied by the state. According to unit they wore red, crimson, dark or light blue or green long coats; only their boots were uniformly yellow. The headgear was represented by a baggy cap. Besides muskets, halberds and sabers, they also carried finely made daggers, decorated according to rank with jewels and diamonds. By regular military exercise and drill, the *Strelzi* soon gained a dominant position within the Russian army; they were the only part of the army which stands comparison with western European contemporaries.

Their special position and *esprit de corps* led to a certain arrogance, a tendency inherent in all elite formations, like Rome's Praetorian Guards. Furthermore, the greater the privileges they gained, the more they wanted. Greed became a pronounced feature among them, and it was supported by a corrupt administration. This, together with their rivalries with the *Boyars*, led to a series of mutinies in the seventeenth century, until their dissolution.

Below. *The election of Mikhail Fyodorovich as czar is proclaimed in Red Square.*

It is difficult to arrive at a satisfactory figure for the early Russian army until the beginning of the seventeenth century. Chroniclers allege that Dmitri Donskoi beat the Tartars at the field of Kulikov with 150,000 men. For its time this represents an immense figure, since western European armies confronting one another hardly made up a tenth of this figure. For this reason, in addition to the fact that the army under Ivan the Terrible amounted to just 90,000 men, this figure must be subject to serious reservation. Even a force of 90,000, however, represents an extremely large body of men, explicable by the fact that there was compulsory national service of all freemen, and men were regularly called up when the need arose. Foreign observers gained rather different, even contradictory impressions of the Russian army: while some praised it highly and emphasized its efficiency, others described it as a disordered rabble. It probably depends on what they had seen. A formation of *Strelzi* was something different to a formation of freemen who had just been called up; moreover the value of the latter in actual battle, even when they were numerically superior, was very low.

During the sixteenth century, the order of battle consisted of the center dominated by the wagon castle and covered by the *Strelzi* and part of the artillery. A thousand horsemen were posted before it. Artillery was entrenched on the left and right wings, flanked on each side by a *Polk*. The rearguard, which also served as the reserve, was intended to be used as a surprise weapon in a battle order which was inherently defensive. When fighting the Tartars, fortresses had to be frequently attacked, though they were hardly the kind that existed in western Europe. In the case of the Siege of Kazan by Ivan the Terrible, it was a systematic and lengthy assault, even though Ivan had 150 pieces of artillery available to him. During these sieges all earthwork, sapping and mining was carried out by the

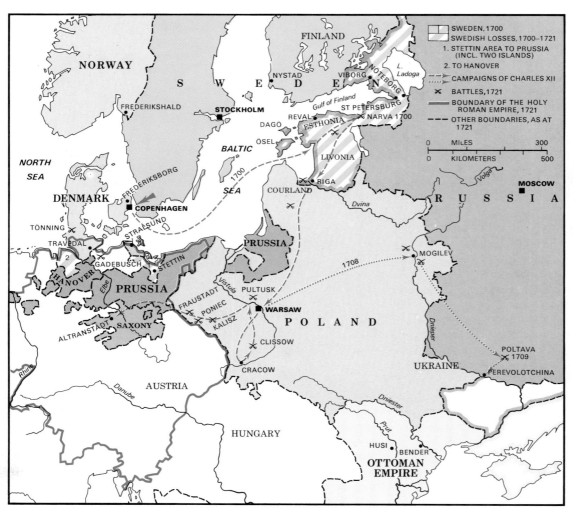

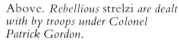

Above. *Rebellious* strelzi *are dealt with by troops under Colonel Patrick Gordon.*

Left. *In 1698 the* strelzi *rose against Peter. He put down their revolt with great severity: here we see* strelzi, *surrounded by sorrowing relatives, being led away to execution. Note the contrast between the bearded* strelzi *and the clean-shaven uniformed soldiers of Peter's army.*

Below. *Czar Peter the Great, whose reign began the European period of Russian history. An energetic and expansionist ruler, Peter imported Western ideas and technology.*

soldiers, something which Russia's contemporaries, the Swiss and the *Landsknecht*, considered to be below their dignity. Russian peasants called into the army did this work without objection, though they were rather reluctant to participate in the general assault. Ivan the Terrible's armies simply dug their way through to the fortress walls, which in most cases were only wooden palisades anyway.

The sixteenth and the seventeenth centuries was the period in which Russia was discovered by the West. Sir Hugh Willoughby and Richard Chancellor set out in 1553 to discover a Northeast passage to China. They had reached the coast of Lapland when one of the ships was carried into the White Sea and finally landed at the mouth of the Dvina, discovering Muscovy. A century later the German philosopher Leibniz wanted to establish close connections between Europe and China; probably because of his deep admiration for Confucius and because he saw in China an alternative model of civilization to that in Europe, he believed that contact between them would yield fruitful results for both. Prussia's good relations with Muscovy meant that the land route to China would be open.

Ivan the Terrible had effectively united the Russian state but, after his death in 1584, a period of great confusion, almost amounting to civil war, ensued until in 1613 the dynasty of the Romanovs came to the throne. Czar Mikhail Fyodorovich (ruled 1613–45) and his very able son, Alexei Mikhailovich (ruled 1645–76), reestablished order more by persuasion than brute force. All the same, they were aware of the great advantage in having a standing army. Without destroying the old army institutions, they established their standing army composed of Russians and foreigners. They were also the first czars to succeed in attracting the Baltic German nobility into the army and administration, where they occupied leading positions until 1917. They patently modelled their army on the western European pattern, taking the old army institution, leaving the external trappings but filling it with new and modern contents. It was reform from above and within, a basis upon which Peter the Great and his successors could continue to build.

The army amounted now to 370,000 men, divided into four branches. Firstly, there were the old traditional troops such as the *Strelzi*, about 113,000 men, of which 49,000 were cavalry (mainly Cossacks) and 64,000 infantry. Secondly, there were the forces modelled exclusively on the Western pattern of about 90,000 men, including 50,000 cavalry and 38,000 infantry. Thirdly, there were the irregulars, mainly cavalry 160,000 men strong, and lastly, the artillery 3600 men strong. Even among the first group, however, western European influences came to the fore. The *Polk*, for instance, was now organized as a regiment. Their leader, the *Golowa*, became the *Polkovnik*, equivalent to a colonel; the leaders of hundreds became captains. The old infantry, made up mainly of freemen and urban Cossacks, was now supplied by the state and received regular pay. It did not increase the combat value, however, and ultimately these men were reduced to a reservoir for recruitment and the replacement of the troops, as in the West.

When war threatened between Poland and Czar Mikhail, Leslie, a Scottish colonel in Russian service, and the Dutchman van Dam were sent to Denmark, Sweden, England and the Dutch Netherlands to recruit a force of 3500 soldiers, which was formed into six regiments: four infantry, one cavalry and one dragoon. Six further regiments were recruited in Russia, each consisting of 1000 men but under the command of foreign officers.

Among the cavalry some troops were equipped with lance, cuirass and helmet – the lance was about 12 feet in length.

Left. *The Empress Natalia Kirillovna, second wife of Alexei Mikhailovich and mother of Peter the Great.*

interest. While still a youngster he recruited his own regiments from village youths and conducted war-like exercises. Fatal casualties did not matter to him. Early in the 1690s he began his famous tour of Europe. In Königsberg he learned the trade of a cannon forger, in Amsterdam that of a ship's engineer, and in London that of a navigator. In 1698, as a result of the last great *Strelzi* rising, he hurriedly returned to Russia, suppressed the rising and ordered many decapitations. None of the survivors was allowed to join any formation of the army.

In place of the *Strelzi*, which had formed the core of the old army, he created his own standing army, though Russian historians often date its origins in the year of his accession to the throne when his guard regiment, the *Preobrazhenski* Regiment, was founded. On 8 November 1699, however, he ordered the recruitment of an army composed of serfs. Church property owners had to provide one recruit for every 25 farms, while secular owners had to provide one only if they possessed between 30 and 50 farms. He also forcibly recruited men who lived in the monasteries without having taken the cloth, and those who attended the residences of the *Boyars*. Many volunteers were recruited as well; they received pay – 11 rubles – and their food. This system remained in existence until 1874, when Czar Alexander II introduced general conscription. In contrast to all other western European armies, the Russian army consisted largely of serf nationals.

In 1700 Peter the Great assembled the *Preobrazhenski* recruits – divided them into regiments and had them trained by foreign officers. While the recruits performed fairly well, the officers proved a disaster. As a result Peter selected a large number of officers from his court officials and had them trained as in Europe. They replaced the foreigners and proved to take the training of their men extremely seriously. After a period of three months Peter had a reasonably trained army of 32,000 men, which he then divided into three divisions, each containing nine regiments. The division was very much the administrative apparatus, rather like the regiment was in western Europe. Each of the regiments contained more than 1000 men. Two of the divisions were stationed around Moscow, the third in the cities on the lower Volga. An additional special unit was formed and stationed in Novgorod. The regiment was divided into 10 companies; two regiments were dragoons.

Early on the color of the uniform depended on the regimental commander. The Imperial guards, the *Preobrazhenski* Regiment, wore dark green, which ultimately became the color for the entire army. In the shape and cut of the uniform and hats, there were strong resemblances to German uniforms. Officers' uniforms were similar to those of the rank and file, but were distinguished by gold braid covering all the seams and the edge of the three-cornered hat. The officers also wore sashes in white, red and green.

All infantry regiments were equipped, like European armies, with the flintlock musket but, instead of the bayonet, they had a very narrow, fine pike which could be mounted on the muzzle; it prevented firing, however, when it came to close combat.

The artillery's commander had been specially sent to the Hague to be trained. The old cavalry, with the exception of the Cossacks and the levies of serfs, disappeared completely. The

Others were equipped first with muskets, later with carbines and two pistols.

It came as a bitter surprise when the foreign contingents hired did not prove themselves in the wars against Poland. What was lacking was the incentive. Some had fought in the Thirty Years' War, and Poland and Russia were hardly areas in which rich booty, comparable with that of central and western Europe, could be made. While dispensing with the foreign soldiers, however, great efforts were made to retain the services of the foreign officers. They were to train the Russian troops, and there was no lack of them. In 1661 alone, four colonels with 90 officers came to enter Russian service, among them Patrick Gordon, the close counsellor of Peter the Great when the latter set about reforming the army.

Patrick Gordon is an invaluable source, as he wrote accounts of his experiences. For instance, about the Crimean campaign of 1687, he wrote that many soldiers had simply ignored their call-up. They had to be fetched from their farms and the distances messengers had to cover were considerable. Once the army was assembled it moved much more slowly than the western European armies of the time. He described the 100,000-strong army as a closely packed mass, one huge square one and three quarter miles long and three quarters of a mile wide. In the middle marched the infantry with the train of 20,000 men; beside it was the artillery covered by the cavalry.

The Russian cavalry did not match those of the Tartars between 1687 and 1689 – only the infantry proved adequate. It was more than obvious that further reforms were needed to bring the Russian army up to western European standards.

This was primarily Peter the Great's task when, in 1689, he, in effect, became sole ruler and began to guide Russia into Europe. Although a giant of almost seven feet he was, like all the Romanovs, a sick man. He was aware, however, of what had to be done. One of his most frequented haunts was the German suburb of Moscow, where he acquired not only a workable knowledge of German but also a more than healthy taste for German beer. There was not a subject which did not excite his

Above right. *Peter the Great strides purposefully through the mud in his new city of St Petersburg.*

Right. *Peter the Great inspecting Dutch ships.*

function of the Cossacks was that of a light cavalry. The ranks of the entire army were also based on the German pattern of Frederick William I.

As elsewhere, the tactical unit was the battalion. Each regiment consisted of two to three battalions, while each battalion contained between three and five companies. Each company was between 100 and 120 men strong. When drawn up in battle line, the infantry was six lines deep, as compared to the three of the Prussians and the four of the French; it was an essentially defensive arrangement.

One new development entirely of Russian origin, and adapted much later by European armies, was the introduction of the brigade which comprised three to four regiments. Several brigades formed an army. They were not units of mixed arms but consisted entirely of infantry. Each brigade was commanded by a general, which eased the complexity of the command structure.

Peter the Great soon had the opportunity to test his new army. The Peace of Kardis in 1661 concluded the Swedish–Russian conflict in the First Great Northern War. It confirmed Sweden's position as the master of the Baltic and so it remained throughout the reign of Charles XI (1660–97). After his successful war with Denmark, he appointed himself autocrat and thereafter attempted to strengthen his country's internal resources. When he died in 1697 he left behind an empire embracing the whole of the Scandinavian peninsula (with the exception of Norway), Finland, Karelia, Ingria, Estonia, Livonia, western Pomerania, the harbor cities of Wismar, Bremen

and Verden, as well as most of the islands in the Baltic. This meant that the Swedes not only controlled the Baltic but (with the exception of the mouths of the Vistula and the Memel) the mouths of all the rivers flowing into it: the Neva, the Duna, the Oder, the Elbe and the Weser. It was, indeed, a most formidable empire, but Sweden's resources were too weak to sustain it for any length of time. Heir to these lands was Charles XII, a mere 15 years old but endowed with considerable military ability – indeed, a warrior king like his ancestors. But, despite his many abilities, he failed to recognize his country's limited resources and that his far-ranging empire was extremely vulnerable, blocked as it was in the east by Russia, and threatened in the south by Brandenburg and the Holy Roman Empire and in the west by Norway and Denmark.

It is against this historical background that the true significance of the military reforms of Peter the Great must be seen, because he trained his army with definite objectives in mind. One of them was to gain access to a warm-water port, since all Russian ports were frozen during the long winters. Two options were open to Peter: to seek it via the Black Sea in the Dardanelles at the expense of the Ottoman Empire or, in the opposite direction, on the shores of the Baltic still in Sweden's hands.

Outside events helped him make a decision. During the reign of Charles XI a Livonian landowner, Johann Reinhold Patkul, had lost his estates and entered service with King Augustus the Strong of Poland, Elector of Saxony. In 1698 he persuaded him to initiate talks between Poland, Denmark and Russia with the aim of forming a coalition against Sweden and then partitioning

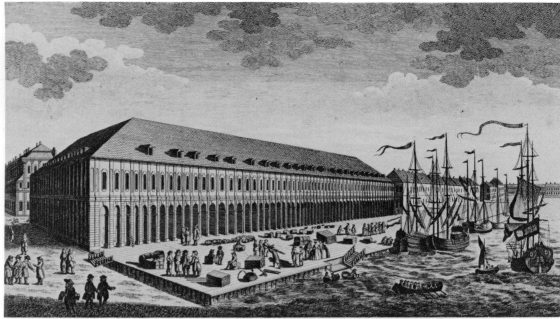

*Above. Obverse of a medal issued
to commemorate the capture of
Notebourg in 1702.*

*Left. The siege of Azov in 1696.
The difficult victory persuaded Peter
to acquire Western military expertise.*

*Right. The new warehouses at St
Petersburg, built as part of Peter's
policy of trade and expansion.*

the Swedish Empire. Geographically, the Baltic region seemed to be more favorable than the distant Dardanelles and Peter agreed to join. The coalition was formed and it was the task of Frederick IV of Denmark to draw the Swedish forces to the west by a diversionary maneuver while Poles, Saxons and Russians would simultaneously invade Sweden's Baltic provinces. That in the meantime Sweden's Charles XI had died made no difference, because Charles XII, in spite of his youth, was as great a military leader. To the allies, however, it seemed a sign of weakness to have a boy on the throne of Sweden. This seemingly favored their scheme.

But, as Fuller wrote in *The Decisive Battles of the Western World*: 'Charles was a knight errant and berserker in one. He lived for war, loved its hardships and adventures even more than victory itself, and the more impossible the odds against him, the more eagerly he accepted them. Wrapped in an impenetrable reserve, his faith in himself was boundless, and his power of self-deception unlimited – nothing seemed to him beyond his reach. The numerical superiority of his enemy; the strength of his position; the weariness of his troops; their lack of armament or supplies; foundering roads, mud, rain, frost and scorching sun appeared to him but obstacles set in his path by Providence to test his genius. Nothing perturbed him, every danger and hazard beckoned him on. High-spirited but always under self-control, faithful to his word and a considerable disciplinarian, from the moment he took the field he became a legend to his men, *un étandard vivant* which endowed them with a faith in his leadership that has never been surpassed. His fearlessness was phenomenal, his energy prodigious, and added to these qualities he possessed so quick a tactical eye that one glance was sufficient to reveal to him the weakest point in his enemy's line or position, which at once he attacked like a thunderbolt. Such was the boy king whose Baltic provinces the self-indulgent Augustus and the boorish Peter over their wine-cups had decided to filch and to divide between themselves.'

The Second Great Northern War began in 1700 and was to last until 1721. In August 1700 Peter the Great left Moscow at the head of an army of 45,000 men and 145 pieces of artillery. He had appointed Field Marshal Golovin as commander. On 4 October 1700 the Russian army reached Narva, which was in Swedish hands and defended by only 1000 men. The Russian army displayed little boldness and, in the words of the Russian historian V O Kluchevsky, 'marched around the fortress even as

a cat might march around a basin of hot soup.' In spite of their massive superiority, the Russians failed to take the city.

This failure was followed by an unpleasant surprise for Peter – Charles XII had rapidly attacked the Danes. Frederick IV of Denmark, relying on his strong fleet to prevent any crossings by the Swedes, had invaded Holstein in the previous April. Nevertheless, Charles managed to slip through the Danish fleet, crossed the narrow channel and invaded Zeeland. This stroke of genius posed a direct threat to Copenhagen and hostilities soon collapsed; peace between the two countries was signed on 18 August 1700 by the Peace of Traventhal.

Having disposed of the Danes, Charles immediately moved eastward. On 6 October 1700 he reached Estonia, intending to move south to relieve the fortress of Riga besieged by Saxon forces. However, on hearing of the siege of Narva, he turned northward again, paused to rest his army and gathered it together again into a compact force. He set out on 13 November, reaching Lagena, just nine miles from Narva. Only at this moment did Peter become aware of the presence of his enemy; he panicked and left after having appointed the Prince de Croy to supreme command.

Battle ensued on 30 November in which the Russians outnumbered the Swedes by five to one. The Swedes had an army of 11,500 men and 38 pieces of artillery; the Prince de Croy had almost 50,000, all well entrenched. Under the cover of a snowstorm Charles attacked at the head of 8000 men, shouting, 'Now is our time, with the storm at our backs they will never know how few we are!' His charisma carried his troops forward. Never before or since has a battle been conducted in which the odds weighed so heavily in favor of the defense. Under the impact of the attack the Russian center, composed of infantry and *Boyar* cavalry, simply took to their heels without firing a shot. The new regiments on the left wing offered stiffer resistance, but in the end gave way. Those who held their ground the longest were the *Preobrazhenski* guards. The Russian leadership at the middle and lower levels, however, was in no way comparable with that of the Swedes. Despite their vast numerical superiority, by the evening the Russians were completely defeated. All guns, the entire camp, many flags, almost all generals, a large number of the officers and 7000 men were captured by the Swedes. Only 23,000 Russians could be collected together again once they had reached Novgorod.

A defeat like this is virtually inexplicable. The only hy-

Right. *This sweeping engraving shows Peter's great victory over Charles XII of Sweden at Poltava in 1709.*

Below. *Prince Alexander Danilovich Menshikov, c. 1670–1729, rose from the ranks of the Preobrazhensky Guards. He was promoted field marshal for his part in the victory at Poltava.*

pothesis which one can put forward is that the Russian rank and file was not firmly enough under the control of their officers. The clumsiness and relative immobility of the Russian army may also have been contributing factors. These were not the reasons put forward at the time, however. It was widely believed that treason must have had a hand in the disaster and the traitors were supposed to be the foreign officers, many of whom were murdered by their own men during the flight. Peter the Great received the news of the defeat rather laconically: 'Is it a wonder that such an old, well-drilled and practical army carried the victory over an inexperienced army?' was his only comment.

Upon his return to Moscow, Peter immediately recruited replacements for his weakened regiments. The lack of a well-drilled cavalry in the battle and to cover the retreat had been a particularly noticeable feature. Thus, in 1701, he set up four new regiments of dragoons. All bells were removed from churches and cathedrals, were melted down and 1268 new guns cast. In addition, he recruited tribal Tartars and Kalmuks.

Peter had learned his lesson – he had left behind General Sheremetiev but with explicit orders to avoid any battle. Instead, with great numerical superiority, he ambushed small Swedish troop contingents and annihilated them completely; prisoners were not taken. Gradually the Russian forces gained confidence. Then, in spite of Peter's earlier orders, he attacked a force of 7000 Swedes near Dorpat in Estonia in December 1701 with 20,000 Russians and defeated them. Other smaller victories followed. Peter the Great was impressed and consequently introduced a new medal, the Order of St Andrew; Sheremetiev

was the first to be decorated. Sheremetiev then set out on a campaign of systematic plunder and devastation of Livland. He also conquered the lands along the Neva on the Baltic. Peter had gained his warm-water port. On Whit Sunday 1703, on an island in the Neva, Peter the Great laid the foundation stone of the city of St Petersburg.

Meanwhile, from 1704 on, Peter once again re-formed his army. Every infantry regiment now consisted of two companies of fusiliers and one company of grenadiers, with a total strength of 1364 men. The size of the army was also increased, reaching, by 1707, 200,000 men, of whom 56,000 were the core of the standing army. Charles XII had in the meantime temporarily retired into Poland and Saxony, from where he renewed his attack against Russia in 1707, and won an initial battle at Smolensk. Peter decided on a strategy of attrition, using the depth of Russia's spaces to draw Charles deeper and deeper into the country, leaving behind only scorched earth. In September 1708 Charles invaded the Ukraine. Peter reacted correctly by sending General Iffland with light cavalry formations, not to meet Charles head on, but to precede his advance with a campaign of complete devastation. Cavalry formations under the command of General Bauer harassed the Swedish flanks by sudden attacks and swift withdrawals. Peter himself, with an army of 15,000 men, cut off Charles' supplies under the command of General Löwenhaupt; that victory was a precondition for the Russian victory at Poltava.

The Battle of Poltava began on 27 June 1709. Peter's forces were encamped behind strong earthwork fortifications. Geo-

graphical obstacles protected his flanks, while woods and bushes obstructed a swift frontal attack, which was a typical Swedish tactic. The Swedes tried to overcome these obstacles under the cover of darkness, but the Russians were alerted and made their dispositions accordingly. In the early hours of the morning the Swedish infantry attacked in four columns with the cavalry following in six columns. Because of the Russian disposition, the battle dissolved into two separate actions. On the left wing, the Swedes seemed to succeed in driving the Russians behind and beyond their earthworks. On the right wing, however, the Swedes suffered heavy casualties and the command became separated from the army. Confusion followed and Peter now drew his 40,000 men supported by 100 guns and formed them into a line of battle. Charles ordered an attack which was met by devastating fire. As the Swedes were mown down, the Russians counter-attacked and virtually swallowed up the Swedish cavalry. By noon the battle had ended with a resounding Russian victory.

Charles was wounded and, together with about 1000 men, escaped and found refuge in the Ottoman Empire, where he successfully drove the Sultan into war against Russia. In 1711 the entire Russian army was encircled by the Turks and was able to secure its freedom only with bribes and the cession of Asov to the Turks. However, the net result of the campaign was the destruction of the myth of the invincibility of 'the last of the Viking Kings' and, at a more practical level, the final gaining of access to the Baltic at Neva. Russia was becoming a European power to be reckoned with.

CHAPTER VII

THE NEW SPARTA:
PRUSSIA AND THE ARMY OF
FREDERICK WILLIAM I

The body of King Frederick I of Prussia lay in state in February 1713 in full Baroque splendor, surrounded by the trappings of an age he had loved, admired and done so much to emulate in his barren kingdom. The chief event of his reign had been his elevation to the title of King in 1701. At his feet, deep in thought, stood the new king, Frederick William I. Rather abruptly he straightened himself, turned on his heel and walked out of the room, leaving behind not only the body of his father, the guard of honor and the dim light of the candles, but also another age. The threshold which he crossed led into an era that he meant to be vastly different from that of his father.

Macaulay has described him as being a man whose 'character was disfigured by odious vices, and whose eccentricities were such as had never before been out of a madhouse . . . the mind of Frederick William was so ill regulated, that all his inclinations became passions, and all his passions partook the character of moral and intellectual disease.' A true reflection of nineteenth-century Whig sentiment, but a nicely turned phrase alone does not make good history, though Macaulay is not the only one to have fallen victim to this superficial impression; after all, it was one shared by many of Frederick William's contemporaries. With utter incomprehension they observed the unfolding of a spectacle that seemed to contradict the very essence of the spirit of the age, the beginnings of the European Enlightenment. The generous and careless rule of the first Hohenzollern king was to be followed by the rule of a man who carefully appreciated the resources of his territories, or the lack of them, a man who reversed the principle of the Baroque Age that revenue had to be adequate to meet expenditure by stating that expenditure should on no account exceed available revenue.

His succession to the crown was tantamount to a revolution against the hitherto prevailing form of princely absolutism. While the art of the Baroque appealed to the senses and dominated not only the Habsburg Empire, Spain and France but also the Protestant courts, Frederick William's Calvinist heritage quickly asserted itself by drastically reducing the pomp and splendor, making way in his kingdom for a functionalism in style and appearance of government hitherto unheard of. No wonder contemporaries viewed him as the 'Barbarian from the North.'

Within hours of his father's death, he assembled his first council and ordered that all valuables such as precious stones, silver and rare furniture in the various royal residences be listed and the latter then sealed. The following day the army swore their loyalty to the new king. For the next eight days his father's ministers were forbidden to approach him about government matters. After that period had elapsed, he confirmed everyone's position and emphasized to them that, while his father had found his pleasure in architectural ostentation and great amounts of jewels, he himself would gain satisfaction by building an army of good troops. Only Rüdiger von Ilgen, who had looked after Brandenburg-Prussia's external affairs up to this time, had two new officials attached to him; together they formed the Cabinet Council, whose members were later to be known as cabinet ministers.

Five weeks later came drastic economy measures. They began with horse fodder: ministers and other notables, who until then received fodder for 20 or even 30 horses, were to receive fodder sufficient for only six. Lesser mortals, such as the court chaplains, received none at all. The royal stables were reduced from 600 to 120 horses. 'My father gave everyone horse fodder so that they would follow him across the country, but I cut it down so that everyone stays in Berlin,' said Frederick William.

This measure was followed by a military reorganization which he had even planned in great detail, when still Crown Prince. The costly and resplendent force of guards, who gave great pleasure to the eye but was of little fighting value, was transformed into regiments of the line; the Swiss guards, introduced by his father, were dissolved completely. All that remained of the guards was one battalion, the king's very own tall grenadiers, which he had commanded as Crown Prince and which he paid and equipped from his own personal income. The cavalry was reorganized into 55 squadrons, each numbering 150 horses, while the infantry was ordered into 50 battalions, or 25 regiments; the artillery, for the time being, was to number two battalions. These economy measures enabled Frederick William to save enough money to increase the total number of his army from 39,000 to 45,000 men. His father's death, from that point of view, had come at a convenient moment; on the eve of the Peace of Utrecht, 1713–15, the Prussian forces, until then tied down in the west to support the Habsburg cause, became free and Frederick William was able to maintain them with his own resources rather than being dependent on foreign subsidies.

The court next underwent royal economies. Its members, that is to say officials, had their salaries cut, in many cases down to 25 percent of what they had received under Frederick I, and in one particular case even down to 10 percent. These were the lucky ones, for the majority of personnel were made redundant and transferred either into the administration or the army 'according to their inclinations to the sword or the pen.' The office of Master of Ceremonies was one that was abolished, making a short-lived appearance only in the form of a practical joke by Frederick William when he appointed his court jester, Gundling, a disreputable historian addicted to drink, to the post. Even as renowned an architect as Andreas Schlüter, the sculptor and architect to whom Berlin owed the Schloss and the masks of dying warriors at the *Zeughaus* (the royal arsenal just beyond *Unter den Linden*, now the Museum for German History in East Berlin), could no longer expect any royal commissions and therefore went to St Petersburg, where he died shortly afterwards.

However, to explain the King's economy measures exclusively in terms of economic motives would show only one side of the coin. Calvin's teaching of divine predestination had played an important part in the King's education. His teacher, Philippe Rebeur, himself a French Huguenot refugee, asked him whether he belonged to the Lord's chosen few, to the elect, and whether he could thus be sure that the House of Hohenzollern

Previous spread. *King Frederick William I of Prussia.*

Left. *The coronation of Frederick William I.*

Below left. *Frederick William I, who established the distinctively militaristic character of the Prussian state. He created the best army in Europe, bequeathing a formidable military instrument to his son Frederick.*

Below. *The Academy of Sciences in Berlin was founded in 1715.*

would be blessed with fortune, the sign of the Lord's divine benevolence. This question was to preoccupy Frederick William throughout his life, causing hours of brooding and searching torment, so much so that, in the education of his own children, he explicitly prohibited the teaching of Calvinist predestination. Upon Frederick William himself it had left its indelible mark. Indeed, one of the vital motivating forces behind Frederick William I was religion, his own brand of reformed Lutheranism. One of the reasons, perhaps, why his personal rule never degenerated into absolute tyranny was his deeply rooted conviction that one day he would have to account for his deeds to his Maker. Of considerable importance in this context is the Pietist movement and its influence upon Prussia.

Though the importance of the personal connection between Frederick William I and August Hermann Francke, the Pietist reformer at Halle, can be overstressed, the Pietist influence as an integrating force within Prussian society in the eighteenth and nineteenth centuries seems to have been frequently underestimated, if not altogether ignored. Basically Pietism was the German 'Puritan' reaction to the Thirty Years' War, with its questioning of the Lutheran faith. The Pietists opposed the Lutheran acceptance of the world as it is and the submission of the individual to it; they accepted Luther's hope for the day of judgment, but they criticized man's social environment. To Luther's call for reform merely of the church, they added the call for the reform of the world and its social institutions. Pietism as a religious and social force was highly complex, and worldwide in its aspirations.

As far as Prussia was concerned, the Pietists aimed to produce responsible subjects: members of society who, irrespective of their station in life, would turn their social conscience toward the common good. Their schools were by far the most advanced in the kingdom and thus, through what at first was a

personal connection between Frederick William I and Francke, the avenue was opened for products of the Pietist schools and academies to enter the Prussian civil service, the army and its officer corps. Pietism produced a social and religious ethos which characterized the Prussia of the eighteenth and early nineteenth centuries. It was a religion suited to civil servants and officers as much as Puritanism was, according to R H Tawney, a religion suited to entrepreneurs. It was a religion sober and hard, drawing into its circle all the Estates of the kingdom. In conjunction with the transformation of the feudal estates of the *Junkers* into private holdings in return for financing and officering the army, Pietism played a major role in the defeudalization of the Prussian aristocracy. In the army Pietists obtained chaplaincies, and the army and the administration therefore became the major channels through which Pietist thought percolated to the lower levels of Prussian society.

Theoretically at least, 1717 saw the beginnings of compulsory elementary education in Prussia, and, among the new schools that were founded, those of the Pietists were the most numerous. The ideal product of their education was not the aristocratic cavalier of the Age of the Baroque, but the businesslike, pragmatic state functionary. This, perhaps, supplies one expla-

Left. *A formal portrait of Frederick William.*

Right. *Frederick William inspecting his giant grenadiers.*

Below. *Frederick William and his cronies at the* Tabak-kollegium, *or Smoking Session.*

nation as to why Germans outside Prussia rarely considered the highly placed Prussian civil servants or Prussian officers worth emulating, but looked rather to the French *grand seigneur* and the English gentleman.

Class lists from 1700 onward supply ample evidence of the great number of Prussian officers and higher civil servants who were graduates of Pietist schools, schools which selected talent from all social classes. Even Prussia's commercial policy was influenced by the Pietist movement, which believed that commerce must be for the benefit of the state and, through the state, for the benefit of all rather than for the enrichment of the individual. There is certainly a case for arguing that, whereas in Britain the rise of Puritanism coincided with the emergence of a modern capitalist economy, the Pietist strain of the Puritan movement in Prussia lay at the foundations of an emerging state socialism – a feature of particular long-term significance when one examines the emergence of liberal institutions in Britain and their absence in Germany a century later.

Actively supported by the dynasty, Pietism permeated all levels of society with an ethos in which all efforts were directed toward maintaining and securing the whole, even if this operated at times at the expense of the individual. The demand of unconditional, unflinching fulfillment of one's duty by all – nobility, burghers and peasants alike – led to situations of which it can well be said that Frederick William I and his son Frederick the Great treated their subjects worse than dogs; it must be added, however, that they treated themselves no better. Duty and the common good were principles enforced at a time when elsewhere their harshness was giving way in favor of comfortable, humane and liberal ideas, in an age inclined more toward Epicurus than Seneca, and when insistence upon the fulfillment of human duties receded and was replaced by the demand for human rights; Prussia meant to catch up, thus causing considerable discomfort all round. The moral implications of Seneca's *vivere est militare* had validity only in Prussia by the end of the eighteenth century.

Frederick William I continued the policy initiated by his father of supporting the Pietists and their institutions, a policy which he realized was yielding immense dividends for the Prussian state. Yet he never became a Pietist himself and, in spite of his reformed Lutheranism, the stern Calvinist streak in him never disappeared. He saw himself and his every action as accountable to God. The prosperity of the state was a sign of divine approval; given Prussia's fragility, positioned in the midst of great powers, the task of the monarch was that his every action be an example to his subjects lest divine approval be withdrawn. It is against this background that one must examine the conflict with his son in later years; it makes the excesses of the king more explicable than through transposing nineteenth-century liberal value judgments.

Frederick William acted in this spirit from the day he succeeded to the throne. It determined his attitude toward his own family as much as it did toward the nobility and his other subjects. His reign also marked the final phase of the struggle between the Hohenzollerns and the Brandenburg and East Prussian nobility over the former's policy of centralization. However, in Frederick William's reign this struggle no longer took the form of personal confrontation, but rather obstruction of the administrative reforms of the king, reforms which whittled away what powers the nobility still possessed in relation to the monarchy. As he put it himself: 'I shall ruin the authority of the *Junkers*; I shall achieve my purpose and stabilize the sovereignty like a rock of bronze.' The provincial Diets, the last strongholds of the *Junkers*, were allowed no other function than that of implementing the king's ordinances. To ensure that, even at that level, no obstacles would be placed in his way, however, he deprived the Diets of their administrative effectiveness by appointing his own officials at all administrative and executive levels of the kingdom. It was that step that really laid the foundations of the Prussian civil service.

In such a predominantly agrarian society, the successful functioning of the bureaucracy required specialized knowledge, an increasing measure of expertise and thus a division of labor. Even an absolute monarchy cannot concentrate all knowledge and expertise in one man or a small group of men. Hence intrinsic in the growth of any bureaucracy is the tendency toward its independence, toward emancipation from an absolutist monarchy. Frederick William I was well aware of this danger, as also was his son, and what he therefore built up was a very dependent, purely technically functioning apparatus which was intended to do little more than to carry out the will of its princely managing director.

Even this was not enough, however; if among other things the bureaucracy was to check the nobility, the danger of the bureaucracy becoming too independent could, according to Frederick William, only be met by recruiting the bureaucracy from the aristocracy as well as from the educated middle class. This would foster rivalry between the two social classes, now side by side within one institution, and prevent an alliance between them against the monarchy. Besides, the religious ethos which permeated Prussian society of the eighteenth century in general, and the army and bureaucracy in particular, was itself a major check against conflicts of interest ever taking on such proportions as to endanger the fabric of the state.

In fact the effective replacement of the remnants of medieval institutions by a centralized monarchic state, run efficiently by a civil service, constitutes the major achievement of Frederick William I. The army and the civil service became the main pillars of the kingdom of Prussia, a kingdom made up of highly diverse components artificially held together by the two institutions which represented most prominently the state community.

A major step toward the consolidation of the Prussian state was taken by Frederick William's ordinance of 13 August 1713,

which declared all royal domains and property as indivisible and inalienable. His father had already abolished the ancient rule allowing a nobleman to do as he liked on the new lands or territories he had acquired. Frederick William's measure constituted a further move toward the transformation of the territories into a unified state. Since for more than a century and a half the nobility of Brandenburg-Prussia had encroached upon the royal domain as well as upon the property of the free peasants, substantial land transfers had taken place without ever having been officially registered. In East Prussia, for instance, this process was not really noticed until Frederick William replaced the multitude of dues and taxes by one general land tax, a tax determined by the size of the holding and the quality of the soil; this in turn required a survey of the lands of the province. In the course of this survey it was revealed that one-third of the land holdings of the Prussian nobility in East Prussia had been illegally acquired from either the royal domain or the peasants.

Upon Frederick William's accession to the throne, the Prussian administration consisted essentially of two main bodies: the General Finance Directory responsible for the administration of the royal domains, and the General War Commissary responsible for the administration of the army and the revenue. Both bodies possessed far-reaching judicial powers in administrative affairs, and each had branches in every province of the kingdom. However, until the reign of Frederick William, these provincial branches had been subject to considerable control by the local notables. From the beginning of his reign, the influence of the Estates in the provincial branches of the central administration was eliminated: most notably they lost any control over the determination of taxation. In other words, what to all intents and purposes had been provincial tax offices became

commissariats, which were staffed and controlled from the center.

The provincial commissaries, now organs of the central administration, extended their influence considerably. Originally part of the military and financial administration, they now acquired many important functions: policing powers over their districts, economic administration, particularly in the towns and cities, supervision of the guilds, and promotion of the manufacturing industries and their protection against foreign competition.

Yet, in spite of this centralized administration, competition between the two major instruments of government and their respective subordinate organs was keen. Ultimately Frederick William could find no other solution to end the feud than to unite the Finance Directory and War Commissary into what became the General Directory. In instructions devised by the king and written in his own hand, he laid down the powers of this new office. It was now responsible for the entire financial and internal administration, including military finance and army supplies. It was composed of four provincial departments, each department headed by a minister under whom were three or four councillors. The first department encompassed East Prussia, Pomerania and Neumark, the second the Kurmark, Magdeburg and Halberstadt, the third the Rhenish provinces, and the fourth the Westphalian provinces of the kingdom. To ensure that the horizon of each department was not limited to

Above. *A trooper of the Prussian Leib Dragoon Regiment, 1740.*

Far left. *Prussian military punishments included hanging, shooting, 'riding the wooden horse' and running the gauntlet between two rows of soldiers armed with sticks.*

Left. *Austrian infantry of the period 1704–10. On the left a grenadier extracts a grenade from his pouch.*

Below right. A Prussian military manual of 1735 shows infantry loading their muskets.

Far right. Soldiers of the Anhalt-Zerbst Infantry Regiment.

Below. Soldiers of the German state of Württemburg. A general is on the right, a grenadier on the left and a cuirassier in the background.

the geographical area under its control, the king delegated to each department specific tasks which affected the whole of the kingdom. Thus the first department was responsible for questions affecting the frontiers of the kingdom and for turning forests into arable land; the second for the maintenance of the main roads, the marching routes of the army, and for military finance; the third for postal affairs and the mint; and the fourth looked after the general accounts.

This fusion also took place at provincial level, the new offices, called War and Domains Chambers, being responsible for the towns and general taxation as well as for the countryside and for revenue derived from the royal domains. As in the central authority, the decision-making process was a collective one, each councillor being head of a particular department or area consisting of towns, country and domains, and decisions being taken after joint discussion.

In order to facilitate their smooth functioning, the chief administrators of each province, the *Landräte*, posts previously filled by nominees of the Estates, now became the king's civil service which the king, without consulting any other body, filled with his own men. Of course changes of this sort were not brought about without resistance; resistance from the nobility and very often from the officeholders themselves. The latter had previously been recruited from the province in which they took up their office; Frederick William insisted that his civil servants should not work in the area of their origin. Two officials who, because of this ruling, were to be transferred from Königsberg to Tilsit and who opposed the move were told by the king: 'One has to serve one's lord with one's life and possessions, with honor and good conscience, with everything except one's salvation. This is for our Lord, but everything else must be mine. They shall dance to my tune or the devil will fetch me!' Note that the emphasis is upon the devil fetching him rather than them!

In a wider European sense, the seventeenth and eighteenth centuries saw the transformation of the state and society based on the power and economic resources of the Estates – their

origins rooted in medieval Europe – into an absolutist state. In Brandenburg-Prussia this period covered the time between the Great Elector and Frederick the Great. Yet not one absolutist monarchy ever had truly absolute power because of the historical accretion of interdependent relationships which no ruler could sever entirely, and which represented checks to any monarch's freedom of action.

In economic terms this change was paralleled by the rise of the mercantilist system, which found its first expression in France under Louis XIV. Economic power was subordinated to the purposes of state. The beginnings of this process in Brandenburg-Prussia can be seen in the construction of an administration serviceable to the whole state. But these were only tentative beginnings which were not developed under Prussia's first king, who had neither the inclination and ability for administration nor the vision to realize the importance of an efficient administration. The accession of Frederick William I brought a resumption of the policies of his grandfather.

One would misunderstand not only the essence of his work but also the character of the man if Frederick William's domestic policies were considered as an imitation of the French example. On the contrary, France, that is to say the French monarchy, had accumulated a serious national debt; Frederick William ended his reign with a surplus. In France the maxim was that revenue had to be created to meet the demands of the monarchy; in Prussia the financial expenditure of the state, including the monarchy, was adjusted to the available revenue. The Age of the Baroque, whether in France, Austria or Spain, was built on credit, credit obtained through banks and increasing taxation. Baroque splendors, whether at Versailles, in Salzburg or the residence of the Bishop of Würzburg, the court of Dresden, were built on the backs of the people – chiefly the peasants. With their sweat and toil, 'culture' was created.

Frederick William's determination to reverse this trend meant that there was no longer any place in Berlin for architectural ostentation. For the first time in Prussian history, an annual budget was established based on the revenue that could be expected, and from that the expenditure for the individual departments or areas was determined.

The pronouncement of the eternal indivisibility of all royal domains and other landed possessions amounted to a proclamation of the indivisibility of the entire territory of the state, thus removing the ruler's privilege of doing what he liked with his territories and subjects. It was the first step toward transforming Prussia from a royal state into a state community.

In his encouragement of trade and manufacture, Frederick William gave considerable support to two young merchants, David Splitgerber and Gottfried Adolph Daum, who in 1712 had set up a small store in Berlin. Since they were not citizens of Berlin but originated from Pomerania and Saxony respectively, the Berlin guild prohibited them from trading in actual goods. They concentrated their activities on buying and selling wholesale and on commission. In so doing they developed connections with Leipzig, Hamburg and Danzig, and even as far as London, Amsterdam, Bordeaux, Venice and Lisbon. The king took due notice of this and soon became a customer. They supplied him with ammunition and rare metals, and soon other members of the royal court and Berlin's society were among the clientele. They expanded Prussian trade into Russia by founding the highly successful Russian Trading Company. They went on to buy arms factories, and established new arms factories in Potsdam. They also purchased ironworks and sugar refineries.

Frederick William's policy toward the textile industry was determined by the requirements of the army. Upon his ac-

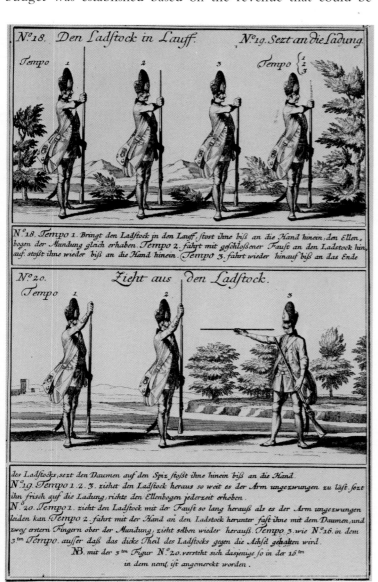

*The evolution of Prussian dragoon
uniform between 1688 and 1845.*

cession to the throne he had his close confidant Johann Andreas Kraut, later to be a minister, found a warehouse and a textile factory in Berlin; it produced the cloth for all the uniforms of the Prussian army. In 1723 it was turned into a state enterprise subject to the General Directory. Toward the end of his reign, almost 18 percent of the Prussian labor force employed in manufacturing trades was concentrated in the textile industry, supplying the home market and feeding an extensive export trade to Prussia's eastern neighbors. The industry was centered in Berlin, Prussia's western provinces – Brandenburg, and, after the Seven Years' War, Silesia.

Neither the Great Elector nor King Frederick I had been in a position to conduct wars, or for that matter even to keep an army of the size they possessed, without subsidies from abroad. At the death of Frederick I the Prussian army had reached a total of 39,000 men. During the reign of Frederick William I that figure was doubled and paid for out of Prussia's own resources. To turn the army into the kind of instrument which displayed such versatility under his son at Mollwitz, or such resilience at Kunersdorf (see Chapter 8), required first of all widespread reforms. First to be affected was the officer corps, which under his predecessors still consisted in part of noble, or allegedly noble, adventurers from all over Europe. Frederick William dismissed all doubtful elements and on principle refused to recruit new members from countries other than German ones. Then, to ensure a supply of officers as well as to tie the bonds between the Prussian nobility and the monarchy closer, he virtually compelled the native nobility to serve as officers. The nobility was also discouraged from serving in armies abroad and although, after granting allodial, or proprietary, rights to their land holdings, there was no longer the medieval feudal tie based on land between the monarchy and nobility, Frederick William I nevertheless insisted on vassalage expressed in terms of service to the crown and state. In that way the Prussian army proved the major institution through which, in due course, the aristocracy was integrated into the state.

Nevertheless, Frederick William's granting of allodial rights

did cause some protest at first, for the higher nobility was deprived of services rendered by the lower nobility; he wanted these services to be commuted into money payments. It caused legal wrangles before the Imperial Court Council which were never resolved. In the meantime, Frederick William proceeded on the basis of the decrees he had issued.

His policy was basically revolutionary in changing existing social relationships, but it was carried out within a very conservative context. This combination of innovation and conservatism was facilitated by Brandenburg-Prussia's social structure. Until well into the nineteenth century Prussia's economic power base was its agrarian economy; the ratio of rural to urban population toward the end of the eighteenth century had been calculated as seven to two. The increase in royal revenue between 1713 and 1786 was not due to increased taxation, specifically land tax or the excise affecting the towns, but was the result of the cultivation of additional land and the maximization of agricultural output. The Prussian provinces supplied by far the larger part of the revenue and the role of the towns, cities and their manufacturing industries at this time has frequently been overestimated, as the result of remarks made by Frederick the Great. Equally, of course, it was neither city nor town which formed the recruiting ground for the army but the land, and it was precisely this relationship between Prussia's military system and its agrarian economy that determined the kingdom's social structure.

The standing army of the Great Elector, a remnant in parts of the private armies of the Thirty Years' War, was an establishment of princely absolutism, 'nationalized' by being turned from a private into a state instrument. The initial heterogeneity of its officer corps was of considerable advantage as the landed nobility was still powerful enough to obstruct the ruler's policies, and particularly because the Prussian *Junker* aristocracy took time to be integrated into the new state. Yet, after the reforms of Frederick William I, the army became the major institution through which the nobility could be absorbed into the state.

The uniforms of Prussian line infantry, 1710–1845.

Until 1730 the army was recruited at random, and frequently by force, from among the German and east European population, substantially from among the peasants of Brandenburg-Prussia. As a result, Prussia's western provinces suffered a great depletion of their population as the peasants simply fled into neighboring German territory – a trend almost as pronounced in Prussia's eastern provinces. Therefore, a decline in agricultural output was inevitable, and with it a decline in state revenue. That prospect was sufficient to compel Frederick William I to seek a compromise between the demands of his military policy and the requirements of Prussia's agrarian economy.

First he endeavored to deal with the situation by prohibiting the forcible recruitment of peasants in Prussia and the escape of his subjects to other territories; neither of these measures proved satisfactory. On the contrary, the regiments had to extend their recruitment then to areas outside Prussia, and expenditure was increased and so, by implication, was the drain of gold away from Prussia. The problem was finally resolved by two expedients. First Frederick William realized that, with its increasing influx into the officer corps, the roles of the Prussian nobility were now military as well as economic – regimental and company commanders alike were also agricultural entrepreneurs, and in order to reduce their recruitment expenditure they tended to look for recruits among the peasants of their own estates. This in turn was bound to affect agricultural production adversely unless the peasant serving in the army was given leave to tend the land during certain periods of the year. Allowing for such leave not only ensured agricultural output, but also meant that the officer/landowner saved the pay he would have given his peasants. This pay could then be used for recruitment outside Prussia. The other measure was that individual regiments enrolled all the young males living in the district in which the regiment was garrisoned. Once enrolled their recruitment by other regiments was forbidden, thus curbing recruitment by more than one regiment in any regimental area.

Frederick William's policy was a combination of these two expedients. He divided the country into clearly defined regimental and recruitment districts, called regimental cantons, and made the enrollment of the youth of each canton compulsory, stipulating at the same time that, after the initial basic training, every soldier would be subject to three months' military service per year. For the rest of the year he would be 'on leave.' Thus a balance was established between the needs of the agrarian economy and the requirements of the army. In addition to the regular soldiers there were now the serving peasants, soldiers who, nine months out of 12, would also be peasants on their masters' estates.

The result of the *Cantonal Règlement* of 1730 was a rapid acceleration in the growth of the Prussian army between 1731 and 1733; not only that, there was a transformation and militarization of Prussia's social structure. The peasant now played an important threefold role, which Frederick the Great clearly recognized when he said that the peasants formed the class 'which deserves the greatest respect of all, because their fiscal burdens are the heaviest, they supply the entire state with essential foodstuffs and, at the same time, the largest number of recruits for the army and also a steady addition to the number of burghers.' A state whose economic strength depended on the maximization of existing agricultural resources and on increasing the amount of land under cultivation could not afford depopulation, and had to 'maintain that species of peasant which is most admirable.' The state of the peasantry was consequently of fundamental importance to Prussia, for 'it represents its foundation and carries its burden, it has the work, the others the fame.'

More than any other action of Frederick William I, this piece of legislation integrated aristocracy and peasantry into the state. The burghers in the towns, as yet too insignificant to matter very much in terms of military potential, were exempt from military service, but they too had to play their part by quartering the troops and, more importantly, by supplying the members of the lower echelons of the growing bureaucracy.

As yet there were hardly any garrisons for the army. Soldiers

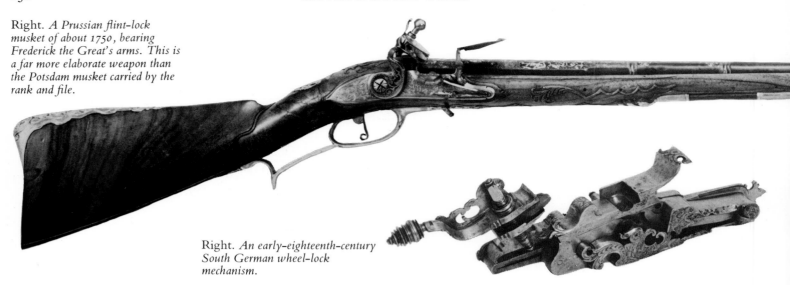

Right. *A Prussian flint-lock musket of about 1750, bearing Frederick the Great's arms. This is a far more elaborate weapon than the Potsdam musket carried by the rank and file.*

Right. *An early-eighteenth-century South German wheel-lock mechanism.*

were quartered in the towns and had to buy and cook their own food; many of them were married and in their spare time pursued a trade. In order to look after children orphaned by war or those who were neglected by their parents, Frederick William founded the *Potsdamer Militärwaisenhaus*, the Potsdam Military Orphanage.

Of the soldier's equipment, only uniform and weapons were supplied; many smaller articles of clothing had to be bought by the soldier himself and paid for through deductions from his wages. This ensured that the army was also an economic driving force within the urban economy. Given the fact that the excise tax was levied on the towns only and that the presence of troops in the towns inevitably increased consumption, then it is understandable that Frederick William once remarked: 'When the army is on the march, then the excise loses one-third.' This primarily economic motivation explains Frederick William's reluctance to deploy his forces in any warlike action; it also goes some way toward explaining his foreign policy.

Frederick William was not simply the commander of his army, he was also its royal drill sergeant, inspired and influenced by his friend Prince Leopold of Anhalt-Dessau, *der alte Dessauer*. The latter's introduction of the iron ramrod, mentioned previously, increased the firepower of the Prussian infantry to a degree unmatched by any other European army at the time. But since an attack was based on linear tactics, that is to say bringing three lines of infantry against the enemy, the bayonet attack remained particularly important, and tall grenadiers were considered the most suitable. For this reason, it has been said, correctly, that Frederick William I, when still Crown Prince, acquired his passion for the tall grenadiers whom he later formed into his own personal bodyguard. This was the one passion on which he was prepared to spend considerable sums quite recklessly. (The source of income which financed this hobby came not from the normal state revenue but from two other sources: the king's own private income derived from his estates, and a specially established recruitment fund to which voluntary contributions could be made. This fund was the chief avenue by which venality in officeholding entered the Prussian bureaucracy.)

In his foreign policy, Frederick William's objective was to consolidate and maintain what had so far been achieved by his ancestors and by himself. In his testament of 1722 he implored his successor: 'I beg you not to begin an unjust war, because God has forbidden unjust wars. You must give account for every man killed in an unjust war. Look at history and you will see that nothing good has come from unjust wars. This, my dear successor, demonstrates the hand of God . . .'

Repetitious though this passage is, it makes clear the intensity of the religious conviction of Frederick William's character. His preoccupation with the state's economy also finds expression when he writes: 'The welfare of a regent is based upon the fact that the land is well populated: population is the real treasure of your land. When your army is on the march outside Prussia, the gate taxes will not be one-third of their usual level when the army is in the country . . . the administration of the domain will be unable to pay rents and that is tantamount to total ruin.' Prussia's army did not only consume two-thirds of her revenue, it also provided a large market for Prussia's young domestic industries and was part of the domestic market that Frederick William so actively fostered.

Upon his accession, Prussia had regained her freedom of action in foreign policy with the conclusion of the Peace of Utrecht on 11 April 1713. But, cautious by nature, Frederick William was loath to involve himself immediately in the confused pattern of the Second Great Northern War. When Peter the Great visited Berlin in 1713 he tried to draw Prussia into an alliance with Russia. For the Prussian king, however, the domestic situation in the kingdom had priority. He said it would take at least a year to get the country's finances in order; after that he would make his decision. Nevertheless, not only did he immediately commence financial reforms, he also simultaneously increased the army by seven regiments.

His major objective was, like that of his father and grandfather, to obtain Stettin and thus have direct access to a major harbor in the Baltic and control of the River Oder. Since Charles XII of Sweden was most likely to die without leaving an heir, the question of the succession to the Swedish throne was uppermost in the minds of the European cabinets. One very likely contestant was the Duke of Holstein-Gottorp, a brother-in-law of Charles XII. Frederick William I promised to support the duke's claims, in return for which he received the promise of Vorpommern up to the River Peene. Nothing came of it; in fact Stettin was conquered by a combined force of Russians, Poles and Danes. This incident was enough for Frederick William to decide whose support he really needed in order to further his aims – Russia's. On 6 October 1713 he concluded a treaty at Schwedt with Prince Menshikov, according to which Prussia was to receive in trust Stettin and Vorpommern up to the River Peene until the conclusion of the hostilities; for the duration of the war Prussia was to undertake the occupation of this territory. To give this arrangement greater permanency, he supplemented it with a secret treaty with the Russians on 12 June 1714 which was to guarantee Prussia the occupied region, while Russia would acquire other Swedish Baltic provinces. Shortly after, in November 1714, Denmark joined this alliance, and also George, the Elector of Hanover.

The sudden return of Charles XII from exile in Turkey introduced further alarm and confusion. Frederick William adopted a reserved attitude, hoping that, by way of negotiations, Sweden would grant the same concessions. These bore no results, however, and on 1 May 1715 Prussia declared war on Sweden. The latter, in a very unfavorable military situation, under strength and no longer enjoying the support of France, had to yield to its opponents. Charles' legendary forced ride across Europe had been in vain. In 1715 he had to capitulate and, three years later, while laying siege to the fortress of Fredriksten, he was killed by a shot through the head. For Frederick William I the net gain was the desired territory of Vorpommern and the city of Stettin, and thus control of the Oder.

Frederick William's close relationship with Peter the Great was not viewed with favor in Vienna, where it was felt that they could no longer rely upon him as unquestioningly as they had been able to rely upon his father. Partly to alleviate this impression and to appease the Habsburgs, he entered into a fully fledged alliance with the latter in 1728, while two years before he had ratified the Pragmatic Sanction which confirmed the indivisibility of the Habsburg crown lands and admitted a female successor to the throne.

Despite his involvement in the web of alliances so typical of

Above. *Field Marshal Prince Leopold of Anhalt-Dessau. The 'Old Dessauer' was a close friend of Frederick William I and had immense influence on the organization of Prussian infantry. Although he never enjoyed quite the same relationship with Frederick, he remained a leading figure until his death in 1747. Three of his sons were soldiers, with varying degrees of success, in the Prussian army.*

BOUNDARY OF THE HOLY ROMAN EMPIRE
TO BRANDENBURG-PRUSSIA
TO AUSTRIA
TO BAVARIA
TO HOUSE OF BOURBON
TO SAVOY
TO FRANCE
TO GREAT BRITAIN

© Richard Natkiel, 1981

the eighteenth century, Frederick William, with the exception of the episode which brought him Vorpommern and Stettin, carefully avoided any aggressive foreign policy. He loved his soldiers too dearly to see them slaughtered on the battlefield. Despite the size of his army, he was one of the most pacific kings of his age. It was a policy which paid handsome dividends.

As the state of the Teutonic Order accomplished in its time, the Prussian kingdom under Frederick William succeeded in an epoch-making achievement, significant not only in the history of Germany but also in that of Europe. With a total population of 2,500,000, it maintained from its own resources an army of 60,000, whose annual budget amounted to about 5,000,000 thalers out of a total state budget of about 7,000,000 thalers. By 1740, the year of Frederick William's death, he had accumulated reserves of about 8,000,000 thalers. In terms of its population Prussia was the twelfth among the European powers, in terms of the peacetime condition of its army the fourth, and in terms of its military effectiveness the first.

By the end of his reign Frederick William could look back on the solid achievement of the consolidation of a state based upon an institutional framework, within which the endeavors of all the elements were directed toward maintaining this artificial structure. The militarization of the agrarian society and the Pietist ethos were well on the way toward combining into a specifically 'Prussian' way of life, which was bound to retard liberalization of Prussia's political, social and economic order. The accent was on stability and conservation, which inhibited the free flow of social forces. By 1740 the God which Hegel was to adulate was already in existence: the God by the name of *der Staat*.

Above. *The young Frederick greets the gouty Frederick William I.*

Right. *Frederick the Great as Crown Prince, wearing the uniform of an infantry officer and the Order of the Black Eagle.*

Left. *Queen Sophia Dorothea, Frederick William's wife and Frederick the Great's mother. Sophia Dorothea showed Frederick affection as a child, and did something to soften the impact of his overbearing father. When she died, in July 1757, Frederick, campaigning near Prague, took to his bed for two days.*

The Battle of Leuthen, 5 December 1757. The bitter fighting around the
walled churchyard of Leuthen, held by the Franconian regiment of Roth
Würzburg and assailed by the 3rd Battalion of the Prussian Guard.

CHAPTER VIII

THE CLIMAX OF ABSOLUTIST WARFARE

C. RÖCHLING
1898

It was rather remarkable that the state founded by Frederick William I was completed by his successor. The fundamentally different personalities and inclinations of father and son gave good cause to expect radical changes of policy.

When he was Crown Prince, and eight years before he wrote his *Anti Machiavelli*, Frederick II, the Great, recognized the geopolitical factors underlying his conception of Prussia's future foreign policy. In his view, a territorially fragmented kingdom stretching across the northern part of central Europe had only two alternatives: the first was to live in harmony with all its neighbors, which would be equivalent to a permanent state of fearful impotence and would lead to a hopeless defensive position in case of conflict; the second was to acquire such territories as would consolidate and secure the kingdom, without too much regard for existing dynasties.

Internally he built on the foundations laid by his father; in his external policy, however, he abandoned the caution and timidity which had characterized the policy of both his father and grandfather, and instead pursued power politics – a little recklessly at first. He made his 'rendezvous with Fame,' a policy which was to take the state to the brink of disaster on several occasions, but from which it managed to emerge victorious. On the battlefields of Silesia the alliance between crown and aristocracy was finally forged which was thereafter to characterize the Prussian state until 1918. In contrast to the Habsburgs, domestic and foreign policy ceased to be subject purely to dynastic considerations, and became instead subject solely to *raison d'état* as Frederick understood it.

The primary focus of his attention was Prussia's position as a significant power and his ambition to turn it into a great power. Although in 1740, immediately after coming to the throne, he dissolved his father's Guard of Giants, he increased the army by seven infantry regiments, which meant that by 1741 Prussia possessed an army of more than 100,000 men.

At the time of Frederick's accession, tension was mounting between France and Britain as a result of a war that had broken out between Britain and Spain in 1739. This situation tempted Frederick to renew the old Prussian claims on the Duchy of Jülich and Berg. By negotiating with France or Britain, both of whom were anxious to secure Prussia's military aid, he hoped to gain decisive support.

While negotiations were still in progress, Emperor Charles VI died quite unexpectedly on 20 October 1740. This had great bearing on the limits of Frederick's ambitions. In Russia the czarina had died, and her death and the ensuing confusion ensured Russia's inactivity for the time being. Habsburg territory, in particular the economically prosperous province of Silesia, would also provide Prussia with an advantageous springboard *vis-à-vis* Poland (if, as it seemed likely, it disintegrated in the near future), and at the same time threaten Saxony. Two days later he called a meeting with Minister Podewils and Field Marshal Schwerin and informed them of his decision to obtain the richest province of the House of Habsburg; he wanted to hear their views as to how he could achieve this, not whether he should attempt it.

Of course claims existed dating back to the sixteenth century, to the time of Elector Joachim II and the treaty of 1537, according to which three Silesian duchies (Liegnitz, Brieg and Wohlau) were to come to Brandenburg after the death of the last of the Piast princes. That line had in fact become extinct in 1675, but the Habsburgs had simply pocketed these provinces without regard to existing treaties. Frederick would now make use of

Right. *Frederick the Great watching the construction of his palace of Sans-Souci.*

Below left. *Frederick the Great as crown prince.*

Below. *Elizabeth Christina of Brunswick-Bevern, who married Frederick in 1733. The marriage was not a success, and she saw little of her husband.*

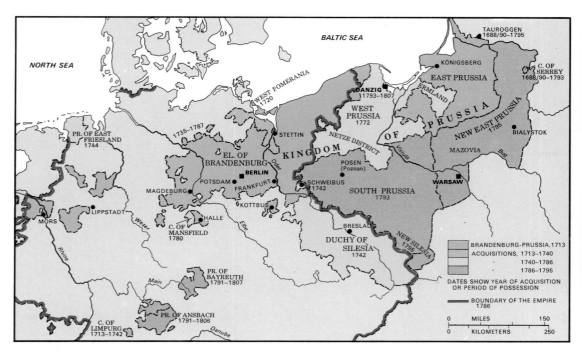

Above . *Kurt Christoph Graf von Schwerin, Field Marshal, 1684–1757.*

these treaties as a pretext to prise the jewel of Silesia out of the Habsburg crown.

Podewils suggested settling the matter by negotiation. Frederick, however, decided to confront Europe with a *fait accompli*: march before the winter, negotiate during the winter, was his motto.

Frederick's generalship was to develop to unexpected heights during the next 23 years, but that does not mean that, on the eve of the First Silesian War, he was a relative novice in the craft of war. For one thing, he possessed the military training every Prussian officer received, for another he was also an avid student of the military writers of the period.

The Prussian army which Frederick commanded may well have been the first of its type in Europe, but as an army it was still inexperienced. The true importance of light cavalry had not yet been recognized, and the infantry had yet to withstand the test of fire. On the whole, there existed general agreement among the tacticians of the period that, with linear tactics of attack and defense, concentrated fire was preferable to general fire, or, as Scharnhorst was to put it later, individual firing was to be avoided, while only entire salvoes would yield any result. Ten men killed or wounded simultaneously would more likely

result in the enemy battalion's withdrawal than 50 killed by a salvo over the entire front of the battalion. Individual fire would lead to wastage of ammunition and excessive wear of the arms, and the officers would lose control over their men.

The ideal way of firing was thought to be to divide each battalion, which in battle would be lined up three deep, into eight platoons; they would fire rapidly one after another, thus maintaining continuous fire and preventing the enemy's cavalry from breaking into the infantry formations. Frederick considered these the ideal firing tactics as well, but was aware that, in practice, they might not be carried out so successfully. What tended to happen was that the first salvo was discharged according to plan, and even three or four platoons might fire in sequence, but, despite the strictest discipline, it would then degenerate into general firing and the officers could do little more than wait until they could advance or withdraw.

It was generally accepted that the attack was to be carried out by the entire line of infantry, which would advance while firing, and would culminate in a bayonet charge. The actual use of the bayonet, however, was relatively rare and it was more of a psychological threat than a real one; in practice, ramming a bayonet into the enemy was one thing, extracting it was another, and quite often could be achieved only with considerable effort, wasting far too much time in the heat of close combat. Once the attacking line met the defense face to face, the latter tended to give way. These tactics corresponded very closely with the composition of the armies at the time. The soldier had no function other than to obey orders, advance in equal step, with an officer at the flank of each formation and one behind. The speed with which the salvoes were fired was a maximum of four per minute, the average being two or three per minute. Salvoes were fired according to command until one had advanced to the enemy's lines, where no real combat was expected. These tactics placed a premium on collective obedience and stifled individual initiative, but were ideal for armies with large numbers of soldiers fighting only for the pay they received, with little personal allegiance to the state or dynasty to which the army belonged.

The most difficult problem was that of firing while moving and, theoretically, an advancing platoon should halt and then fire. Again it was an exercise that could be nicely demonstrated on the parade ground but was hardly feasible in battle. The development that took place during the wars of Frederick's reign was to let the infantry storm forward without firing, using fire only in pursuit and defense; preparatory fire was carried out by artillery. Yet it was a development not uniformly followed in the Prussian army, and throughout the three Silesian wars it varied from battle to battle. More often than not the Prussian army attacked accompanied by rapid musket fire; this resulted in heavy enemy losses which, however, were matched by the losses inflicted by the defenders. In the end, all that was gained by these tactics was the maintenance of what Delbrück calls 'the stability of the tactical body.'

One of the problems of linear tactics was that a line of infantry three deep could be broken through all too easily. The tacticians of antiquity had already realized this weakness; they tried to meet it by introducing a second line whose function it was to strengthen the weak points of the first and ward off attacks from the flanks and the rear. Particularly because of the vulnerability of the flanks, battalions were positioned facing outward to repel an attack from the sides. The aim of most generals was to place their troops on as wide a front as possible so that, as a result of the length of one's own line, it was possible to

Left. *Frederick, wearing his familiar snuff-stained blue uniform, arrives to inspect the progress of a building project.*

carry out a flanking movement, enveloping one of the enemy's wings and causing him to falter from the side rather than being defeated by means of a frontal attack. The disadvantage of this was that the longer the line, the thinner it was, and therefore the forces attempting the maneuver lacked that superiority of numbers necessary to bring it to a successful conclusion. Topographical factors introduced immense difficulties, particularly when the battlefield was hilly or undulating.

In effect this maneuver was hardly ever successfully deployed, but the problem which gave birth to it seriously occupied Frederick and resulted in the 'oblique' order of battle. That is not to say that Frederick was its inventor, however; the significance of the flanks had been recognized for centuries, and Frundsberg, for instance, the 'father of the *Landsknecht*,' always barricaded his flanks. During the Battle of the White Mountain, 1620, in the Thirty Years' War, similar precautions were taken by the Imperial and Protestant forces. In the Wars of the Spanish Succession attacks were already no longer carried out with equal intensity over the entire front, but tended to be weaker on one wing in order to strengthen that one which was to envelop one of the enemy's wings. Blenheim, Ramillies and Turin are appropriate examples. The origin of the oblique battle order was found in the classics, in the writings of Vegetius, while the first modern military theoretician to take up the problem was Habsburg's Montecuccoli, with whose writings Frederick was very familiar; he advised that the best troops should be positioned on the flanks. The initiative in the battle should then originate from that wing which qualitatively and quantitatively was the stronger.

The French writer Folard, from whose works Frederick ordered extensive extracts to be made, paid considerable attention to the importance of the oblique order of battle, while from the writings of another French military theoretician,

Right. *The consecration of Maria Theresa as Archduchess of Austria, November 1740.*

Below left. *Marshal de Puységur, whose military theories had an important influence on Frederick the Great.*

Below right. *The title page of de Puységur's influential book on the art of war.*

Below. *Raimundo Montecuccoli, 1609–80. An Italian nobleman who fought for the Imperial Army in the Thirty Years' War and subsequently had a distinguished career fighting the Turks and the French.*

Feuquières, whose views were identical with those of Folard, Frederick adopted entire passages to include in his instructions. In short, the concept of the oblique order of battle had existed among military theoreticians and generals for some time. Frederick was quite familiar with it; his contribution is that, after several attempts which involved at least one complete defeat, he applied it successfully.

Actually, to strengthen one wing more than another was fairly simple, but as soon as the enemy recognized this he did the same thing, strengthening his wing that was opposite the weaker one. In theory the result could well have been a battle in which one wing chased the other, the opposing armies revolving like a cartwheel. For the oblique order of battle to become fully effective, one would have had to envelop the enemy flank with one's attacking flank. Since no enemy was fool enough, however, to expose his flanks deliberately, he therefore positioned himself at right angles to the direction of the expected attack, and the attacking force was faced with the major task of wheeling around. This was a movement of considerable complexity because the traditional linear tactics had made little allowance for that degree of mobility. Marshal Puységur, another formative influence on Frederick's military thinking, suggested breaking up the linear formation into battalions. However, this carried the intrinsic risk of multiplying the number of flanks, each battalion now having its own flanks instead of being part of a continuous line. Consequently, it was of the utmost importance to keep the intervals between the battalions as narrow as possible, yet large enough to allow for greater mobility. It was one of the tasks of the cavalry to protect these spaces, in addition to the protection of the flanks.

Furthermore, the oblique order of battle was only an

ART
DE LA GUERRE,
PAR PRINCIPES ET PAR RÈGLES.
OUVRAGE DE M. LE MARÉCHAL
DE PUYSEGUR.
Mis au jour par M. LE MARQUIS DE PUYSEGUR fon Fils,
Maréchal des Camps & Armées du Roy.

DEDIÉ AU ROY.
TOME PREMIER.

A PARIS, QUAI DES AUGUSTINS,
Chez CHARLES-ANTOINE JOMBERT, Libraire du Roy pour l'Artillerie
& le Génie, à l'Image Notre-Dame.

M. DCC. XLIX.
AVEC APPROBATION ET PRIVILEGE DU ROY.

advantage when the attacking wing was stronger, while the rest of the line tied down the maximum number of enemy troops; speed was of the essence to prevent the enemy from taking countermeasures. In other words, the attack had to come as a surprise, and success would be achieved the moment the enemy's front had been enveloped on one of his wings.

The oblique order of battle is therefore what the German historian Delbrück quite rightly called 'a tactical work of art,' which Frederick developed not at one stroke but over the years, putting into practice at least eight different variations of it. Just because it won Frederick some spectacular victories does not mean that, by itself, it was a guarantee of success; it could very well happen, as it did at Kunersdorf, that, if not thrown at the first attempt, the enemy would hold his position; this would ultimately lead to both lines meeting head on and thus to a battle with all the available forces deployed, with none in reserve. That such an order of battle could be defeated by other tactics

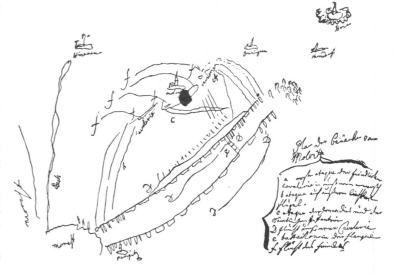

Above. *Field Marshal von Schwerin, 1685–1757, was an educated and humane man, whose feud with the Old Dessauer divided the Prussian officer corps for the first years of Frederick's reign. A brave and capable commander, he was killed at Prague in May 1757 while striving to rally his own regiment.*

Left. *The Empress Maria Theresa of Austria, who reigned from 1740–80, improved the administration of widespread accumulation of lands and tried to better the lot of her subjects.*

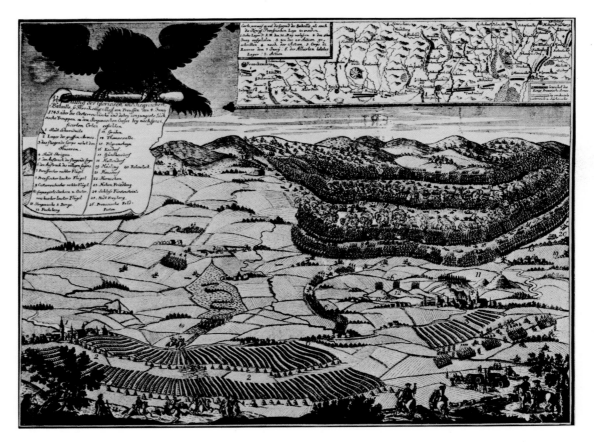

Left. Frederick's own sketch of the Battle of Mollwitz, 10 April 1741. Things initially went so badly for the Prussians that Frederick was advised to leave the field. His solid infantry saved the day, and Frederick reappeared the following evening.

Right. Frederick the Great's victory over the Austrians and Saxons at Hohenfriedberg, 5 June 1745.

was amply demonstrated when it was carried out by the Prussian army against Napoleon's forces in 1806.

The best definition of the oblique order of battle is that supplied by Delbrück, who describes it as 'that form of battle in which the entire line of battle represents a little interrupted or uninterrupted front. It is a characteristic of the wing battle that one wing is advanced while the other is withheld, and that the attacking wing is strengthened to catch the enemy in the flank or even in the rear. . . . The oblique battle order is a subform of the wing battle which was adapted to the elementary tactics of the epoch. The reinforcement of the attacking wing can consist of infantry in the form of preliminary attacks preceding the main attack, or adding reserves during the battle as well as cavalry or artillery.' This approximately represents the body of ideas on military tactics which Frederick the Great possessed on the eve of the outbreak of the First Silesian War.

Without knowing or foreseeing the ultimate consequences of his action, Frederick was determined to annex Silesia. 'Who would have thought that destiny had chosen a poet to topple the political system of Europe and to turn upside down the political combination of its ruler!' he wrote to his friend Jordan. 'My youthfulness, the burning embers of passion, my thirst for fame, yes, even curiosity admittedly, a secret instinct, have torn me from the joys of tranquillity. The satisfaction of seeing my name in the gazettes and later in history has seduced me,' he admitted on another occasion.

The First Silesian War was undoubtedly a *Blitzkrieg*; the army was in a state of complete preparedness, utter secrecy was maintained and all stratagems of diplomacy were exploited. Frederick was still making diplomatic proposals to Maria Theresa when his troops entered Breslau. He rallied France to his side, while the Habsburgs were supported by Britain and the Netherlands; even Russia seemed to range herself against him.

Just at that point Frederick gained an impressive and temporarily decisive victory at Mollwitz on 10 April 1741. In order to occupy Silesia, Prussian troops had been scattered widely over the province. Meanwhile Austria's forces, some 14,000

strong under Field Marshal Count Neipperg, managed to cross the Sudenten passes from Bohemia into Silesia and were about to cut the Prussian army into two, forcing Frederick to accept battle. At Mollwitz the Prussian army, under Field Marshal Schwerin, gained its first major victory. It was not Frederick's personal victory, though he had drawn up the plan of battle, which envisaged a tentative application of the oblique order of battle. Although superior to the Austrians in infantry and artillery, the Prussian cavalry was inferior in quality as well as in quantity and the Austrian cavalry virtually swept them from the battlefield. Defeat stared the Prussians in the face. On Schwerin's urging, the king left the battlefield for his own safety. Schwerin, grabbing hold of the colors of the First Battalion of Guards, then rallied the Prussian infantry and artillery again and, in one massive effort, attacking as though he was on the Potsdam parade ground, threw the Austrians. The Austrian attempt to separate the Prussian forces had miscarried. Parts of Silesia remained in Austrian hands, however, with only the small part of Brieg going to Prussia.

The result was an alliance with France and the support of Elector Charles of Bavaria for the Imperial throne instead of Maria Theresa's husband. In 1742 he was duly elected in Frankfurt as Charles VII.

In the meantime Frederick had learned the lesson of Mollwitz and reorganized his cavalry. Cuirassiers, who had been the dominant part of the cavalry on heavy horses, were retrained on lighter horses that were quicker and less clumsy to maneuver; the hussars under General von Zieten were expanded, as were the dragoons. The Prussian cavalry earned its first laurels at the Battle of Chotusitz on 17 May 1742 in which the Austrian army was again defeated, a defeat of sufficient impact to persuade Maria Theresa to make peace with Prussia at Breslau on 28 July 1742. Silesia in its entirety was now in Prussian hands.

The peace was not of a very long duration; Maria Theresa was determined to regain Silesia. Austrian forces had expelled the French beyond the Rhine and a new coalition, this time between Austria and Russia against Prussia, seemed to be in the making. In the light of this prospect, Frederick decided to take the initiative in the form of a preemptive strike and in August 1744 broke the Peace of Breslau: the Second Silesian War began.

Frederick's armies moved into Bohemia and captured Prague, compelling the Austrians to leave Alsace. They returned from the Rhine by forced marches and threatened to cut Frederick's lines of communications; this compelled him to withdraw from Bohemia into Silesia. Now the Saxons, supported by British subsidies, joined the Austrians and added another 20,000 men to Frederick's enemies. A war of attrition followed; at no stage was Frederick able to force his enemy into battle, and time and again he was outmaneuvered. Doubts about his ability as a military leader began to be voiced within the Prussian officer corps, the example of Mollwitz being invoked. Even more drastic consequences could be seen among the rank and file of his army, of which 17,000 deserted either to the enemy or simply just out of the army. Maria Theresa, seeing herself on the threshold of the liberation of Silesia, proclaimed that the citizens of the province no longer owed any allegiance to the king of Prussia.

A quality now began to show in Frederick which was the basis of the claim to greatness that his contemporaries and posterity made on his behalf. This claim does not rest on the brilliance of his victories, for they are matched by the severity of the defeats he suffered. It rests in part on his capacity, when threatened and when near to the point of defeat, to generate unexpected resources and, despite great odds, to force fortune in his direction.

Since the middle of March 1745, the king had been with his army, relentlessly training and drilling his troops. Instead of guarding and defending the mountain passes that led from Bohemia into Silesia, Frederick decided to meet the Austrians on Silesian ground. All avenues into Silesia were kept under close observation during the spring of 1745, and every move of the Austrian forces was reported to Frederick in his headquarters in Schweidnitz. On the evening of 3 June 1745, reports were conclusive. Seventy thousand Austrians and Saxons formed into eight columns moved from the Sudenten passes into Silesia between Hohenfriedberg and Pilgramshain. The commander of the Austrian army, Prince Charles of Lorraine, finding the mountain passes unoccupied, had no doubts about the outcome of any battle: 'There would be no God in heaven if we should not win this battle.' Apparently there was not.

Contrary to Austrian expectations, Frederick attacked their left wing. First the Saxons, then the Austrians were thrown. For the first time the Prussian cavalry proved vastly superior to Austria's. The dragoons of the Ansbach-Bayreuth regiment rode into attack sweeping everything before them, their 10 squadrons destroying six battle-hardened Austrian infantry regiments and capturing 66 flags. The enemy lost 10,000 men killed and wounded. In military terms it was a splendid victory for Prussia's soldiers, the air of triumph still captured in the stirring tunes of the *Hohenfriedberger Marsch*, the composition of which has been attributed to Frederick himself, and probably rightly so. This result reestablished confidence in his leadership; it was his first personal military victory. Mollwitz had been that of Schwerin, Chotusitz was argued by the Austrians not to have been a victory at all, but there was no doubt as to who had been the victor at Hohenfriedberg. Frederick had triumphed with a concept that ran contrary to established military thinking; instead of taking the initiative himself he had left it to the enemy, thus tempting Austria into Silesia. Once there he had attacked and inflicted a resounding defeat. Frederick pursued the enemy for another three days. Then the fronts came to a halt again, for the Austrian army in Bohemia still represented a formidable

force and, in the light of the experience of the previous winter, Frederick did not venture beyond Königgrätz.

If Frederick could have had his way now, he would have made peace, provided that he could have retained Silesia. But his great opponent Maria Theresa was still prepared to fight; George II in Britain, behind the backs of his ministers, also advised Austria against making peace. In the meantime Emperor Charles VII had died and Maria Theresa's husband was crowned Emperor Francis I, with the Elector of Brandenburg and the Palatinate dissenting.

In the early autumn of 1745 Frederick was preparing to withdraw from Bohemia to take up winter quarters in Silesia. Mistakes had led to numerous mishaps; Frederick's cabinet secretary Eichel, the man entrusted with all of Frederick's political secrets, had been captured by the Austrians, as had his baggage. The threat of the Saxons diverted a substantial part of the army, the main part of which was now 22,000 strong in Silesia. Prince Charles of Lorraine now attempted to impose Hohenfriedberg in reverse on Frederick. Frederick's army was encamped at Soor, which Charles intended to attack by surprise with a numerically much superior force of 39,000 men. On 30 September 1745 at five in the morning, Frederick received the first news while already convening with his generals. Frederick was trapped, withdrawal or evasion being made impossible by geographical factors. He decided that the only salvation lay in attack. This unconditional readiness to accept battle and attack with a fervor decided the battle, as though all the odds were in favor of the Prussians. Again the Prussian cavalry made the ultimate and decisive contribution. Frederick's military contribution was again significant, but still no sign was discernible that peace could be obtained. He therefore turned against the weakest link of his enemy, the Saxons.

To prevent the Austrian and Saxon armies from uniting, Frederick attacked the Saxon forces at Kesseldorf near Dresden on 15 December 1745. The Prussian Army was commanded by the very man who had given it its decisive shape, the close friend of Frederick's father, Prince Leopold of Anhalt-Dessau, *der alte Dessauer*. While his battalions lined up in battle formation, Prince Leopold, on horseback in front of his troops, took off his hat, drew his sword, raised it to the sky and loudly prayed: 'Oh Lord if today you should not bless us with victory, please make sure that the scoundrels on the other side will not get it either!'

The Prussian infantry advanced as they had done on the parade ground, salvo following salvo accompanied by the concentrated fire of the artillery. Even before the Prussians encountered the Saxons in close combat, the latter took to their heels. It was a battle conducted almost to the letter of the instruction manual for infantry tactics. The battle was won, the Saxons were beaten, and were prevented from uniting with the Austrian army. The immediate consequence of this victory was that Frederick entered Dresden, the Saxon capital, and this was the point at which Maria Theresa decided to terminate a venture which had brought her armies serious reverses, while raising Prussia's military glory to hitherto unknown heights.

On Christmas Day 1745, Austria and Prussia concluded peace in Dresden; Prussia retained Silesia. Frederick returned to Berlin, and for the first time the title 'the Great' made its appearance in the popular vocabulary. Believing, if only for a short time, that his career as a general had come to an end, he decided to devote himself to more peaceful pursuits. The consequences of his actions at the beginning of his reign, however, had not yet run their full course.

Nevertheless he did not neglect his army. The tasks of civilian administration were even closer coupled with the requirements of the army than had been the case under Frederick William I.

Right. *A mounted trooper of the Hesse-Darmstadt Lifeguard, with a dragoon and drummer of the Dragoons of the Guard, 1750.*

Bottom left. *A Prussian grenadier presents arms to an officer of the Foot Guard.*

Bottom right. *Hungarian hussar and infantryman in Austrian service.*

Below. *Officer and hussar, Hesse-Darmstadt, 1763.*

Supply depots were established throughout the kingdom, and the system of mobilizing supplies was improved to the extent that, whereas each regiment had previously required 12 days to be fully mobilized, it now took only six days. Civilian and army administration was transformed into a precision machine to meet any eventuality. The *Landräte* were now to a very large extent also responsible for supplies and quarters being available at any time for troops on the march, each quarter having at its door a shield on which the number of soldiers to be billeted was listed. In contrast to his father, Frederick also took recourse to recruiting foreigners to the extent that they could make up to two-thirds of each company; however, this measure was not fully implemented until in the later stages of the Seven Years' War. In the border territories, fortresses were improved and extended.

All the Prussian army maneuvers during the 10-year period between 1746 and 1756 were conducted with the aim of perfecting the oblique order of battle. Frederick has often been de-

scribed as a representative of the battle of annihilation, a kind of precursor of Napoleon. This was hardly the case, for he was in principle wedded to the system of his time, the strategy of attrition. He was never able to annihilate his enemies – his forces were too small. All he could do was to weaken them to the point at which they were prepared to enter into a negotiated peace settlement.

He acted carefully and cautiously most of the time, and gave battle to serve as a deterrent effect upon his enemies. During the Seven Years' War, pressed on many fronts, he hoped to shake off his enemies through decisive battles, and he could afford to risk battle because his army possessed superior tactical mobility, which gave it a good chance in the attack. But the dependence on his supplies always necessitated protecting vital provinces so that he could never appear on the battlefield with his entire army. While his victories on the whole did not help him very much, defeat never brought him to his knees. Many of his battles were sudden reactions or responses to the enemy's

Right. *The Austrian statesman Wenzel Anton, Prince von Kaunitz, 1711–94. Kaunitz, the most agile diplomat of his age, helped bring about the Diplomatic Revolution of 1756.*

Below. *The Battle of Lobositz, 1 October 1756. Lobositz was something of an accidental battle, won by the dogged determination of the Prussian infantry.*

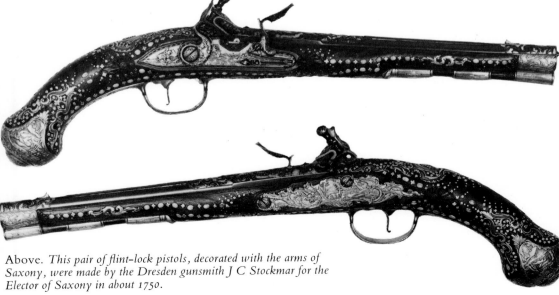

Above. *This pair of flint-lock pistols, decorated with the arms of Saxony, were made by the Dresden gunsmith J C Stockmar for the Elector of Saxony in about 1750.*

Above. *The able Austrian commander Leopold Joseph von Daun, 1705–66, Frederick's adversary on many battlefields.*

Left. *Frederick launches his army against the overextended French at Rossbach, 5 November 1757.*

Right. *The Battle of Prague, 6 May 1757.*

Below. *General Frederick William von Seydlitz, Frederick's hard-living, hard-riding cavalry commander who led the decisive charge at Rossbach.*

initiative, the consequences of which he averted by giving battle almost immediately. Frederick fully realized his limitations: 'With such troops one could conquer the world, if the victories were not as disastrous to the army as they are to the enemy.' The decision to give battle he described as a 'means to vomit which one gives to a sick man if no other course of salvation exists.'

By 1755 dark clouds were assembling on Prussia's horizons. Since 1746 an Austro-Russian defensive alliance had existed, potentially directed against Prussia. Britain, increasingly engaged in war with France over colonial predominance in North America, concluded in September 1755 a treaty with Russia according to which the latter was to protect Hanover. The specter of encirclement stared Frederick in the face, so in January 1756 he concluded the Convention of Westminster with George II, guaranteeing the neutrality of Germany in the imminent Anglo-French conflict. Meanwhile, France was busily negotiating with its former archenemies, the Habsburgs. The Convention of Westminster gave Frederick the hope of having neutralized the Russians, whom he feared most, and he was consequently highly alarmed by news of extensive Russian military preparations. His suspicion of being encircled was further confirmed when, in May 1756, Maria Theresa's chancellor, Count Kaunitz, brought about the 'diplomatic revolution' by inducing the French to reverse their alliances. In April 1756 the existing Franco-Prussian alliance expired, but it was primarily the Convention of Westminster which caused France to join the Habsburg camp.

Frederick believed, to the end of his days, that the initiative for his encirclement came from Vienna. Yet in fact it came from the Russians, who pressed the Austrians to take action, and threatened that they would act on their own if necessary. A plan

'to wipe out Prussia' did exist and it was drawn up in Russia. British alarm at Russia's military preparations was allayed with assurances that these were being made in order to keep her treaty with Britain. Frederick assumed that the British could keep the Russians under control, but what he did not realize was that Russia was rather more anxious to make war on Prussia than Austria. 'From the start it set out to produce a plan for the reduction of the power of Prussia, and it continued in existence almost to the end of the Seven Years' War, dealing with all aspects of that conflict, diplomatic, military, financial and administrative. It was a council especially intended for the direction of what we call the Seven Years' War – only it began that work in March 1756, five months before Frederick attacked Saxony.' (Sir Herbert Butterfield).

Russia was the driving force; it offered 80,000 men to Maria Theresa and both Russia and Austria were making political preparations 'to goad Prussia into making the attack.' Frederick was only partially, if at all, aware of all this. He believed the center of the conspiracy to be in Vienna, and now decided to arm himself with all speed and as much noise as possible to show his neighbors that he was not to be caught unawares. He inquired in Vienna several times about the purpose of Austria's military preparations, but, receiving evasive answers, he put himself at the head of his army on 28 August 1756 and occupied Saxony.

His main army consisted of 61,600 men and, with the occupation of Saxony and the capitulation of the Saxon army in the fortress of Pirma on 16 October 1756, Frederick had gained a secure base for the further conduct of his operations; with the onset of winter, however, the attack on Bohemia had to be abandoned. Frederick took the Saxon troops which had capitu-

lated into his army, a serious error because, at decisive moments, they were to desert *en masse*.

On 18 April 1757, after abandoning his winter quarters, he assembled his army in four groups near Chemnitz, Dresden, Zittau and Landeshut, a total force of 116,000 men, while 30,000 Prussian troops covered East Prussia. He operated on external lines, meaning his army was widely spread out, and entered Bohemia. The Austrians, equally strong, were to the southeast of him. The aim of the operation was to penetrate to Leitmeritz with two army groups to get at the rear of Prague, while the other two groups were to march upon Prague directly. The plan succeeded, but now came the siege of Prague, which could be achieved only by starving out the garrison of 50,000 troops. At the same time he had to ward off the Austrian relief army under Field Marshal Daun. Time was pressing, and so were supply problems. The French, Russians, Swedes and the army of the Reich were also about to attack. Daun's forces gave cause for concern since there was no defensive position Frederick could take, whilst Daun, in his position west of Kolin, cut off the Prussian lines of supply. Frederick attempted first to storm Prague; he applied his oblique battle order but lacked the strength to envelop the enemy's flanks. Signs of rout were evident among the Prussian army when Schwerin, as at Mollwitz, took hold of the regimental colors and at the head of his battalion stormed the Austrian positions. Under murderous Austrian defensive fire, the aged field marshal was killed, his body entwined with the colors. The infantry attack was decisively supported by the Prussian cavalry under General von Zieten. It was the bloodiest battle so far in the history of warfare, and the Austrians lost over 15,000 men. However, though a breach was made, Prague was not taken and the bulk of the

Above. *Von Schwerin surveys the ground.*

Left. *Frederick rides forward across the snow-covered ground at Leuthen.*

Below left. *Menzel's unfinished painting shows Frederick addressing his generals before Leuthen, telling them of his intention to attack a numerically superior and strongly positioned enemy.*

Austrian army withdrew into the fortress; Frederick held it under siege, expecting in vain that it would shortly fall.

Frederick now had to turn to Daun. Lacking the element of surprise, Daun expected Frederick at Kolin, with his army of 54,000 pitched against Frederick's 33,000. Daun's men waited for the Prussian attack; Frederick again decided in favor of the oblique order of battle, but the premature action of one of his generals, who initiated a cavalry attack, turned it into a battle over the entire front. Time and again the Prussian infantry lines advanced agaist the volleys of the Austrian army, and time and again they were thrown back. When the Saxon cavalry regiments from Poland rode a devastating attack against the weakest link in the Prussian line of battle, the Prussian troops would no longer go forward. Frederick in person had gathered 40 men of the Anhalt regiment to attack when an Englishman, Major Grant, called to him: 'But Sire, do you intend to conquer the batteries on your own?'

The battle was lost for the Prussians, and it could have been a disastrous defeat had Daun pursued them. But being cautious, the idea did not appeal to him. The defeat at Kolin on 18 June 1757 gave Frederick's plan of campaign an entirely different face. He now had to give up Bohemia altogether, and the siege of Prague was raised. Within his family, doubts were voiced about Frederick's generalship: his brother, Prince Henry, wrote a letter on the evening of the battle to his sister Amalie: 'Phaëthon has fallen, we do not know what will become of us.'

Moreover, problems emerged elsewhere. The French had beaten the Hanoverian forces of the Duke of Cumberland; Frederick dealt with that problem at once by returning to the tactic of the strategic defensive but combining it with the tactical offensive. A French army under Prince Soubise, sup-

ported by troops of the Empire, moved toward the River Saale intending to attack Frederick in Saxony. Frederick anticipated this with a force of 20,000 against the enemy's 50,000. On 5 November 1757 at Rossbach, the Prussian army attacked the enemy while it was still on the march. The attack demonstrated the high degree of mobility achieved by the Prussian army, which, while marching parallel to the French columns, formed itself into attacking echelons without the slightest difficulty. The Prussian attack threw the French into a state of utter confusion, confusion which was turned into a rout by the Prussian cavalry under General von Seydlitz, which scattered the enemy in all directions. Thereafter the French army ceased to play a significant part in the Seven Years' War in central Europe.

'That battle,' said Napoleon, 'was a masterpiece. Of itself it is sufficient to entitle Frederick to a first place in the rank among generals.' The French guns, their colors, baggage and mistresses had fallen into the hands of the Prussian army. The victory of Rossbach had an immense psychological impact upon Germany: 'Never since the dissolution of the empire of Charlemagne had the Teutonic race won such a field against the French. The tidings called forth a general burst of delight and pride from the whole of the great family which spoke the various dialects of the ancient language of Arminius. The fame of Frederick began to supply, in some degree, the place of a common government and a common capital. It became the rallying point for all true Germans, a subject of mutual congratulation to the Bavarian and the Westphalian, to the citizen of Nuremberg. Then first was it manifest that the Germans were truly a nation . . .' (Macaulay).

Rossbach also symbolized the beginning of Germany's literary and cultural emancipation from the French – in spite of a Prussian king who culturally was rather more a product of France than of Germany. Rossbach was the Agincourt of the German people.

But it was not only in Germany that the effect was felt. In Macaulay's words: 'Yet even the enthusiasm of Germany in favour of Frederick hardly equalled the enthusiasm of England.

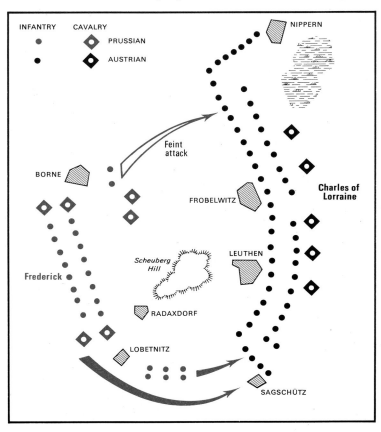

The birthday of our ally was celebrated with as much enthusiasm as that of our own sovereign; and at night the streets of London were in a blaze of illuminations. Portraits of the hero of Rossbach, with his cocked hat and long pigtail, were in every house. An attentive observer will, at this day (April 1842), find in the parlours of old-fashioned inns, and in the portfolios of printsellers, twenty portraits of Frederick for one of George II. The sign-painters were everywhere employed in touching up Admiral Vernon into the King of Prussia. This enthusiasm was strong among religious people, and especially among the Methodists, who knew that the French and Austrians were Papists, and supposed Frederick to be Joshua or Gideon of the Reformed Faith.'

Frederick had no time to enjoy his victory, however – Rossbach had given back to him his operational freedom. After having invaded East Prussia the Russians had been thrown back again. Prince Charles of Lorraine, though, had deeply penetrated into Silesia with his main army; the Duke of Bevern had not been able to resist this advance and encamped himself in a defensive position awaiting Frederick to retrieve the situation. Frederick's aim was to reconquer the whole of Silesia before the winter put an end to campaigning. He required the province to resupply his army and to give it a rest, as well as an operational base against Bohemia and Moravia. If he could not beat the Austrians decisively, there was little chance for a peace settlement.

On 13 November 1757 the king set out with 18 battalions and 29 cavalry squadrons, roughly 14,000 men. He had to cover well over 200 miles in the shortest possible time, and abandoned the route along which his supply depots were established. The troops lived off the land. *En route* one piece of bad news chased the other. The Austrians had conquered the fortress of Schweidnitz, then inflicted a defeat on a Prussian contingent near Breslau and occupied the city. Zieten was sent out to stabilize the situation, in which he partially succeeded; by 2 December he returned to the main army with 20,000 men, while Frederick had been encamped since 28 November at Parchwitz. There, in the camp, almost miraculous changes were brought about: the

discouraged and exhausted Prussian troops transformed themselves again into a military force seldom seen in the eighteenth century. Virtually free from deserters, it was again the old core of the Prussian peasant infantry. Frederick did all he could to encourage his soldiers. Then, on the evening of 3 December, he assembled his officers, generals and commanding officers and addressed them:

'Gentlemen! . . . I have prepared a plan of battle that I shall, and must, wage tomorrow. I shall, against all the rules of the art, attack an enemy which is nearly twice as strong as ourselves and entrenched on high ground. I must do it, for if I do not, all is lost. We must defeat the enemy, or let their batteries dig our graves. This is what I think and how I propose to act. But if there is anyone among you who thinks otherwise, let him ask leave here to depart. I will grant it him, without the slightest reproach. . . . I thought that none of you would leave me; so now I count entirely on your loyal help, and on certain victory. . . . Now go to the camp and tell your regiments what I have said to you here, and assure them that I shall watch each of them closely. The cavalry regiment that does not charge the enemy at once, on the word of command, I shall have unhorsed immediately after battle and turned into a garrison regiment. The infantry regiment which begins to falter for a moment, for whatever reason, will lose its colors and its swords, and will have the braid cut off its uniforms. Now gentlemen farewell; by this hour tomorrow we shall have defeated the enemy, or we shall not see one another again.'

The Austrians were spread out over a front stretching a mile and a half, in a defensive position, while Frederick's forces occupied a considerably shorter front, at the village of Leuthen. The Prussians succeeded in concentrating their main effort against the left wing of the Austrians, who, instead of attacking the Prussians while they were still in the process of forming up, were content to wait and let them come. They also failed to recognize until it was too late where Frederick would place the main emphasis of his attack. At first it seemed to the Austrians that the main force of the Prussian attack would be directed against their center; then, before they realized what was hap-

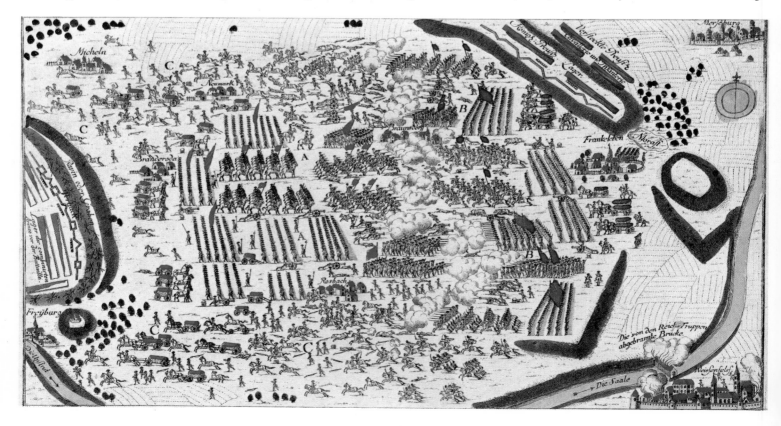

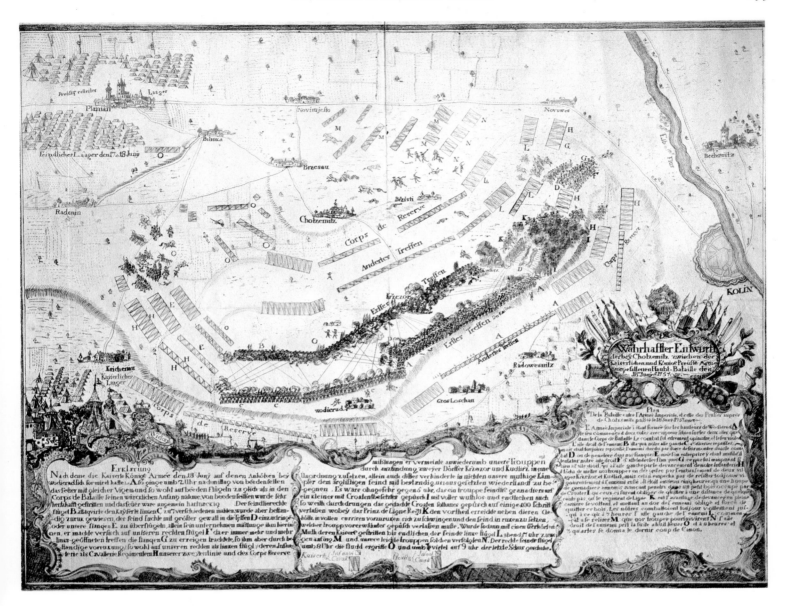

Left. *A contemporary artist's view of Rossbach.*

Above. *The Battle of Kolin, 18 June 1757. Frederick's attempt at a flanking attack went badly wrong, and the ensuing battle cost his army 15,000 casualties (contemporary Austrian plan).*

Right. *The German artist Knotel's view of Frederick addressing his generals before Leuthen.*

Left. *Another contemporary view of Leuthen.*

Below left. *A panoramic view of Leuthen, looking along the length of the Austrian position. The Austrian left flank (bottom) is already in trouble, and a fierce fight is developing for the village of Leuthen itself.*

Below. *On 30 June 1758 the Austrians ambushed a large ammunition convoy bound for Frederick's siege lines before Olmütz. The raid was so successful that it led to Frederick's abandonment of the siege.*

pening, the Prussian troops re-formed and attacked the Austrian left flank. The oblique order of battle proved a complete success and Leuthen became a resounding defeat for the Austrians. In a state of disorganization and chaos they left Silesia and withdrew into Bohemia. True, they had fought bravely, the village churchyard had been defended by them like lions. But still they were overcome by the Prussians; Frederick had once again secured his prize. On the evening of that day on the snow-covered, bloodstained ground of Leuthen, dimly lit by camp fires, a voice began to sing among the groaning of the dying and wounded and within seconds the entire Prussian army took up the hymn: 'Now Thank Thee All Our God' – *der Choral von Leuthen*. Even Frederick, the religious sceptic, was deeply moved.

Rossbach and Leuthen also paid dividends in the realm of foreign policy. In April 1758 an agreement was signed between Prussia and Britain in which both powers promised not to enter into a separate peace and Prussia was given an annual subsidy of £670,000. For Frederick things seemed to look up again; he could return to his original plan of attack against Austrian territory. In 1758, however, he chose Moravia rather than Bohemia as his area of operations. He hoped to force Maria Theresa to make peace by conquering the fortress of Olmütz, but it was not to be taken and this compelled him once again to abandon the strategic offensive. The Russians had returned to East Prussia, conquered Königsberg and compelled the city to pay homage to the czarina. There was little that Frederick could do about East Prussia, but when the Russians advanced into Neumark, bombarding Küstrin with their artillery, their objective became clear, namely to link up with the Austrian forces. This he had to prevent at all costs. On 25 August 1758 at Zorndorf, the main Prussian and Russian armies encountered

F. Weigand. X.A.

Left. *Ragged Russian prisoners receive donations from the ladies of Berlin.*

Right. *As night fell across the battlefield of Leuthen a Prussian grenadier began to sing the old hymn Nun danket alle Gott. Soon more than 25,000 men were singing it in gratitude for survival and victory.*

Center left. *Frederick's brother, Prince Henry, defeated the Austrians at Freiberg on 29 October 1762. Here we see the Prussian cuirassiers crashing into the Austrian infantry.*

Below right. *An English engraving shows the Prussian lines rolling forward at Leuthen.*

Below left. *Austrian cavalry cut up retreating Prussian infantry at Kunersdorf, 12 August 1759.*

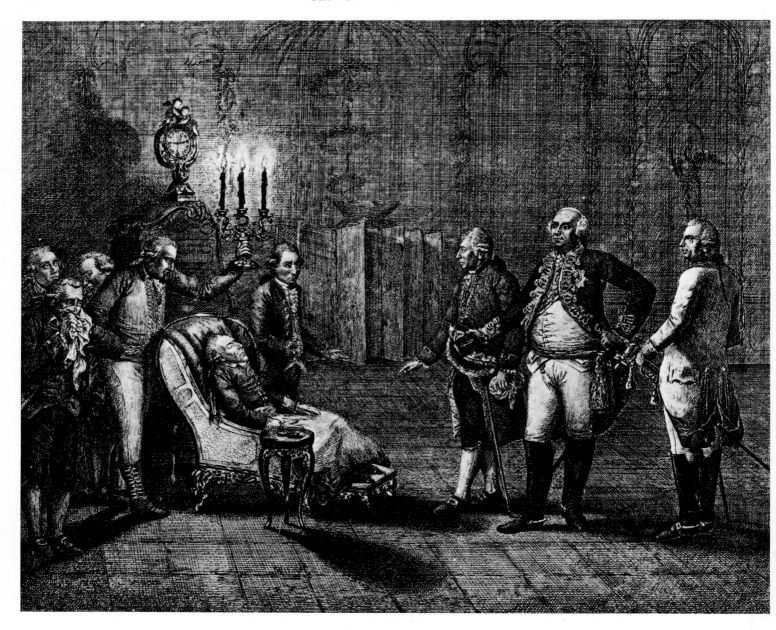

each other for the first time in major battle. It lasted all day. The Russian infantry fought with steadfastness and bravery, and with a defiance of death that made even Frederick shudder. The Prussian battalions showed signs of exhaustion and at one point Frederick personally led his men into attack. The Prussian cavalry under General von Seydlitz, riding attack after attack, once again stabilized the situation in favor of the Prussian army. The battle ended not because the Russians had been defeated, but because night intervened. Short of ammunition, the Prussian army looked forward rather apprehensively to the renewal of the struggle on the following day, but next morning they were relieved to find that the Russians had withdrawn, leaving behind 20,000 casualties, half of the original strength. Frederick had secured his objective of preventing the Russians from linking up with the Austrians. When the British envoy, Sir Andrew Mitchell, congratulated Frederick on the battlefield for his victory, Frederick pointed toward Seydlitz and said: 'Without him we would have fared badly.'

Using the advantage of interior lines of communication, Frederick now turned toward the River Lausitz, where Daun seriously threatened the Prussian army commanded by the king's brother, Prince Henry. The Austrian surprise attack upon Frederick's unfortified camp at Hochkirch during the night of 13 October put an end to his underestimation of Daun. The Austrians captured more than 100 pieces of Prussian artillery.

Hochkirch also, however, provided a demonstration of the discipline of the Prussian army. As Field Chaplain Küster records in his memoirs: 'Here in the complete darkness, in which the watching eye of the officers could not supervise his men and command them to form up into their ranks, nor call back those that had been separated from their units, here the bulk of the musketeers demonstrated that they knew their duty even without the command of an officer.' In this battle Frederick's soldiers performed the impossible, a withdrawal in exemplary order, and Daun did not venture to pursue the Prussians. Daun's failure to exploit his success allowed Frederick to grasp the initiative again, and in the end maintain control of both Silesia and Saxony.

By the beginning of 1759 Frederick came to accept that, because of limited resources of men and materials, he could fight only a defensive war to maintain Silesia and Saxony. A shortage of manpower slowly made itself felt, and a number of the best generals had been killed; in the Seven Years' War more than 1500 officers were killed, including 33 generals in the years between 1756 and 1759. In his personal life Frederick had also suffered tragedy; his favorite sister had died of gout, the family disease of the Hohenzollerns. He himself was suffering from it, and it was taking its toll of his own personal stamina. In the spring of 1759 the Russians renewed their attack, beating the Prussian forces under General Wedel in the Neumark, and

Left. The death of Frederick, early in the morning of 17 August 1786.

Right. The Empress Maria Theresa.

Below. The Seven Years War in northwestern Germany: In July 1761 Ferdinand of Brunswick defeated the Duc de Broglie at Vellinghausen.

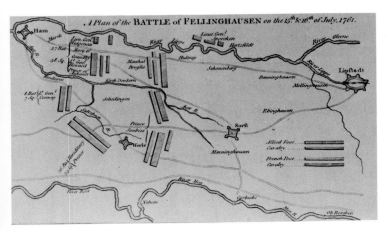

approached Frankfurt-an-der-Oder. Frederick decided to attack them at Kunersdorf near Frankfurt. On 12 August 1759 he had 53,000 men under his command; the combined force of Russians and Austrians numbered 70,000. The Prussian army concentrated its attack on the Russians, who were in well-entrenched positions with their artillery positioned on the commanding heights to the northeast. Frederick again took recourse to the oblique order of battle, but the resourceful Russian commander, General Shaltikov, made a riposte. By fortifying his forces at the center heavily, he made them virtually invulnerable to attack, and made them available for use as reinforcements in either the left or the right wing. Frederick attacked the Russian left wing across extremely difficult ground, and the attack soon got bogged down in the Russian defensive fire. Attack succeeded attack, each suffering the same fate, and the intervention of the Prussian cavalry was cut short when Seydlitz was wounded. Two horses were killed under the king. Then the Austrian cavalry commanded by Marshal Laudon, an officer whom Frederick had once rejected for service in the Prussian army, attacked and routed the Prussian forces. As at Zorndorf, Frederick took up the colors of Prince Henry's regiment and, shouting to his soldiers, 'Lads, do you want to live eternally?', took them into attack. When that failed he tried to form a defensive line, but the Prussian army was in disarray, fleeing back toward the River Oder in the west; the king himself was nearly captured by Cossacks.

The Prussian army was beaten, and soundly at that. For the next 24 hours Frederick thought that his end, and the end of his state, had come.

While the king was in a state of despair, however, Prussian discipline reasserted itself. His adjutants collected what remained of the army. It had lost 25,000 men, the Russian army

19,000. Instead of the Austrians and Russians venturing upon a common pursuit of the Prussian army, however, they followed their different aims. Shaltikov had overestimated the Prussian resources and, after the losses he had sustained, was not prepared to sacrifice much more for Austria's benefit, while Daun was more interested in reconquering Silesia than in marching into Berlin; Russians and Austrians moved off in different directions. Frederick had also lost Dresden, and Saxony now became the theater of operations again. But Prussia's prospects seemed gloomy; shortages of every kind increased his wish for peace. Jointly with England he proposed peace negotiations in November 1759, but Austria, encouraged by her successes, rejected the proposal. Frederick failed to achieve his campaign objective for 1760, namely to recapture Dresden, and consequently had to give up Saxony and withdraw into Silesia, while Prince Henry kept the Russians in check in the northeast. At Liegnitz Frederick achieved his first major success against Laudon since Kunersdorf. Confidence resurged among the Prussians. Frederick

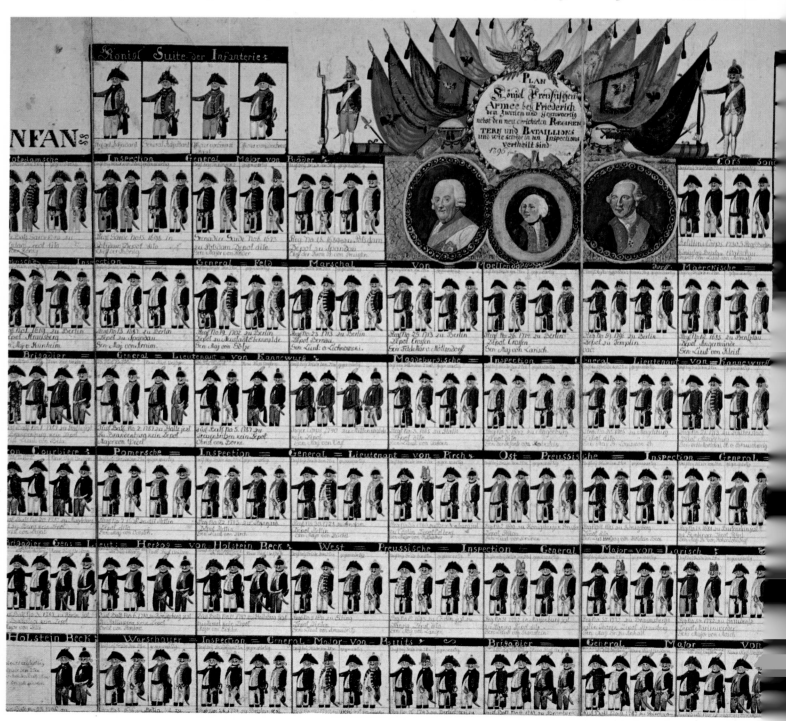

thought he could now force fate and attempt one more bid for Saxony. On 3 November 1760 he fought and won the Battle of Torgau, but the weakness of his forces did not permit him to follow up this victory and achieve his actual objective, the capture of Dresden.

Since the death of George II in 1760, Pitt, Prussia's most faithful ally, had been hard pressed in the Lords and Commons by a faction demanding peace, in the light of Britain's recently acquired supremacy in Canada. That desire for peace was shared by France, Russia and Austria, who now agreed to Frederick's earlier suggestion of convening a peace congress at Augsburg. However, because Frederick made Prussia's participation conditional on the acceptance of his demand that Prussia should not lose any of its territory, the congress was never convened. Britain's ally now became the most serious obstacle to peace.

Frederick's lack of manpower was approaching dangerous proportions. Volunteer regiments were set up, while in the regular army two-thirds of the men were foreigners; even

Left. *An invaluable source of uniform detail, this colored drawing by von Muhlen shows the uniforms worn by Frederick the Great's infantry.*

cadets from the age of 14 were called into active service. With such devices he increased his army again to 100,000 men. Encamped at Bunzelwitz in Lower Silesia, he awaited the enemy attack, an attack which could well have been the *coup de grâce* for his forces had not Daun overestimated the Prussian strength and refrained from attacking. On 5 October 1761 Pitt resigned, and Britain virtually abandoned Prussia.

Then on 5 January 1762 a miracle happened that Frederick had not expected: Czarina Elizabeth died and her nephew, the Duke of Holstein-Gottorp, Peter III, became her successor. An ardent admirer of Frederick the Great, he declared Russia's disinterest in all conquests and recommended to the allies a speedy end to hostilities. Peace between Russia and Prussia was signed on 22 May 1762, and the Russian forces received orders to return home. Thus most of the campaign of 1762, with the exception of the Battle of Freiberg on 29 October when the Austrians were defeated again, had followed the traditional eighteenth-century pattern of warfare, the strategy of attrition.

Austria, facing financial ruin, felt that the war was exacting sacrifices hardly justified by the reconquest of one province. Dire economic necessity compelled Austria and Prussia to agree on an armistice for the winter of 1762–63. Britain concluded its separate peace with France at Fontainebleau on 3 November 1762; it precipitated the initiation of discussions between Prussia and Austria. Frederick gave assurances that he would return to Saxony whatever he held, without indemnities. Ultimately, these negotiations led to the conclusion of the Peace of Hubertusberg in 1763 by which Frederick retained what he had had in 1740 – namely Silesia. His rendezvous with fame had led him along avenues which he had hardly expected in 1740; indeed, on several occasions during the Seven Years' War he expressed regret over this youthful folly. Frederick the Great, the Prussian army and Prussia as a whole were totally exhausted, but Prussia had been established as a major power in Germany as well as in Europe.

Right. *Frederick the Great: the warrior king in old age.*

CHAPTER IX
WARFARE IN THE
NEW WORLD: NORTH AMERICA

Since the late sixteenth century North America had been the object of European colonization, primarily by the British, Dutch and French. The Dutch colonial empire in North America was the most short-lived. Ever since the days of Cromwell and the rise of his navy, Britain and Holland had eyed one another distrustfully, envious of each other's commerce. This state of affairs did not change after the Restoration in 1660. Conflict usually began among the trading companies overseas, after which the respective mother countries then intervened. Hostilities between Britain and Holland began in this way in West Africa in 1664. After subduing the Dutch there, an English squadron set out for North America and seized the Dutch settlement of New Amsterdam, changing the name to New York. All this took place before any formal declaration of war between the two countries was issued – in fact war was not declared until February 1665. Such action was highly popular in England; Cromwell's former confidant, General Monk, said, 'What matters this or that reason? What we want is more of the trade which the Dutch now have.'

France had been established in Canada since 1603, moving into the interior and then southward along the Mississippi where, in 1682, she established the territory of Louisiana. France's colonial policy was not dissimilar to that which had been pursued by Spain in South America. Its emphasis lay mainly on commercial exploitation, the search for minerals and the beaver trade, all with the intention of producing additional revenue for the empty coffers of Louis XIV's treasury. These ventures were also accompanied by intense missionary activities by the Jesuits among the Indian tribes. Virginia had been in British hands since 1584, Massachusetts since 1620, Maryland since 1632 and the former Dutch colonies of New York, New Jersey and Delaware since 1664. In 1683 William Penn founded the Quaker colony of Pennsylvania and in 1713 Britain also gained Newfoundland and Nova Scotia, which brought them, of course, into sharp conflict with the French.

British settlements were established with the intention of territorial expansion and were therefore much more densely populated than those of the French; this was particularly the case in New England, where the influx of immigrants came in two major phases, before 1640 and after 1660 – in other words, at times when life for the Puritan sects was rather uncomfortable, during the reign of Charles I and after the restoration of Charles II. The French Huguenots emigrated to Canada for similar reasons, but Louis XIV was not prepared to tolerate what he considered heretical settlements in Canada. Therefore they had to find another place of refuge much farther to the south in the Carolinas, where they made a permanent residence – incidentally, side-by-side with the Roman Catholic communities which had already established themselves there. By the time the Treaty of Utrecht was signed in 1713, there were 158,000 British colonists in New England and 20,000 French colonists in Canada. By 1748 the French had increased their number to 80,000, but the British colonies outstripped them by well over a million.

By the Treaty of Utrecht the French lost Newfoundland and Nova Scotia to the British. To compensate for this the French established the fortress of Louisburg on Cape Breton Island controlling the entrance to the St Lawrence River, and tensions increased anew between British and French settlers. In 1745, when France and Britain were at war, New England settlers under the command of William Shirley, Governor of Massachusetts, assisted by five British men-of-war under Admiral Warren, laid siege to Louisburg and, after five weeks, captured it. However, it was only a temporary gain. By the Treaty of Aachen in 1748, Louisburg was returned to the French.

Previous spread. On 4 October 1777 Washington made a surprise attack on British headquarters in the village of Germantown. The attack was foiled by a fog which threw the assaulting columns into confusion.

Right. A French view of Louisburg.

Far right. King George II 1683 – 1760, succeeded to the throne 1727.

Right. Forces from the New England colonies forced Louisburg to capitulate in 1745. The subsequent peace treaty returned the town to France. This contemporary British print emphasizes the role played by British forces, which was in fact relatively minor.

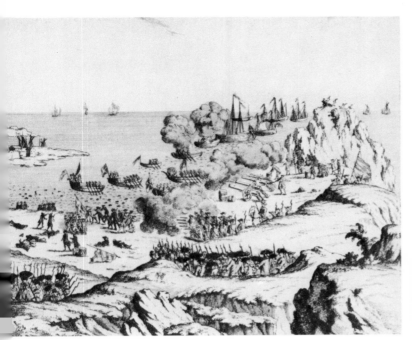

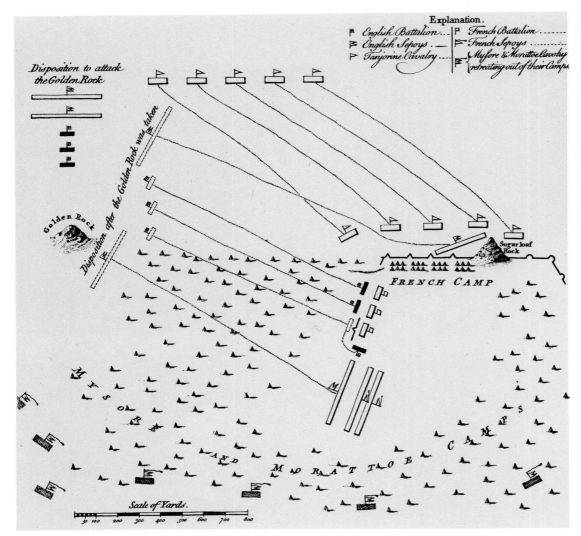

Disposition to attack
the Golden Rock

Golden Rock

Disposition after the Golden Rock was taken

FRENCH CAMP

Sugar loaf Rock

MISORE AND MORATTOE CAMPS

Scale of Yards.

Explanation.

English Battalion .... French Battalion ....
English Sepoys .... French Sepoys ....
Tanjorine Cavalry .... Mysore & Morattoe Cavalry
                                  retreating out of their Camps.

Above. *William Pitt the younger, 1757–1806, denounced Britain's struggle with her North American colonists.*

Left. *British troops were active on the plains of India as well as in the backwoods of North America. A contemporary plan of Major Stringer Lawrence's attack on the camp of the French and their Indian allies, September 1754.*

Below right. *The mortally wounded Major General Edward Braddock retreating with the remnants of his force.*

Below. *Braddock was ambushed by the French and Indians near Fort Duquesne on 9 July 1755.*

Hardly had the treaty been concluded than the French Governor of Canada, de la Gallisonière, initiated a scheme which attempted to cut off the British settlements from the rear. He sent out an expedition into the Ohio region and claimed it in the name of Louis XV. The objective was to link Canada and Louisiana by a chain of forts and contain the British to the eastern seaboard; the British colonists, however, had already begun their westward expansion. In small groups they penetrated the Appalachians, some of them settling in the fertile valleys, others making their way to the southwest into Tennessee or to the northwest into the bluegrass region of Ohio. In 1753 the British Governor of Virginia, Robert Dinwiddie, sent out a young man by the name of George Washington, supported by a small number of soldiers, to establish a fort at the point where the Alleghany and Monongahela rivers joined. In 1754 Washington was sent out again, this time supported by 400 soldiers and Indians; a series of minor skirmishes ensued between the French and the British, but the French, far superior in numbers, compelled Washington to surrender.

So far Anglo-French relations in North America were characterized by 'mutual pestering,' but Washington's surrender changed all that. In the spring of 1755 two regiments were sent to North America from Britain. From Alexandria in Virginia they were sent out under the command of General James Braddock, accompanied by Washington, who had since been released by the French, with the objective of capturing Fort Duquesne, which had been built on a site which Washington, in fact, had selected as suitable for a fort a couple of years earlier. The military expedition consisted of 1400 British regulars and 600 members of the Virginia militia. The regulars advanced as though they were on a European marching route; Braddock ignored all advice given to him to the effect that North America was not a theater of war to be compared with Europe, and that traditional forms of advance and tactics did not apply. He

marched on in a column of three rows, drums rolling and fifes blaring, with the result that, in the forests along the Monongahela River, he was ambushed by the Indians, mainly Iroquois, supporting the French, 863 soldiers being killed including Braddock. James Fenimore Cooper, in his *Leatherstocking Tales*, has left us a very graphic account of this ambush. However, hardly one of the Virginia militia was killed, for they knew how to exploit the geographical advantages the country offered and were not prepared to act as foolhardily as Braddock and his troops. But then, from the point of view of the British regulars, the colonial militias were hardly considered to be soldiers: at best they were good support forces, at worse a disobedient rabble who cared little for taking orders from regular officers.

When the French and Indian War officially broke out in 1756, the French sent out the Marquis de Montcalm to Quebec to take over command of the French forces in Canada, which were under the governorship of the Marquis de Vaudreul.

Actually Montcalm's arrival had been preceded by that of Lord Loudon and General James Abercromby, the former to take over as commander-in-chief of the British forces. 'I do not augur very well of the ensuing summer; a detachment is going to America under a commander whom a child might outwit or terrify with a popgun,' was Sir Horace Walpole's comment on the commander and his expedition. In fact, Loudon and Abercromby both lacked drive and initiative. Decisive action was not their *forte* – first they procrastinated the entire summer in taking Fort Ticonderoga, an objective which they abandoned when they thought that the capture of Louisburg would prove less arduous. Arriving near the fortress, they found out that the French fleet was superior to their own, so they abandoned the project altogether. Montcalm, meanwhile, was given time to assemble his 8000 French Canadians and Indian tribes at Ticonderoga undisturbed and then march upon Fort William Henry, which they quickly forced to surrender.

Only a change at home had any effect on circumstances in North America. When William Pitt joined the Newcastle administration he virtually ran the country. Relying on Prussia to deal with France in Europe, he concentrated all British efforts to defeat and expel the French army from Canada. With a shrewd eye for talent, political and military, he selected the best soldiers and sailors and replaced Loudon by Abercromby. Then he recalled General Amherst from Germany and sent him out to North America. Pitt's instructions were to capture the three pillars of French power in Canada in 1758: Fort Duquesne, Ticonderoga and Louisburg.

Louisburg was the first objective because it controlled the St Lawrence River. Since 1748 it had been further fortified and contained a garrison of 3000 soldiers under the command of the Chevalier de Drocour; they were also supported by 12 warships. Pitt in turn raised 22 warships of the line, 15 frigates and 120 transports; they were to carry and support 14 battalions of infantry as well as artillery and engineers, all under the command of Amherst.

He set sail for Halifax accompanied by Brigadier General Lawrence and Brigadier General James Wolfe. Sailing from Portsmouth on 19 February 1758, they arrived at Halifax on 28 May. They found all necessary preparations had been made and put to sea again, anchoring in Gabarus Bay on 2 June. The British immediately destroyed the major French batteries and Wolfe, advancing round the harbor, captured Lighthouse Point. Having got that far, the siege of Louisburg could now be pressed home. On 26 July Drocour surrendered to the British and the St Lawrence River was now open. Amherst tried to persuade Admiral Boscawen, in charge of the naval forces, to

sail up the river to Quebec, but he considered the obstacles too serious and the project was abandoned.

The capture of Fort Duquesne, which was the gateway to the west, was entrusted by Pitt to Brigadier General John Forbes. With a backbone of 1500 Highlanders supported by 4800 men of the colonial militias, including Washington, he set out early in July. Forbes made a number of errors, similar to Braddock's, but he managed to patch them up. The French had already realized that they were in an untenable position, so they evacuated the fort and burned it down; all that Forbes found were the smoldering remnants. The site is now part of Pittsburgh.

The capture of Ticonderoga was important because it opened the land route for the British to advance upon Montreal and Quebec. The operation was initially commanded by Abercromby but, being unsure of himself as usual, he handed over command to his deputy, Lord Howe. Howe was one of the few British officers who was prepared to forget all he had learned about traditional tactics – indeed, he had been trained by the American ranger Robert Rogers. He assembled the largest British force yet seen in North America: 6350 regulars and 9000 militiamen. At the end of June 1758 he broke camp at Albany and advanced to the ruins of Fort William Henry. There, on 5 July, his army began to cross Lake George in over 1000 vessels. On the next day he landed to head a reconnaissance party, but was almost immediately killed by a rifle shot. This put command back into the hands of Abercromby, who had little will and courage left.

Three days later the army encountered the first French obstacles which Montcalm had erected. Abercromby ordered a frontal assault without waiting for his artillery to come up. The

Left. *Lieutenant General Sir William Pepperell at the siege of Louisburg.*

Right. *Jeffrey, 1st Lord Amherst, 1717–97. This formal portrait, after Sir Joshua Reynolds, shows Amherst overlooking the heights of Abraham in 1759. Armor was by now out of date, and was depicted only as a convention in such portraits. This is particularly ironic in Amherst's case, for he was an enterprising, forward-looking officer who had little use for the stiff formality which had contributed to Braddock's defeat.*

Below. *Raising the British flag at Fort Duquesne, 1758. George Washington, seen in the center of this nineteenth-century print, took part in the expedition as an officer of colonial militia.*

British mounted seven assaults but were mowed down by the defending French infantry. The British troops retreated in disorder, making their way back as best they could to the landing place. Ticonderoga held firmly under Montcalm, though overall the balance sheet for the British in 1758 was not bad: they had captured Louisburg and Fort Duquesne. Also, in a brilliant sortie carried out by Colonel Broadstreet, British forces crossed Lake Ontario and burned down Fort Frontenac. The main gates into Canada were open.

Pitt decided that in 1759 the attack should be mounted on a broader front from the mouth of the St Lawrence River to Lake Erie. In the meantime, Amherst had also succeeded where Abercromby had failed – he drove the French from Fort Ticonderoga. Amherst's orders were now to move on to Montreal and Wolfe, supported by the Royal Navy, was to take Quebec. A third army under General Prideaux was to advance up the Mohawk River, clear Lake Ontario, occupy Niagara and so clear the trade route to Lake Erie.

Wolfe had already had a distinguished career: he had fought in Germany in the 1740s and had been present at Culloden. He disdained the colonial militia, however, and believed that the Red Indians were fit only to be exterminated. But he took immense care about every detail, and had learned from Braddock's disaster: 'The regiment will march by files from the left, and is to be formed two deep; if the front is attacked, that company that leads is immediately to form to ye front two deep and advance upon the enemy; the next is to do the same. Inclining to ye right of the enemy, the next to ye left if the ground will permit of it, and so on to ye right and left, until an extensive front is form'd, by which the enemy may be surrounded. And as an attack may be sudden and time lost in sending orders, these movements are to be made in such a case by the several officers without waiting for any. If the column is attack'd on ye left, the whole are to face to ye left and attack ye enemy, on ye right ye same; if in ye rear, the rear is to act as the front was order'd, the whole going to the right about; if on the right and left, the two ranks are to face outwards, if in ye front and rear, ye first and last companies front both ways.'

Pitt, aware that the first problem was not land but sea power, selected Admiral Saunders, Admiral Holmes and Admiral Durrell. The first two were to cooperate with Wolfe's army and the third was to carry an expedition to block the St Lawrence River against any French attempts to bring supplies to their troops.

Wolfe was given *carte blanche* to appoint his own subordinates; they were mainly under 30 years old. 'It was a boy's campaign,' as one cynical contemporary observed. Wolfe made his preparations while Montcalm, who had no idea where the major blow would fall, tried to resist Amherst at Lake Champlain and Fort Niagara. His position was not an enviable one: Canada had a population of only 82,000 to the American colonies' 1,300,000. He was also insufficiently supported from France, where the funds for royal consumption at Versailles were considered more important than those needed for the defense of Canada against the British onslaught. Inevitably, corruption flourished within the Canadian administration, leading to economic stagnation and decline: 'Agriculture and trade were paralyzed, loyalty shaken, while diminished resources, and discontented people, hastened the inevitable catastrophe of British triumph.' Yet a stroke of luck did come Montcalm's way – the British Admiral, Durrell, because he feared the tide of the St Lawrence, did not enter it, allowing 18 French vessels to pass up the river to Quebec. The French had also intercepted a letter from General Amherst which contained details of the British plan. Montcalm had rushed to Quebec and made all necessary preparations, nearly foiling Wolfe's plans.

Quebec as a fortress was considered impregnable, and had been modelled on Vauban's pattern of fortifications. Moreover, standing on a rocky hillside between the St Lawrence and St Charles rivers, there was access by land only on one side. At first Montcalm played for time, hoping that the storms and fog of the autumn would drive the British naval forces away. The British navy, however, withstood the weather and in the spring of 1759 Wolfe could make his advance. On 9 June the fleet entered the Gulf of St Lawrence, had come upstream by the 26th, and the Isle of Orleans was occupied. Having now seen Quebec for the first time, Wolfe had to devise a plan; in the meantime, however, both Wolfe and Montcalm played a game of wits. Montcalm was now running short of supplies, and Wolfe intended to force him out of Quebec and give battle. Wolfe ferried his army on flat-bottomed boats and landed near a little-known path which led the British troops up to the heights of the Plains of Abraham; this was a serious threat to Montcalm's lines of supply. The Plains of Abraham consisted of a plateau of grassland about a mile wide.

Montcalm was forced to accept battle. His total strength amounted to approximately 5000 men, Wolfe's actual battle

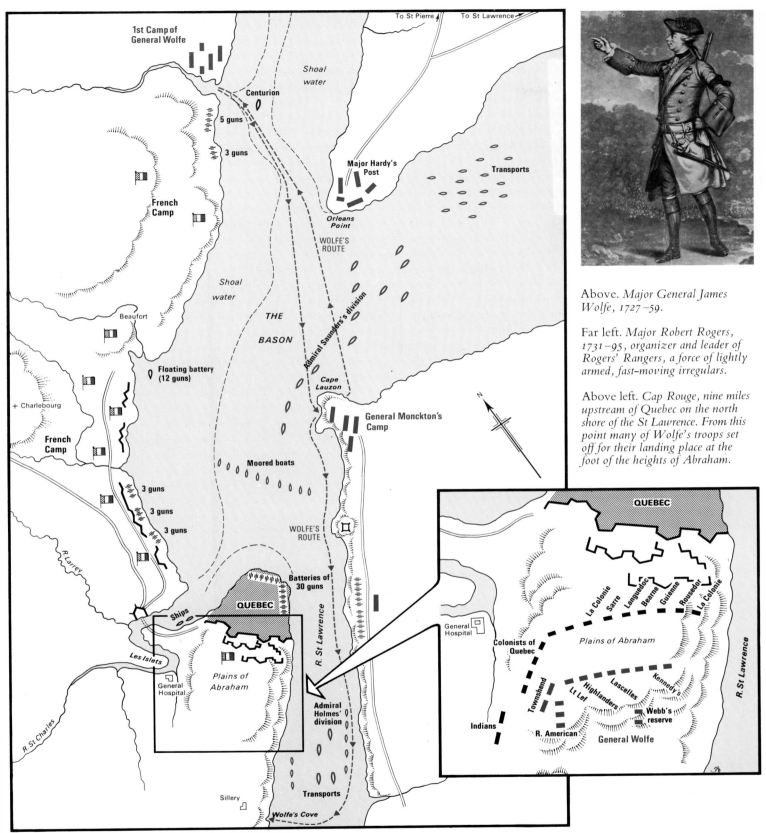

1st Camp of General Wolfe

Centurion

5 guns

3 guns

Shoal water

To St Pierre *To St Lawrence*

Major Hardy's Post

Transports

French Camp

Orleans Point

WOLFE'S ROUTE

Admiral Saunders's division

THE BASON

Shoal water

Beaufort

Floating battery (12 guns)

Cape Lauzon

General Monckton's Camp

+ Charlebourg

French Camp

Moored boats

3 guns

3 guns

3 guns

R. Larrey

WOLFE'S ROUTE

Batteries of 30 guns

QUEBEC

Ships

Les Islets

General Hospital

Plains of Abraham

R. St Charles

R. St Lawrence

Sillery

Admiral Holmes' division

Transports

Wolfe's Cove

General Hospital

QUEBEC

La Colonie   Sarre   Languedoc   Bearne   Guienne   Rousedor   La Colonie

Colonists of Quebec

Plains of Abraham

Townshend   Lt Lef   Highlanders   Lascelles   Kennedy's

Webb's reserve

Indians

R. American   General Wolfe

R. St Lawrence

N

Above. *Major General James Wolfe, 1727–59.*

Far left. *Major Robert Rogers, 1731–95, organizer and leader of Rogers' Rangers, a force of lightly armed, fast-moving irregulars.*

Above left. *Cap Rouge, nine miles upstream of Quebec on the north shore of the St Lawrence. From this point many of Wolfe's troops set off for their landing place at the foot of the heights of Abraham.*

strength just over 3000. Both armies formed up and, at one o'clock on 13 September 1759, the battle began with the French advancing. Wolfe, his line two deep, issued 'express orders not to fire till they [the French] came within 20 yards of us . . . the General formed the line of battle, he ordered the regiments to load with an additional ball.'

The French advanced 'briskly in three columns, with loud shouts and recovered arms, two of them inclining to the left of our army, and the third towards out right firing obliquely at the two extremities of our line, from the distance of one hundred and thirty – until they came within forty yards; which our

troops withstood with the greatest intrepidity and firmness, still reserving their fire, and paying the strictest obedience to their officers.'

When the lines were 100 yards apart, Wolfe's men marched forward until only 40 yards separated them from the French lines. They then fired their volley: 'With one deafening crash the most perfect volley ever fired on battlefields burst forth as if from a single monstrous weapon, from end to end of the British line.' Under the cover of the smoke the British advanced again and again, each time firing their volley. As the smoke began to clear 'we observed the main body of the Enemy

retreating in great confusion towards the Town, and the rest towards the River St Charles.' The battle had lasted little more than a quarter of an hour; the British pursued the enemy and entered Quebec.

As in every battle, a great price had to be paid; on the Plains of Abraham it was the death of Wolfe and Montcalm. The struggle for supremacy in North America, however, had been decided in favor of the British. The following year Montreal capitulated and Britain's aims had been achieved, duly recognized three years later when, on 10 February 1763, France ceded the whole of Canada to Britain. The Anglo-French struggle for supremacy had also been conducted in India, and here France was left with only five towns. That Britain could place its major effort overseas was in no small measure due to Frederick the Great's campaigns in central Europe, and there is more than an ounce of truth in the assertion that North America, the West Indies and India were conquered on the plains and hills of Europe.

However, Britain's problems were not over yet. Its treasure was depleted – the cost of warfare had been immense since Britain also paid heavy subsidies to Prussia. Consequently, it faced financial problems which had to be solved by means of taxation, taxation to be applied not only to the motherland but also to the colonies overseas. In 1760, when the French and Indian War was closed in America, the British colonists were fairly satisfied with the existing compromise between home rule and imperial control exercised by Britain. They were happy for Parliament to control Imperial commerce so long as it allowed the North American colonies to prosper, and they had no quarrels with British foreign policy which had yielded such splendid results.

There was considerable dissatisfaction in Britain, however.

Among the politically articulate sections of the population, the opinion was voiced that financially the colonies had not carried their proper share in the war. The colonists disagreed. Britain's possessions in North America had virtually doubled in size, but this also meant that the territory had to be secured and British troops stationed there, a garrison of about 10,000 men. The colonists were to be taxed for the upkeep of this protective force. Various taxation laws were introduced and, at the same time, the mercantile system was tightened by strengthening the Acts of Trade and Navigation.

So far the colonists had not objected to the mercantile system since it left plenty of loopholes; some Acts had, in fact, never been enforced. Yet the Revenue Act, the first of these new measures – and novel chiefly in its rigorous enforcement – created trouble among the colonial lawyers, who feared that a

Above. *The death of Wolfe, 13 September 1759.*

Above left. *British troops land at Montmorency, July 1759, covered by the fire of HMS Centurion (after a drawing by Captain Henry Smith).*

Left. *The death of Wolfe's gallant adversary, the Marquis de Montcalm. The French artist has been too imaginative: Montcalm did not die on the battlefield, and there are no palm trees in Canada.*

Right. *The British struck at the French nearer home: here British troops land on Belle Isle in the Bay of Biscay, 1761.*

precedent had been created, to the detriment of the American colonies. They pointed to the preamble of the Act because it proclaimed that the new duties were levied for revenue purposes. This was the thin end of the wedge and, as in Britain 120 years before, the cry was raised: 'no taxation without representation.' While colonial opinion was mobilized, Parliament passed the Stamp Act on 22 March 1765, which extended to the colonies, as it laid a tax on all legal documents, newspapers, pamphlets, etc. Considering the number of land transactions that were always taking place in the course of territorial expansion, the stamp duty on a contract selling land, for instance, was bound to be a considerable irritant. From the colonists' point of view, the Stamp Act was even more annoying than the Revenue Act: it was direct taxation and had nothing to do with the regulation of commerce. Virginia led the opposition with

Henry's speech; the Stamp Act Congress followed in New York, the first intercolonial meeting summoned by local initiative. The Congress questioned the constitutionality of the Act, pointing to the fact that the colonies were not represented in Parliament at Westminster. Whether direct representation would solve the problem was left as an open question.

The Stamp Act united colonial opinion as nothing before had done, and Britain repealed it. However, the repeal was coupled with the assertion that 'King and Parliament have full power and authority to make laws and statutes of sufficient force and validity to bind the colonies.' Tranquillity seemed to return to the colonies. In 1767, however, the Townshend Acts were introduced, a return to the policy of raising revenue through customs duties. The administration in the colonies was reorganized to ensure their enforcement, and the additional taxes

LIBERTY TREE

STAMP ACT

Left. *A popular cartoon shows Bostonians tarring and feathering an excise man and forcing him to drink tea. It was Lord North's grant of a temporary monopoly of selling tea in America that led to the Boston Tea Party, when Bostonians disguised as Indians threw a cargo of tea into the water.*

Right. *The Boston Tea Party.*

Below right. *British troops land at New York, July 1776 (contemporary French print).*

thus raised were not only to support the garrison but were also funds for the creation of a colonial civil list; this meant that royal governors and judges were made independent from the colonial assemblies. The public outcry was less severe than over the Stamp Act but still strong enough for these measures to be repealed in 1770. Tempers calmed again – except in Boston, the seat of the British administration.

However, taxation was not the only problem – there were also problems related to the Indians, the fur trade, public land and politics. The Indian problem was whether Indian hunting grounds were to be reserved for the Indians in the interest of humanity, thus stopping westward expansion. The problem of the fur trade was a question of control: who should exercise it, imperial, federal or local officials? Regarding public land, the issue was how land acquired from Indians should be disposed of and by what authority. Finally, the political difficulties arose concerning the degree of self-government to be allowed to new settlements and their relationship to the older colonies.

The urgency of these problems was highlighted by Pontiac's uprising, which showed that the colonists had, as usual, mismanaged their Indian affairs, and that British regulars were required to protect the colonists.

To find a temporary solution to the problem, the Royal Proclamation of 7 October 1763 announced a provisional western policy; this aimed to placate the Indians and prevent over-

expansion and a consequent further drain of Britain's treasury. The Appalachians formed the western frontier and the boundaries of Canada and the Floridas were settled. It was not meant as a permanent barrier to westward expansion, though a subsequent British administration declared it a permanent frontier.

Constitutional calm had followed the agitation of 1767 to 1770. Only in Massachusetts, where Governor Hutchinson took a very high hand with his assembly, did agitation continue to ferment. Samuel Adams argued that the people were 'paying the unrighteous tribute.' To mobilize Massachusetts' public opinion, he made clever use of the Boston Town meeting and had a Committee of Correspondence appointed which drafted a statement of 'rights to the colonists' with a 'list of infringements.' Over 75 towns replied and appointed in turn their Committees of Correspondence – the forerunners of a similar institution in the French Revolution and culminating in the Council movement in central Europe in 1918–19 and, of course, the Russian 'soviet.' The Committees of Correspondence were a political machine to be of service when a real issue arose. Such an issue appeared in the form of the Boston Tea Party and the consequences led to the invitation by the Virginia House of Burgesses to the other 12 colonies – or rather Committees of Correspondence – to meet in Philadelphia in September 1774. From then on the way led directly to the American Revolution, or the War of American Independence.

But what sort of army did the colonists have? It consisted of the militia, the forerunner of the United States Army. Originally the militia organization was based on the English Muster Law of 1572, when the English Parliament, in the face of the Spanish threat, wanted to ensure that all counties had an immediate military reserve at hand just in case a Spanish invasion should occur. The colonists in North America continued with it, necessary as it was in view of the Indian threat. In the course of time the law was adapted to the various changing requirements to mobilize forces at any point of the 13 colonies. It was also supposed to enable the various colonies to concentrate within the shortest possible time militia regiments at any given point in cases of emergency. From the militia originated the 'Snow Shoe Men' in 1702 and the 'Picket Guards' in 1755, whose function was to act as vanguard to the regular troops, and ultimately the 'Minutemen' in 1774, troops consisting of militiamen who could be ready for combat within a minute. In addition to these elite units, which had proved their value in the French and Indian War, there was the militia itself, consisting of the able-bodied men of each community or settlement. They were divided into companies, whose strength, however, was rarely greater than 30 men. The companies were part of regi-

Above left. *Two Mohawk Indian chiefs, circa 1744.*

Below right. *The first engagement of the war took place when British troops set off from Boston to destroy an arms dump at Concord. The march turned into a running battle against armed colonists.*

Below. *British officers, in their quarters at New York, discuss the forthcoming campaign.*

Die Generals und Officiers der Königlich Englischen | Les Royalistes ou les Officiers du premier Rang de l'Armée Armee und derer Hülffs Truppen zu Neu Yorck. | Engloise et des Trouppes auxiliaires a Novelle York.
Printed for Carington Bowles in St Pauls Church yard London.

ments, but each regiment varied in strength depending on the number of people available in each county. The militia elected its own officers and non-commissioned officers after those loyal to the crown and appointed by the colonial governors had been removed in more or less free elections. The newly elected leaders were, of course, supporters of the cause of independence.

Military exercises, or rather drill, were carried out three times a week on the village common. The men were familiar with the tactics of fighting in the wilderness, but now they had to train themselves in the close battle order of the British troops whom they ultimately would have to confront. British officers were rather amused by these attempts, which were bound to look rather clumsy at first. In fact, when the British were encountered in open battle by the 'Continental Army,' the latter at first proved inferior. They were much better fighting the way they knew, which provided the first example of new infantry tactics before the age of absolutist warfare came to an end.

Battle commenced on 19 April 1775, when British units were ordered by Governor Gage of Massachusetts to destroy a secret arms dump which the colonists had established at Concord near Boston. As the British troops approached Lexington, about 70 riflemen barred their way. They were quickly driven off, but their numbers were increased by armed inhabitants from nearby settlements. Instead of meeting the British as on a European battlefield, they conducted a running battle against both flanks of the British troops, the colonists being well protected by the trees, bushes and general topography of the countryside. The British were forced to withdraw and, although well trained to carry out this maneuver in an orderly fashion, they were con-

tinuously harassed by the colonists and had great difficulty in making their way back; the colonists fired from all sides and evaded any direct engagement with the bulk of the British troops. Losses among the British were severe and they returned to Boston in a state of exhaustion. Neither their weapons nor discipline had had any effects upon the colonists – they just could not be driven back like an army fighting according to the conventional pattern.

The colonists could hardly have been aware that, by the use of their tactics, they were actually ushering in a new type of warfare, and a new phase in military history; even after Lexington, they tried to emulate the British in their exercises. Apart from the militia, the colonies did not have a regular military force, nor did they possess arms manufacturers or an administrative apparatus to supervise logistics and ensure supplies. When, on 15 June 1775, George Washington was appointed by the Confederate Congress as supreme commander of the military forces, his initial task was one of vast improvisation. Of course he had the militia, but the militia had its own inherent limitations. As the American Revolution was to show time and again, militiamen were loath to fight outside their state. There was as yet no awareness of a common identity – people were Virginians, New Englanders, Pennsylvanians, etc, first and foremost. The militia consisted mainly of volunteers or local levies, capable of fighting in the wilderness, but without the discipline of the regular soldier. They initially rejected notions of subordination as incompatible with the rights of a free man. Their advantage consisted in knowing their territory and in fighting individually in loose formations as *tirailleurs*, not as a closed

body of well-drilled soldiers. In open battle their numerical superiority over the British, who never had more than 40,000 men in the colonies, did not confer any advantage. At first, wherever American and British contingents met in open battle, the Americans were beaten back, frequently with disastrous consequences, namely that the militiamen simply made off home.

As individual fighters, however, they were superior to the British; they also had greater experience of war – after all, they had been fighting the Indians virtually since their arrival and the French since the late seventeenth century. They were good guerrilla fighters. Man for man the militiaman was superior to the British regular, but unit for unit inferior.

They also enjoyed another advantage, and that was in the area of supplies. Because of the militia system, arms, mainly muskets and ammunition, were stored in adequate quantities in all towns, villages and frontier outposts. It was the task of the leaders of the local militia and the Minutemen, and was accomplished successfully. Also, since, like any army, the militia marched on its stomach, the question of food supplies was imperative, and here, too, adequate stores were kept. By comparison, British troops encountered immediate hostility when they went to requisition supplies and the British army had to rely very largely on supplies from the mother country, where the naval lines were continuously threatened and interrupted by the French navy, since the conclusion of the Franco-American alliance.

The main weapon of the militia, as well of the British army, was the Brown Bess flintlock musket. One British officer described it as follows: 'A soldier will hit his man at a range of about 80 yards, perhaps even 100 yards. But a soldier must really have bad luck if at a distance of 150 yards he is even wounded. Firing at a range of 200 yards is like shooting at the moon, hoping to hit it.' It had a corn, but not a notch, for aiming. The recoil was light but the emission of gunpowder smoke was rather strong. Still, it was a usable musket, a weapon supplemented later among the colonists by the long musket known as the Kentucky rifle, which was far superior to the existing musketry. The militia also possessed artillery, but quantitatively and qualitatively inferior to that of the British. The same applied to the artillery crews. Neither the Americans nor the British had much cavalry; it was not really suited to the battlefields of North America, as had already been demonstrated.

If the Americans were to have success against the British, then it could hardly be achieved by the skirmish and combat actions of individual militia units, but by their combined force. The Confederate Congress established a Committee of Safety, which appointed the individual commanders and the supreme commander George Washington. It was due to his toughness and strength of character that the American Revolution would be brought to a successful conclusion. He was fully aware that he could never beat the British in a war of annihilation, but only by expelling them from the territory of the new republic. Washington managed to hold on until the fate of the former colonies changed through French intervention. This was despite great disadvantages: the worst of defeats inflicted by the British; the opposition of many of his fellow commanders; a lack of any significant funds; and less than unanimous support from a political leadership which was more often divided than united. The Confederate Congress entrusted him with the setting up of an army as a core of troops for open field battle, but, distrustful of any standing army, limited its number to 22,000 men. This army was made up of the militia troops.

Washington's task was to transform these troops into something like a regular army. The Continental Army had to be brought in line with the organizational and tactical conditions of troops of the line, inspired by a common desire to further the democratic common good. Looking for officers with great military experience, he met the man who assisted him in accomplishing this task: Friedrich Wilhelm von Steuben (1730–94). It is often maintained that Steuben was not a 'baron,' implying that he was not of noble origin. This is only partially true, however. Steuben was not a baron because this title was not used among the Prussian nobility; its equivalent was *Freiherr* and that is what Steuben was. As an officer in the Prussian army he had a highly distinguished service record in the Seven Years' War; he was the wing adjutant of Frederick the Great's General Quartermaster and left the Prussian army almost immediately after the Peace of Hubertusburg. He then served on the court of the Duke of Hohenzollern-Hechingen – the Roman Catholic line of the Hohenzollern family – and then as a colonel in the forces of the Margrave of Baden. Upon French recommendation he came to America via Paris and arrived in Washington's camp at Valley Forge in March 1778. There he was received with open arms and appointed Inspector General.

Above right. *At Lexington, on their way to Concord, the British drove off some local militia. This spirited painting gives an excellent impression of the action from the American side.*

Left. *This view of the Battle of Concord shows the British column under heavy fire from the flanks,*

Right. *A contemporary print shows the Battle of Bunker Hill and the burning of Charlestown.*

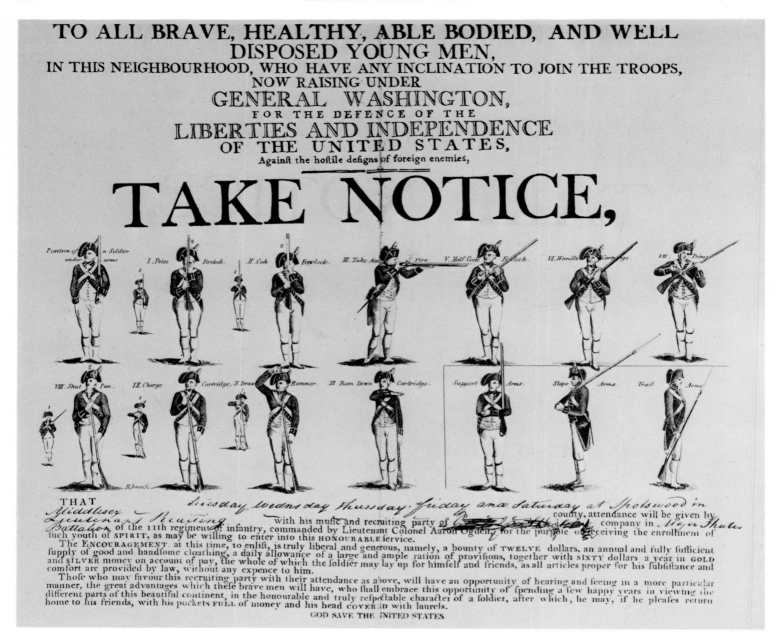

He immediately set about the task of forming an efficient army from one which had been depleted and demoralized by several defeats. In contrast to the Marquis de Lafayette, who had joined the American cause out of youthful enthusiasm and in order to serve France at the same time, Steuben completely broke with his past. He had decided to become a free American and fight for the liberty of his newly adopted country.

During the severe winter of 1778–79, he wrote his famous *Regulations for the Order and Discipline of the Troops of the United States*. Comprising 25 chapters, the manual contained the rules for exercises, field service order, general service and administrative regulations. He wrote it virtually off the top of his head, for books and other sources were hardly available at Valley Forge. In essence the product was based on his memory of the Prussian Infantry Field Manual, whose author had been Frederick the Great. The Potsdam example, though not the spirit, was the foundation of the subsequent field exercises of the American army. Of course, the manual first required approval by the Confederate Congress, which it gave to the 'Blue Book,' as it was called, on 29 March 1779. For the duration of the war, next to the Bible it was the most important book for the American soldier. Thus, in a very curious way the ideas of Frederick William I, Prince Leopold of Anhalt-Dessau and Frederick the Great had made their way to the New World. To this day, if one

wants still to see truly Prussian infantry drill, one has only to visit either East Germany or West Point.

The British, overestimating their own position, left the Americans sufficient time to reorganize themselves. Steuben created a training establishment, which drilled and trained militia soldiers at considerable speed but with great thoroughness, though complaints by the men, who were quite unaccustomed to Steuben's often draconian measures, were frequent. He first established a teaching and training company, which represented the cadre force. When they drilled in public, spectators came from far and wide to see, for it was a new and strange phenomenon to see American soldiers perform exercises and maneuvers just as the Prussian army had conducted them during the Seven Years' War. The impressions left on the observers were mixed: the majority saw in them the means by which, ultimately, the British would be defeated; others voiced their concern over whether a military establishment of this kind could not become a danger to the freedom of the new republic. However, since the new republic had to deal with its external enemies first, they dismissed those doubts, for the time being at least.

Before the beginning of each exercise, Steuben inspected his men with great care, being fairly liberal with admonishments and reprimands, but also praise where praise was due. The

TEUCRO DUCE NIL DESPERANDUM.

First Battalion of PENNSYLVANIA LOYALISTS, commanded by His Excellency Sir WILLIAM HOWE, K. B.

ALL INTREPID ABLE-BODIED

HEROES.

WHO are willing to ferve HIS MAJESTY KING GEORGE the Third, in Defence of their Country, Laws and Conftitution, againft the arbitrary Ufurpations of a tyrannical Congrefs, have now not only an Opportunity of manifefting their Spirit, by affifting in reducing to Obedience their too-long deluded Countrymen, but alfo of acquiring the polite Accomplifhments of a Soldier, by ferving only two Years, or during the prefent Rebellion in America.

Such fpirited Fellows, who are willing to engage, will be rewarded at the End of the War, befides their Laurels, with 50 Acres of Land, where every gallant Hero may retire, and enjoy his Bottle and Lafs.

Each Volunteer will receive as a Bounty, FIVE DOLLARS, befides Arms, Cloathing and Accoutrements, and every other Requifite proper to accommodate a Gentleman Soldier, by applying to Lieutenant Colonel ALLEN, or at Captain KEARNY's Rendezvous, at PATRICK TONRY's, three Doors above Market-ftreet, in Second-ftreet.

I. MILTON F.

Far left. *A poster seeking recruits for the newly formed United States Army.*

Left. *This recruiting poster sought recruits for a loyalist unit.*

Above. *A bronze medal depicting Washington's abortive attack on the British headquarters at Germantown.*

Below. *Washington and some of his senior officers at Valley Forge.*

officers were his most willing and dedicated pupils, as were the noncommissioned officers, whom he always questioned in great detail when on parade about the condition of their men. Also he found enough time to keep in close touch even with the common soldier, who in Steuben always found an ear willing to listen to his difficulties and complaints; he was always ready to help and intervene on behalf of the individual soldier wherever this was possible. This cadre force, once brought into proper shape, then provided the model for the rest of the forces. In that way Steuben speedily supplied Washington with the kind of army he really needed.

But of course, one of the problems which even Steuben could not overcome was that the Americans possessed no military tradition in the European sense of the term. In a letter to a friend he wrote: 'But, my dearest General, you must not believe that in our army the Prussian elementary school, war training, tactics and discipline have been introduced by me. If I had tried to do that I would have been stoned to death; it is something which under the prevailing conditions I simply could not have accomplished. . . . In the first instance much is lacking in this people which is remotely comparable with the warlike spirit of the Prussians, Austrians and French. To your own soldiers you simply order do this and he does it. To my soldiers I have first to explain: this and that are the reasons why you should this and that, only then will they do it. Your army has already existed for over a century; mine for a day. My officers and noncommissioned officers were as good recruits as were my soldiers. My army renewed itself after every campaign . . . in short I had to train everything, I had to supply everything, together with my aides and deputies. All of them were first shaped by my

Far left. Jean Baptiste Donatien de Vimeur, Comte de Rochambeau was sent, by the French government with 6000 men to support the American cause. This aid proved to be most effective at Yorktown in 1781.

Below left. Despite their primitive uniforms, these American soldiers have already been transformed into an efficient fighting force by the efforts of Steuben.

Right. American troops enter one of Cornwallis' redoubts at Yorktown, October 1781.

Below right. American soldiers of 1781. On the right a lieutenant wears the buff facings of troops from New York and New Jersey. An artillery private stands to his left.

very own hand. . . . Now judge for yourself whether it was possible for me to occupy myself excessively with formal rifle drill and military parades. Against my original intention and against my better judgment I was forced to start much from the end rather than from the beginning. After all that you will surely admit that my task has not been an easy one . . .'

In spite of the underestimation of his troops expressed in his letter, Steuben's success was nevertheless surprising considering the innate dislike of the American soldier for arms drill. Another specifically Prussian element which Steuben introduced was the relative silence with which every maneuver and action, from loading the rifle to advancing, was carried out. Generals and staff officers were admonished not to shout, or to occupy themselves with minor details which could be delegated to subordinates. He instilled inner discipline into the army, and gradually it began to function like a smoothly oiled piece of machinery. It could carry out all forms of combat in closed formation, became a master in the closely coordinated salvo, as well as in dissolving from a closed formation into small individual units which, protected by what cover the countryside afforded, could hold off the enemy and, upon order, immediately reassemble into the original formation. And they learned how to attack *en masse* with bayonets fixed and levelled.

Obviously, the perfection which Steuben aimed for could never be achieved in the short time available to him. Next to the regular battalions fought the untrained musketeers as *tirailleurs*, but they could fall back on the former for protection if necessary. Indeed, the combination of closed combat with *tirailleur* tactics was one of the factors that resulted in victory over the British troops. Steuben therefore placed great emphasis on training the light infantry and expanding its numbers. He recognized that Prussian regulations and drill could not be transferred lock, stock and barrel to the American continent – not only was the geographical environment different but, as already

BATTLE SITES OF THE
AMERICAN WAR OF
INDEPENDENCE, 1776-1781

Above. *A proclamation announcing the end of the war.*

Above far left. *General Tadeusz Kosciuszko, 1746–1817, a Polish soldier of fortune whose knowledge of fortification and military engineering was of great value to Washington.*

Left. *The surrender of Cornwallis at Yorktown, October 1781 (contemporary French print).*

mentioned, so were the attitudes of the American soldiers. A well-trained light infantry could exploit all the advantages which a bush war had to offer, while the linear tactics of the regular army could be employed wherever territory and other conditions allowed it. The light infantry did not fight statically, it conducted a war of continuous movement and its rules were adapted to the prevailing conditions. Increasingly Steuben transferred the best of his soldiers to the light infantry battalions. The wide American spaces favored operations conducted by independently acting formations. They were given a specific task; how to accomplish it was up to them. From Steuben's point of view, this represented a clear break with his own military background. He simply adapted himself to the new environment. Long before the armies of the French Revolution introduced such tactics, Washington's army already practiced them. Steuben combined two infantry brigades, each comprising two regiments, with a light battalion, two squadrons of cavalry and two companies of artillery, into a division. As the principle of total war made its appearance in the American Civil War, so the new kind of warfare which displaced that of the *ancien régime* was first practiced, not in Europe, but in North America.

It can hardly be said that Steuben's personality and innovations were received with undivided approval. As far as his personality was concerned, he was too much a Prussian and too impulsive to be easily accepted, and he found resistance, particularly among members of the Confederate Congress, far removed from the firing line. Also he did not want to function forever as the educator and trainer of the army. He aimed at a command in the field, and succeeded in becoming Washington's chief of staff. His operational plans provide ample evidence that he estimated correctly the strategic difficulties of conducting a war against the superior British forces. Although he had forged an efficient army, its actual strength was by no means sufficient to accomplish bold, decisive strokes. In the autumn of 1781 he received the much-desired independent field command at Yorktown, where Lord Cornwallis was besieged with the bulk of the British main army. As the only officer with experience in dealing with fortifications, Steuben, now a divisional commander, directed the practical and engineering aspects of the siege with such success that, on 19 October 1781, Cornwallis and his troops capitulated.

The fall of Yorktown broke London's determination to continue the war; less than two years later, in September 1783, Britain recognized the independence of its former 13 colonies with the Treaty of Versailles.

That the Americans could in the end achieve decisive military successes was also due partly to the support of the French navy and a French expeditionary corps under General Rochambeau. However, in any overall assessment of the reasons for the defeat of the British army – which largely consisted of Hessian mercenaries (of which one-third were killed, one-third were taken prisoners, and one-third deserted to the Americans and settled in the United States) – one fact is certain. The British army remained bound by the static forms of linear tactics; this applied particularly to the hired German formations. By contrast, Washington's soldiers adapted Prussian military rules to their specific environment. The most important factor, however, was that the war was not between two professional armies but that, as far as the Americans were concerned, it could be described as a 'people's war.' This, combined with other factors such as the geography of the country, was to ensure ultimate victory. From the point of view of military history, the American Revolution inaugurated the beginning of the end of the tactics and warfare of the *ancien régime*.

CHAPTER X

THE "GENERAL WILL"

The Reformation had pulled God down from His high pedestal and turned Him into a subject of public discussion and controversy. It was almost inevitable that eventually those secular powers who claimed their office by divine right, especially the monarchy, should become subject to similar scrutiny. In other words, if there was no God, what point was there in having a king? John Locke with his two *Treatises on Government* did not initiate this process of debate, but he was perhaps the most widely influential advocate of it. He laid great emphasis upon the theory of contract; Locke really secularized Puritan theology – his ideas were not particularly original. According to him, the individual came and comes before society, and human dignity is innate and independent of society. Hence human dignity must not be injured or infringed – on the contrary, it must always be respected. Before forming himself into a community, man was in his natural condition, a condition in which he enjoyed complete freedom, and in which the ground he tilled was his very own. The family he founded was his domain. He owed obedience to only one law: Natural Law. That later on men formed themselves into societies does not do away with this Natural Law, he claimed, nor with those individual rights which man exercised from time immemorial. Men have formed themselves into societies out of their own free will, and they must therefore strictly control the government of that society, control it so strictly as to make any infringement of man's natural rights impossible. If a government should infringe these rights and duties, then it is on the way to becoming a tyranny. Resistance against tyranny is thus not only a right, it constitutes a major duty.

These ideas were part of the intellectual foundation of the American Revolution, and, together with the body of ideas which the Enlightenment had produced in Europe, they were also at the root of the French Revolution. This revolution was more than just a change in the form of state, it demolished royal absolutism and put into its place a bourgeois republic. The French Revolution was a consequence of economic changes which had brought material wealth and cultural influence to the upper bourgeoisie of the urban centers, resulting in greater political rights. It was fomented by a financial crisis into which France had been sinking steadily deeper for a long time, but was also the immediate consequence of widespread hunger. Shortages of bread caused deep unrest at the bottom of the social scale, while the immense national debt gave the people the opportunity to demand political concessions.

The decisive mistake made by the French monarchy was not to reform the state with the assistance of a bourgeoisie equipped with equal political rights, the Third Estate or *tiers état*. Thus the *ancien régime*, the absolutist feudal state with its barriers between the Estates, each of which had separate privileges, collapsed under the assault of its subjects. The monarchy became a constitutional one. With the Declaration of the Rights of Man on 26 August 1789, principles were proclaimed which drew the conclusion that the state was the responsibility of its citizens; the bourgeoisie would no longer be a mere tool for other purposes. In reality, however, the revolutionary state was, for the time being, the domain of the upper bourgeoisie, which alone possessed the vote. During the course of the Revolution, elements of inter-class struggle emerged, and the lower orders of society demanded equal rights. This period provides what is often seen as a classic example of the structure of revolutionary forces: their social composition, their motives, their ideology, psychology and organization. It is an example of the escalation of force: of how a radical minority, carried by widespread dissatisfaction, could bring about a political explosion.

Aware of the need for mass support, the leaders placed great emphasis upon creating a favorable public opinion. Samuel Adams' example of the Committees of Correspondence were

Previous spread. *The mob fights its way into the château of Versailles, 10 August 1792, overcoming the Swiss Guard.*

Above. *This 24-pounder is mounted on a special carriage to permit it to fire downwards.*

Left. *The opening of the Estates-General in 1789.*

Right. *A plate from an eighteenth-century English military manual showing cannon and their accessories.*

GUNNERY.   PLATE CCXLIX.

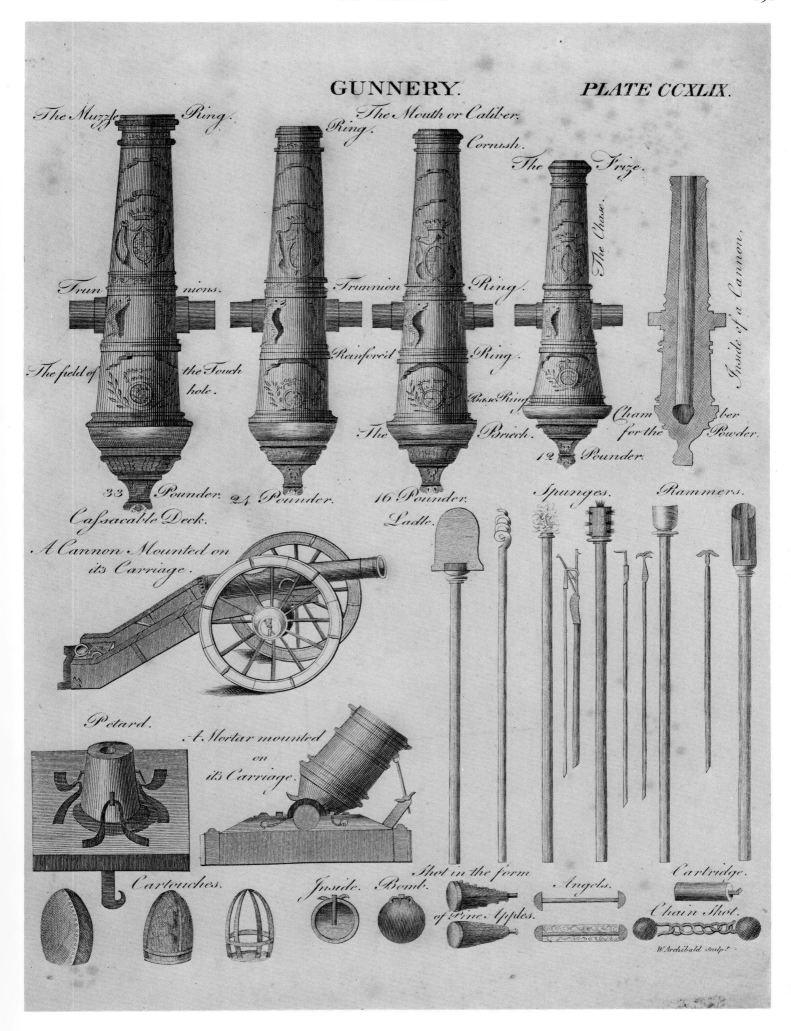

The Muzzle Ring.   Ring.   The Mouth or Caliber.   Cornish.   The Frize.   Inside of a Cannon.

Trunnions.   Trunnion Ring.   The Chase.

The field of the Touch hole.   Reinforct Ring.

Base Ring.   Cham ber for the Powder.

The Breech.   12 Pounder.

33 Pounder.   24 Pounder.   16 Pounder.

Cassacable Deck.

A Cannon Mounted on its Carriage.

Ladle.   Spunges.   Rammers.

Petard.

A Mortar mounted on its Carriage.

Cartouches.   Inside. Bomb.   Shot in the form   Angels.   Cartridge.

of Pine Apples.   Chain Shot.

W. Archibald Sculpt.

emulated, committees which emphasized aims of almost utopian proportions. In contrast to America, however, these committees gave rise to party factions. After the fall of the Bastille, the intellectuals of the Revolution created 'The Society of the Friends of the Constitution,' which covered the whole of France with its network of branches. Its core was the wealthy bourgeoisie, though its doors were opened to artisans, small merchants and traders. Under the leadership of Robespierre, Danton and Marat, the Jacobin Club became the driving force of republican agitation, promoting an 'educational' democracy, an imposed 'democracy' and the inevitable terror. The entire French population was politicized and, when in course of the Revolution France became involved in war, the military consequences were equally far-reaching; the national emergency produced a national mass army, a new type of soldier – the citizen in arms – and a new officer caste.

This first European mass army brought fundamental alterations to the methods of warfare and the principles of leadership, as well as the whole supply structure of armies. While the absolute monarchy had used its standing army in military conflicts to extend its power, the leaders of the French Revolution used force to impose its ideas and ideals upon others. Subsequently ideas, missionary zeal and propaganda determined the course of war as much as new weapons and column tactics or the system of requisition and the strategic principle of annihilation. Operations expanded over wide areas, using structured armies. The strict discipline characteristic of the Age of Absolutism made way for the excesses of a revolutionary *élan*, with all that this implied in terms of psychological incitement of the fanatical potential of the masses. The partisan, or guerrilla fighter, emerged to become one of the key figures in military history.

As we have had cause to observe before, nationalism was a key force. The Revolutionaries imbued their nation with the faith that its principles and its civilization would serve as models

Far left. *Maximilien Robespierre, 1758–94.*

Above. *Fighting in the streets of Paris in April 1789.*

Below. *A revolutionary poster proclaims Liberty, Equality and Fraternity.*

for the whole of mankind. The idealistic universalism of the intellectual currents of the French Revolution were thus transformed into an egotistical nationalism. Once the Republic had been achieved in France, territorial conquest was pursued in order to expand the ideological base of the revolution.

The development of the French Revolution can be described in terms of a geometric curve, at the start of which stood the Bourbon dynasty and at the end of which lay the Napoleonic Empire. The zenith of the curve marked Robespierre's dictatorship. Its beginning was the irreversible victory, the victory of the people over the monarchy and feudal rule. A bourgeois constitution was written whose supporters at first still shared their power with supporters of the *ancien régime*, and which at that stage did not grant equal rights to all citizens. Under the impact of the continuing economic crisis, the starving, the suffering and generally underprivileged rose against what they considered counterrevolutionary machinations. The Revolution reached its height in the form of mass hysteria directed against the church and the monarchy. The monarchy could hold the little ground left to it for a very short time. When conflict followed with the Habsburg and Hohenzollern dynasties, who had combined against the Revolution, the democratic Left in France gained the upper hand and, with the majority support of the National Assembly, called for a crusade against the monarchs of Europe. The first alarming news of the defeats sustained by the Revolutionary armies precipitated the second revolution, which destroyed not only the monarchy but also the initiators of the first revolution; they became the victims of a totalitarian democracy.

Above. *The Paris mob storms the Bastille, 14 July 1789.*

Above left. *Queen Marie Antoinette, 1755–93, executed during the Reign of Terror.*

Left. *The Tennis Court Oath, 20 June 1789. When the chamber of the Third Estate was closed by Louis XVI, its members met in an indoor tennis court and declared that they formed a National Assembly, and would not disband until they had framed a constitution.*

In January 1793 after the king and queen were executed, the hour of the Jacobins had arrived. They united the nation by force in order to withstand the threat from outside and did so successfully. Internally, they proclaimed a new constitution of 1793, which was submitted for ratification to the people. Of 7,000,000 entitled to vote, however, only 2,000,000 chose to do so, and less than a third in Paris. Nevertheless, the executive power residing in Paris' Committee for Public Welfare, though nominally responsible to the National Convent or Assembly, pursued the cause, which meant action against its internal and external opponents. Internally those were the days of the guillotine: 'The guillotine should remain in action in France in permanency. Five million inhabitants in France are quite enough,' proclaimed Guffroy, the editor of one of the Jacobin gazettes. From that moment onward, the French Revolution lost the widespread sympathies which it had so far enjoyed abroad. The total number of victims of this phase of the Revolution is difficult to assess – at a conservative estimate, in 1792 there was a total of 1700 suicides, over 5000 'counterrevolutionaries' were drowned in the Loire River at Nantes, 2000 Royalists were butchered at Lyons and 900 in Toulon, and almost 14,000 were guillotined in Paris and other cities, having 'to sneeze into the sack.' These figures do not include tens of thousands butchered in the civil war. The Revolution ate its own children. Extremists began to express concern at the wave of murder.

In the spring of 1794 the Revolution entered the phase of 'total democracy,' upheld for the best part of three months by the personality of Robespierre. The shedding of blood was directed into more 'orderly channels.' Terror was now subjected to law in the service of public virtue. There is little doubt about Robespierre's personal integrity, and there can be no doubt that he was an absolutely committed fanatic. He was determined to establish the rule of 'reason' and Rousseau's 'General Will' and *Social Contract* by force; the revolutionary tribunals were everywhere, denunciation prospered and suspicion was cause enough to lose one's head.

Soon the Terror was being used in the interests of a total social revolution. Ideas which we would now describe as Communist made their appearance in the legislative consultations. The confiscation of church property had raised enough cash to finance the war. Peasants had gained proprietary rights over their soil, but the demand arose to bless the poor of land with the property of the enemies of the republic. This required the full support of the people and raised the alarm among the bourgeoisie. Once the foreign armies had been repelled, Robespierre stumbled over his own policies. On 28 July 1794 he too ended under the guillotine.

The forces of reaction gained ground again. Although for the time being government remained in the hands of the Revolutionary committees, the reservoir of fanatical tyrants seems to have been exhausted. When royalist reaction, however, began to set in no less brutally than the red terror of the Jacobins, the republican spirit reestabished itself from 1789 in the form of the Directory of Five. They set out to prevent any further misuse of democracy and stabilize internal conditions in France.

But the revolution had not yet run its full course. Royalists as well as members of the radical left planned their coups. The government vacillated between left- and right-wing options and opinions were divided, as they were in the National Assembly. Corruption prospered. When the threat from abroad was renewed, it seemed as though the fanatical energy of the Revolutionary army was on the decline. France was growing tired of upheaval; we may suppose that it longed for the strong man who would finally establish order.

Napoleon Bonaparte was that man and, with his *coup d'état* of 9 November 1799, he brought the chaos under control with a compromise between the old nobility and the new nobility (which he was yet to establish) and the *haute bourgeoisie*. Under his hands a strongly centralized government was established. That the First Consul became the Emperor bothered the French little; law and order had returned. The spirit of 1789, however, had not died.

For the military historian the question of particular interest is how the victory of the Revolution was brought about and how it was possible for such chaos to ensue. The old army failed almost totally, not simply because the majority of its numbers

Left. *The Marquis de Lafayette, 1757–1834, a liberal aristocrat who had served with distinction in the American War of Independence, was appointed commander of the Paris National Guard (contemporary French engraving).*

Below. *The philosopher Jean-Jacques Rousseau, 1712–78, whose* Social Contract *spoke of a 'general will' invested in the people.*

abandoned the king, but because its structure dissolved and discipline disappeared completely. Even during the pre-Revolutionary period, the French army was no longer the reliable instrument it once had been. The officer corps, however, was still the domain of the nobility, and venality in the purchase of commissions was not only widespread but almost customary – the crown needed the money. In fact, it needed the money so much that it appointed more officers than it actually required. Compared with the numerically stronger Prussian army of Frederick the Great with 80 generals, or the Austrian army with 350 generals, the French army had 1171 generals on the eve of the Revolution. The lower nobility was barred because it did not have the necessary funds for the purchase of a commission; it was represented in the army only as the lower charges, which led these ranks to oppose the monarchy.

In contrast, the noncommissioned officer corps consisted of able and experienced soldiers; many of them had participated in the American Revolution. Upon them rested the burden of the daily military duties, though they had no prospects of ever being rewarded. The bad example provided by the officer corps caused the NCOs to assume, and probably rightly so, that qualitatively they were its equal, if not even superior. Their influence upon the ranks was infinitely greater than that of the officers.

The common soldier, of course, was worst off – his pay was negligible and, to add to his grievances, the Minister of War, the Comte St Germain, introduced corporal punishment. Given the dissatisfaction among both NCOs and the rank and file, it is not surprising that they were highly receptive to revolutionary suggestions. Discontent was aggravated by divisions between the French generals and the decay of the principle of subordination. Colonels no longer always obeyed generals – hardly something that would encourage discipline in the lower ranks. The result, however, was that, at the outbreak of the Revolution, the French army was no longer an instrument upon which the king could rely unconditionally. The attitude of the army in the main was one of indifference or outright support for the insurgents. They joined the newly formed citizens' guard in large numbers; in Paris alone 6000 soldiers joined the ranks of the Revolutionaries.

The old French army largely dissolved with the Revolution. Many of its noble officers took to their heels after the storming of the Bastille, seeking refuge abroad, from where they conducted their counterrevolutionary agitation and propaganda. Therefore, only the National Assembly could reorganize the army. At first reform of the old army was attempted, but before 1792 the purpose of maintaining an army was held in doubt; it was considered more important to concentrate on the National Guards, who were founded by the National Assembly. The purchase of officers' patents was abolished – access was opened to all with talent – and the rate of pay for NCOs and guards was to be increased. All this, however, could not prevent the complete politicization of the military forces. In all regiments, radicals of various colors continued their agitation and created their Revolutionary committees. The members of the committees considered the orders the military formations received, debated them and decided whether they should be carried out or not; officers trying to enforce their orders risked their lives. National Guards and the remaining members of the regiments of the line fused. In the summer of 1790 mutinies broke out in several garrisons; the report about them submitted to the National Assembly culminated in the observation: that 'there was now no longer any power of the state which would be respected . . . the evil grows from day to day, it is not limited to certain individual formations who debate and decide what is in their interest, in Strasbourg seven regiments have formed a military congress, each represented by three deputies. Representatives of France, hurry in order to counteract the torrent of military insurrection with your entire strength, do not wait till new storms make it even more powerful breaking the strongest of dams.' The military committee tried to introduce countermeasures but they were too weak to bring about a consolidation of the army. On the contrary, at Nancy, where three regiments of the old army were still stationed, they ill-treated their officers and plundered the regimental funds; they immediately fraternized with the National Guards who had been dispatched to establish order. The leader of the mutiny, however, was arrested, tried and sentenced to serve as a galley slave. This caused such an outcry from the radicals that the sentence had to be reversed; the man was released and, upon his arrival in Paris on 9 April 1792, the city provided him with a triumphal entry.

Louis XVI's attempt to escape demonstrated dramatically that there were no more troops in any number loyal to the king; it also cost him his head the following year. Given the reaction of the foreign powers, France confronted them with what remained of a military force. It was under the command of generals who could never be sure of their support in the National Assembly; any military misfortune might cost them their lives.

At the outbreak of Revolution few thought of war – indeed, the National Assembly publicly promised never to use a French army against the liberty of another nation. It decreed the setting up of a regular army consisting of volunteers, if necessary reinforced by the militia, for the protection of *la patrie*. The political interest in forming a new army concentrated on the National Guard, as a democratically organized force. It represented the early constitutional phase of the Revolution, and the role it played exemplifies and reflects the political organization of the new France. It was divided in 83 regional *départments*, all roughly equal in size and population, with 574 subdistricts and 4730 cantons. Their representatives were elected by those entitled to a vote, in other words by the bourgeoisie. They were also to provide the National Guard. This limited recruitment of the National Guard from members of the bourgeoisie added fuel to an already explosive situation, since it emphasized the class divisions between those who owned property and those who did not. The more the Revolution turned to the left, the more strongly the radicals fought the National Guards, demanding a universal franchise and the general armament of the people as the safest means to take over power.

It would be too much to expect military efficiency from the National Guard, and members of the National Assembly expressed their concern about France's military safety. As a consequence 100,000 National Guard members were formed into volunteer battalions and integrated with the remnants of the old army. Volunteers, however, were hard to come by and the old soldiers resented the privileges which the National Guard enjoyed. In this highly confused situation, France declared war on Austria on 20 April 1792. The patriots believed that this would regenerate the Revolutionary *élan* and divert attention from internal difficulties. When Prussia joined Austria, France was totally unprepared for war. There were to be three French armies, but actually only 100,000 men could be mobilized. The *Marseillaise* had a catchy tune, but it could not make up for a trained army.

Lafayette was given an army command and General Rochambeau ordered to carry the main strike into Belgium toward a line between Brussels and Namur, where they confronted 40,000 Austrians and were beaten badly. Panic broke out among the Revolutionary forces, who made their way back to Lille. Officers who tried to control and rally them were

Volontaire partant pour les frontières, en Septembre 1792.

Allons Enfans de la Patrie
Le jour de gloire est arrivé;
Contre nous de la Tyrannie
L'étendart sanglant est levé; &c...

killed. A number of hussar squadrons, including their commanders, also deserted and joined the enemy, among whom
were small contingents of troops made up of French emigrants.
Austria and Prussia now planned a march directly upon Paris.

The second revolutionary phase began in Paris under this
threat. The Jacobins held the existing government responsible
for the disaster; they executed the king and proclaimed the
Republic. They were not impressed by the proclamation of
Field Marshal the Duke of Brunswick that, should any harm
come to the French king and queen, Paris would be subjected to
severe punishment. Lafayette tried to save the king but most of
his soldiers would not follow him. With a few supporters,
however, he saved himself by crossing over to the allies. It was
an action which broke the last barrier between Robespierre and
the establishment of a regime of terror.

The military side of the second phase of the Revolution,
however, was a different picture, one that demonstrated that
Frenchmen were still able to expel the enemy from French soil.
Volunteers then came forward, increasing the army by late
September to 60,000 men, reinforced by many old and experienced former soldiers. On 19 September 1792 about 35,000
Prussian troops penetrated to the rear of the French forces who,
with 50,000 men, held a well-secured position between the
River Aisne and the marshland southwest of St Ménéhould
facing west. When, on the morning of the 20th, Prussian vanguards had reached the foot of the Valmy Ridge in heavy rain,
the Duke of Brunswick left them there totally inactive. He
wanted to take no risks until the bulk of his army had arrived.
The French General Kellerman exploited this delay to the full.
His battalions, representing the left wing of the French forces,
occupied the ridge near the village of Valmy and he positioned
his artillery there. However, even after both French and
Prussians had completed their battle formation by one o'clock,
no real fighting had taken place. The battle was limited to

artillery fire. The cannonade of Valmy achieved very little because of the wet ground. The French expected the Prussian attack and General Kellerman rode up and down his formations shouting '*Vive la nation!*' The soldiers responded by singing the *Marseillaise*.

The Duke, however, considering that the wet conditions would make an advance extremely difficult, decided that any attack would involve heavy losses and did nothing. Both sides shot about 20,000 rounds of artillery ammunition at each other. The Prussians lost 173 men, the French 300. When darkness fell, Kellerman withdrew from the ridge unhindered. The affair caused deep depression among the Prussians – the army of Rossbach had refrained from attacking the French revolutionary army! Among the French, who considered Valmy their victory, a feeling of elation and superiority prevailed.

In the spring of 1793 the war with Prussia and Austria was formally transformed into a war of the Empire against France. The Duke of Brunswick, who after Valmy had withdrawn, once again took the offensive and recaptured parts of the left bank of the Rhine, but, through lack of coordination in the planning of their operations, every one of the allied armies acted as it thought fit without consultation with the others. By the end of the year the French were again on the offensive. In 1794 the Duke of Brunswick was replaced by Field Marshal von Möllendorf, one of the veterans of Frederick the Great's army. However, the second Polish partition, a rising of the Poles in Prussia's Polish provinces in 1794, established different priorities for Prussia, and the Peace of Basle ended Prussia's participation in the war against the French at the time.

After Valmy the French Revolutionary army went on the

Above left. In 1798, a French army led by General Humbert unsuccessfully invaded Ireland.

Far left. This French print of 1792 shows a volunteer on his way to the frontier.

Right. Marshal François-Christophe Kellerman, Duke of Valmy, 1735–1820. The oldest of Napoleon's marshals, he made his military reputation at the Battle of Valmy in 1792, before Napoleon came to power.

offensive, capturing Landau, Speyer, Mainz and Frankfurt-am-Main. In Belgium General Dumouriez defeated an Austrian corps on 6 November 1792, the first genuine battle which the Revolutionary army won. At that point the national and basically cosmopolitan spirit of the Revolution began to take on the characteristics of imperialist expansion, and occupied territories were annexed.

This policy alarmed Britain, which tried to raise a major coalition against France. In 1793 the allied armies had been successful in their operations, Belgium being reconquered, as were the cities along the Rhine. General Dumouriez suffered a severe defeat at the hands of the Austrians, his army left him and, like Lafayette, he had to find refuge among the enemy with 800 men.

The murderous battle at Fleurus, near Charleroi, decided the revolutionary war for France. The Austrians withdrew, the French followed on their heels and, by the end of 1794, they occupied the whole of the left bank of the Rhine again; they conquered Holland and defeated at the other end the Spaniards at San Sebastian. Only Britain and Austria were interested in continuing the war. After Prussia had made its peace with France, Austria followed in 1797 with the Treaty of Campo Formio. The counterrevolutionary war of the coalition had come to an end.

One can now step back and examine the changes the Revolution brought to the armed forces. The *levée en masse* was a notable innovation. Shortage of troops was still a general problem and on 20 February 1793 Robespierre decided to introduce mass compulsory service carried out by lot; the *levée en masse* was born. All able males between the ages of 18 and 40 were eligible for military service, 200,000 men being required for the volunteer battalions, 100,000 for the regiments of the line.

The immediate impact was shattering. It gave the signal to a counterrevolutionary rising among the peasants of the western provinces – a republic which forced them into military service, more readily than the old monarchy had done, was to be fought to the death. The entire Vendée was in uproar, as was Brittany and the swamplands of Poitou. Lyons, Marseilles, Bordeaux, Toulouse, Nîmes, Grenoble, Limoges and Toulon rebelled against Paris. Civil war raged and the Jacobin dictatorship, supported by the *Sans-Culottes*, formed Revolutionary praetorian guards who moved into the rebellious areas, but it took a considerable period of time and even greater bloodletting before the rising was quelled.

Even in other parts of France where rebellion did not rear its head, eligible men left the villages and took to the woods. Of the 300,000 men required, 180,000 were recruited, the major proportion from France's eastern provinces.

The *levée en masse* was a slogan that, at the time, did not become reality; instead of being a decree ensuring national service for every able-bodied man, it became a means of raising urgent replacements for the army. It was not accompanied by patriotic fervor, and had to be enforced using the threat of the guillotine. Ultimately, by 1794, 1,200,000 men were raised, including the work forces for the armaments factories. A mass army such as this was to become a dangerous instrument in the hands of a man capable of using it. It also took society a further step toward the radicalization of warfare.

In France the *levée en masse* was modified after the death of Robespierre, and in 1798 it was decreed that every Frenchman from the age of 20 to 25 was compelled to do military service, with younger men having precedence over older ones. A precondition was a state of war, and Consul Bonaparte modified it in March 1800 with the introduction of the principle of replacements. Every conscript who did not wish to join the army had

Above far left. *Fighting in Flanders in 1795.*

Above. *This engraving, produced in 1818 when Waterloo was a recent memory, shows a heroic episode from the fighting in Flanders in 1792: a French hussar trooper captures a color single-handed.*

Left. *The Duke of York defeats a French force at Landrecies in 1793.*

to pay 2400 francs and provide a substitute who would serve on his behalf.

Thus the French Revolutionary army was composed of highly diverse forces. Firstly, there were about 100,000 men of the former Royal Army, soldiers and officers who drifted back into the army from about 1792 onward, then there were the volunteers of 1791 and 1792 and the conscripts from 1793 onward. The troops which repelled the first invasion belonged mainly to the first category. The core consisted of the artillery with its mainly bourgeois officers; they were wedded to the ideals of the Revolution and, together with the cavalry units created in 1792, formed the elite of the army. From the spring of 1793 they fought in five different operational theaters: on the Belgian frontier, in the Ardennes, along the Moselle and the Rhine, in the Alps, where they fought mainly Austrians and Sardinians, and in the western and eastern Pyrenees. The entire force comprised 11 armies of varying sizes, totalling about 800,000 men, of which 600,000 were used in actual combat. Another 150,000 men must be added to this, being the men the forces used to crush the rebels in the Vendée.

Initially the internal conditions of the army were deplorable. The volunteers of 1791 were full of enthusiasm. This soon wore off, however, and their usefulness became increasingly variable. In their place came men motivated rather less by idealism and more by the prospect of booty; confronted by the enemy, a few volleys were enough to scatter them in all directions. Yet they received more pay than the old soldiers, a source of widespread

friction. Service in the volunteers was limited to 12 months, and there were battalions with 120 men and companies with only nine. France therefore owed its salvation in 1793 not to her army, but to the indecisiveness and disunity of her enemies. The provision of personal equipment was poor, many soldiers dressed in rags, and many had no shoes, let alone overcoats: '. . . whole battalions were without trousers, just covered with a cloak held together by pins; when the 7th Paris Battalion marched past Danton in this condition, he remarked, "Now those are real *Sans-culottes*!" . . .' complained one female member at the National Convent.

The new Minister of War, Bouchotte, a radical, insisted that the traditional military hierarchy must never be established again. His suspicions were directed against the officers, and he fanned the embers of growing suspicion between men and officers into full flame. The bourgeoisie was not to be transformed into soldiers, but all soldiers into militant *Sans-Culottes*. The Convent appointed commissars to serve with the officers and keep an eye on them. More often than not, when a commander had ordered punishment for an offense against military discipline, the commissar annulled it under pressure from the men. Officers considered unreliable were arrested upon the merest suspicion. Commissar Billaud, during his mission to the northern army, arrested six generals on one day, and Commissar Ronsin four generals and 17 staff officers. Most of them came under the guillotine. Hardly anyone was prepared to assume command for fear of suffering the fate of his predecessor.

At the top level of command, conditions were equally desperate. The appointment of a general was a political matter, and a captain of the dragoons became Commander of the Rhine army. The goldsmith journeyman Rossignol became Divisional Commander after he had denounced his predecessor General Biron and sent him to the guillotine. The pamphleteer Ronsin climbed the ladder from captain to general in four days – he was a friend of Bouchotte. On the other hand, the young major of the artillery, Bonaparte, who was chiefly responsible for the conquest of Toulon, was made a brigadier general. The customs officer Hanriot, commander of the National Guard of Paris in 1793, was a renowned drunkard. In 1794 he ended his career in a drunken stupor by being thrown from his horse and landing on a garbage heap. Hardly had a man joined the army than he demanded promotion; it seemed that everyone wanted to order, none to obey. The Convent noted with dismay that the army had in excess of 20,000 officers. The army had been thoroughly democratized.

In 1791 foreigners who had served in the old French army and who did not wish to return home were all naturalized; they too developed into a willful instrument of terror and formed bands of thieves and robbers. Ordered to collect taxes, they often collected but pocketed the money themselves.

Right. *Karl Wilhelm Ferdinand, Duke of Brunswick, 1735–1806.*

Below. *The heights of Valmy, 20 September 1792.*

With the end of the Terror in France in late July 1794 after the fall of Robespierre, conditions began to stabilize again in the army. The revolutionary rabble developed into a professional army again, who fought not for the dynasty, but first for the defense and then for the expansion of France. The idea of liberty, equality and fraternity released immense emotional powers. 'It is a pleasure to see, how seriously the soldiers perform their duties. . . . We have a new disciplinary manual which we have sworn to obey point by point. It is strict, but the men know that as long as they stay on the path of honor they have nothing to fear,' wrote one volunteer.

But it was a will to order affairs that saved France, and the country owed much to the enormous efforts of one man, the former engineer Captain Lazare Carnot (1753–1823). Called to head the department of defense within the Committee of Public Welfare, he immediately established a central office for army administration, supervised troop recruitment, and gave the *levée en masse* a practical shape. He was not concerned about the political opinions of his subordinates as long as they followed his instructions. He was also incorruptible, and after every journey of inspection he handed back any surplus funds to the treasury. He had immense courage and publicly opposed Robespierre. The radicals would have preferred to see him under the guillotine had they had someone else to provide the organization for a war. Carnot supported the Terror as long as it served the principle of victory against the external enemy. The citizen in arms was his aim, the effective fusion of the old regiments of the line with the volunteers in order 'to turn every Frenchman into a soldier.'

The army's structure was in need of reform. He began work

Left. *A French* tirailleur *of 1805.*

Below. *This contemporary French engraving shows the recapture of Toulon by the Revolutionary forces in December 1793.*

Above. *Lazare Carnot, 1753–1823, a regular engineer officer who cobbled together the Revolutionary armies in 1793–34.*

in late 1793. He dissolved the most recently recruited troops, and then reorganized them through his personal selection of their officers and NCOs, to establish first a reliable core. Appointments were to be made according to talent as well as on length of service, and the election of officers and NCOs was abolished. '*Carrière ouverte aux talents*' (Career open to talent) was his motto. He appointed many new army commanders, and Napoleon had him to thank for his command over the army operating in Italy. The right of volunteers to terminate their service after 12 months was abolished, and desertion was punished by death. Officers had to share tents with their men and received the same food supplies.

A new military school, the *École de Mars*, was established in which 1800 sons of *Sans-Culottes* received their training as future officers. It was closed, however, with the demise of the Jacobins. When Robespierre was executed, Carnot remained and, in 1794, founded the *École Polytechnique* for the training of artillery and engineer officers. Nine years later followed the *École Spéciale Militaire*, the future St Cyr. In time Carnot sorted out the wheat from the chaff, and Europe would soon be familiar with the names of Marceau, Kléber, Moreau, Bernadotte and Ney, to name but a few of the future eminent commanders.

Carnot completely reorganized France's arms manufacture and had it working at full capacity. Tailors and shoemakers worked day and night to provide uniforms and footwear for the army. Within months he accomplished a task which normally would have taken years. However, on the whole, technical advances were few. The Chappe brothers had invented optical telegraphy in 1792 with the aid of large mirrors, and by August 1794 the first line of optical telegraphs had been built between Paris and Lille consisting of 22 stations, relaying 60 signals per minute. In the following years the network was extended all over France, but it came fully into its own only during Napoleon's campaigns. The hot-air balloon, fixed to the ground by ropes, did valuable service at Maubeuge and Charleroi, but, with the advent of Napoleonic warfare and its rapid movement, subsequently fell into disuse.

In 1797 Carnot opposed a *coup d'état* from the left and had to escape abroad, but was called back later by Napoleon, who needed an able minister of war. But he was not prepared to come until after the disastrous Battle of Leipzig in 1813, when he realized that the country needed him again. One important

Below. *On 3 March 1795 an Austrian force under the Prince of Saxe-Coburg routed a French army at Aix-la-Chapelle.*

consequence of the military revolution was general reorganization. The vast army created by conscription necessitated a
new type of structure and organization, enabling simpler and
more mobile forms of combat. The old army had been tied to
linear tactics – was a fairly rigid body. Now it was a matter of
structuring the army into individual formations, each consisting
of infantry, cavalry and artillery, capable of operating independently from one another as well as jointly. Greater mobility
and cooperation between the three main branches was the
objective. The idea was not new, as it harked back to the
Romans. Prince Moritz of Saxony had experimented with it,
and other writers had put forward the idea of dividing the army
into divisions in order to increase mobility. However, it was
only during the course of the French revolutionary wars that the
ideas were put into practice.

The half-brigades had been the first step, though Napoleon

Left. *A trooper of the Lambeth
Cavalry, one of the many
volunteer units raised to combat the
menace of French invasion
(engraving by Thomas
Rowlandson).*

Above right. *A British long
6-pounder field gun crossing a ditch
(plate from William Congreve's
notebook).*

Left. *The young Bonaparte at the
Battle of Arcola, November 1796.*

Right. *George III and the Prince
of Wales at a review, 1799.*

changed them back into regiments. The half-brigade was the work of Carnot in 1793 – it was formed from one battalion of the line and two battalions of volunteers. Early in 1794 the Revolutionary army consisted of 250 half-brigades, of which 40 were light infantry deployed as *tirailleurs*. The infantry was armed as it had been throughout most of the eighteenth century, and its rate of fire was two rounds per minute. The cavalry maintained its old formations – 29 regiments of heavy cavalry, 20 regiments of dragoons, 23 regiments of chausseurs and 11 regiments of hussars – all in all about 500 squadrons of 140 men each. The artillery was divided into companies and attached to the infantry, while heavy artillery was maintained as a separate unit.

Carnot established the division, consisting of four half-brigades. Each brigade was commanded by a general and, according to need, each half-brigade or brigade could operate

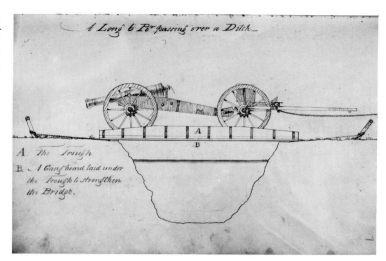

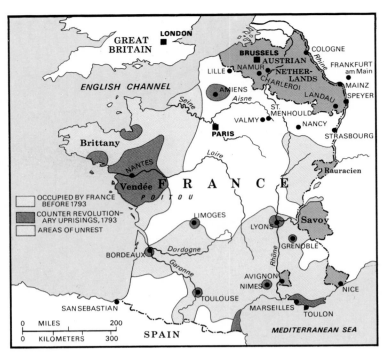

GREAT BRITAIN
LONDON
BRUSSELS
AUSTRIAN
NETHER-LANDS
COLOGNE
FRANKFURT am Main
LILLE
NAMUR
CHARLEROI
MAINZ
SPEYER
LANDAU
AMIENS
Aisne
ENGLISH CHANNEL
Seine
ST. MENHOULD
VALMY
NANCY
PARIS
STRASBOURG
Brittany
Loire
NANTES
Rauracien
Vendée
F R A N C E
Poitou
LIMOGES
Savoy
LYONS
Rhône
GRENOBLE
BORDEAUX
Dordogne
Garonne
AVIGNON
NIMES
NICE
TOULOUSE
MARSEILLES
SAN SEBASTIAN
TOULON
SPAIN
MEDITERRANEAN SEA

OCCUPIED BY FRANCE BEFORE 1793
COUNTER REVOLUTION-ARY UPRISINGS, 1793
AREAS OF UNREST

MILES 0 — 200
KILOMETERS 0 — 300

into specific departments. One of its main functions was to conduct the operation of the army, organizing billets on the march, security and so on. It was also to obtain military intelligence and to evaluate it, organize transportation and the supply of arms and materials, as well as food, and organize the engineering branch for sieges and fortress operations. Each branch coordinated its results and submitted them to the army commander, who, with the aid of the Chief of Staff, then drafted a basic concept for the operations to be conducted. Napoleon's staff in Italy in 1796–97 comprised five personal adjutants, 26 general staff officers, including their aides, three military administrators and a commissioner responsible for civil affairs. Corps staffs amounted to between 10 and 18 officers.

New tactics also appeared on the scene. Reference has already been made to the *tirailleur* tactics, but they could never be decisive except in conjunction with larger formations. Linear tactics always involved the risk of the line, three or four deep, being broken through. The Chevalier de Folard, whose influence on Frederick the Great has already been mentioned, was one of the first to question whether a column on the march, instead of being formed up into a line of battle, could not become an offensive formation itself. If the *colonne d'attaque* of 760 men attacked in a formation 32 men deep, it was bound to break through any linear formation and then roll up its flanks. In the French Revolutionary army, however, the column tactic developed more out of necessity than design. Masses of citizen soldiers could not be trained quickly enough to master linear tactics, so they attacked in bulk, or in what was to become the column. These new tactics were applied for the first time at the Battle of Jemappes, when General Dumouriez stormed the Austrian entrenchments, though it was more a horde of infantry than a disciplined column. Improvements, however, were already noticeable in 1793 in the Netherlands, Flanders and among the Moselle and Rhine armies. The terrain was more favorable to the column tactics of the French, who were surprised by their speed and penetration. *Tirailleurs* were used to initiate the battle, testing the enemy's nerve, until the column went in to attack, massively supported by artillery fire and cavalry.

separately. It took some time for this transformation into divisions to be achieved; once established, each division contained infantry, cavalry and artillery. Napoleon let his divisions operate separately until the moment had come to regroup them and bring about a decisive defeat. He also combined divisions into independently operating army corps. Again this took time, and was achieved while Napoleon prepared for the invasion of England, during which he carried out operations with army corps until the system worked. To each army corps belonged three to four cavalry regiments, each of four squadrons. Beside the light artillery, army corps were also equipped with two heavy batteries of eight guns each, engineers, sappers and a train battalion.

That part of the cavalry which had not been detached to the brigades and divisions maintained its own organization. It was still an arm of great tactical significance as an instrument of reconnaissance and pursuit, and for rapid penetration in battle. Dragoons and cuirassiers were combined into subdivisions supported by four pieces of light artillery. The strength of a subdivision consisted of 2500 horsemen.

The headquarters of the army of the *levée en masse* was at first in a state of confusion into which only Carnot had managed to bring order. This also applied to the command structure of the individual armies. In such a large army a commander could not concern himself with each and every detail as could be done in a small army, the size of Frederick the Great's; he had to delegate tasks to other officers trained in specific military skills. What emerged was a general staff strictly rationalized and subdivided

The column was essentially a formation of infantry units one behind another, each 50 yards wide and 12 deep and divided from the next unit by a gap of 50 yards. Naturally, there were numerous variations to this basic plan, depending on the topographical conditions, and the traditional battleground, the plain, became less significant. The column was quicker and more mobile than previous infantry formations and could be changed and adapted to the situation. The old fear of gaps between the formations disappeared, as they could be covered by the faculty of greater maneuverability and by *tirailleurs* or cavalry. Moreover, upon command they could immediately change

Left. *On 6 November 1792 Dumouriez drove the Archduke Albrecht's Austrians from a strong position on the heights above Jemappes.*

Right. *General Jean-Victor Moreau, 1763–1813. A talented general who lacked political acumen.*

Far right. *Marshal Jean-Baptiste-Jules Bernadotte, 1763–1844, Prince of Pontecorvo, left Napoleon's service to reign as Charles XIV of Sweden.*

Above. *The bravest of the brave: Marshal Ney, Duke of Elchingen and Prince of the Moscowa, 1769–1815.*

Above. *General Jean-Baptiste Kléber, 1753–1800. A brilliant general, he was assassinated in Egypt in 1800.*

Left. *One of Rowlandson's prints from a series showing infantry drill.*

Below left. *A Gilray cartoon pokes fun at privilege and influence in the army.*

Above. *A recruiting sergeant of the 33rd Regiment.*

Right. *Bonaparte, a former artillery officer, laying a gun with his own hand at the Battle of Lodi, 10 May 1796.*

Top right. *A humorous print shows the antics of volunteer units.*

Below. *Another print from Rowlandson's infantry series shows a private of the Lambeth Volunteers.*

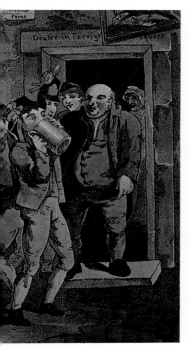

direction, something which previously could be achieved only by taking recourse to the oblique order of battle.

In actual battle the first column would attack, spread out if necessary and subsequently re-form, while the second column would remain behind in column formation until it was called into action. When facing an enemy attack, the column remained in a closed formation as a tactical body or square to repel it by concentrated fire.

From an auxiliary weapon, the artillery developed into a fully fledged and highly respected arm. The guns had been much improved: cannons and howitzers were made lighter and more mobile, the barrels were shortened, iron axles introduced, and the charge reduced to a third of the weight of the missile. The bulk were eight and 12 pounders and the siege guns 16 and 24 pounders. Ammunition consisted of metal balls and grapeshot. The engineers, who in the French army had at first served together with the artillery, were established as a separate corps, divided into mining companies and sappers. Despite genuine improvements ballistic efficiency still had its limitations. As column tactics developed, the divisional artillery was divided

and detached to the infantry wings of the second column, which were within range of the enemy. As the attack advanced so did the artillery, always trying to get close enough to subject the enemy to intensive grapeshot fire. The artillery fired simultaneously to maximize surprise and impact.

The new infantry and artillery tactics were bound to affect the cavalry as well; if they did not take care they could come into the firing line of their own *tirailleurs*, and a well-ordered and entrenched enemy position provided few opportunities for a cavalry attack. Success could only be achieved by surrounding the enemy while at the same time subjecting him to intense artillery fire. Individual attacks by small formations were pointless; only the massive use of cavalry could achieve success. During the age of linear tactics, the cavalry was an integral part of the battle order, securing the vulnerable flanks of the infantry; now, column tactics combined with operations taking place over much wider areas provided new opportunities for the cavalry. It gained greater flexibility and could easily adjust to the changing tactical situation. It could directly support the infantry columns as well as operate independently.

Left. *A romantic print shows an officer taking leave of his wife and child before going overseas.*

Right. *A sharp fight between a Franco-Dutch and a Russo-British force in Holland in September 1799.*

Below. *British and Russian troops are evacuated from Holland, November 1799.*

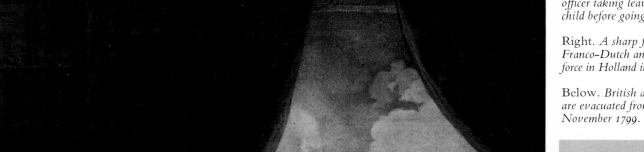

CHAPTER XI
THE NEW AGE
I: NAPOLEON

Napoleon was the master of the column tactic and he handled it with virtuosity, although some of his generals did not always fully understand it, especially when it concerned its application in large formations. He abolished the half-brigades and reintroduced the regiment, which now, in contrast to the eighteenth century, was an operational and not an administrative unit. Until his reforms of 1808, his infantry regiments moved into the field with two battalions, while the third remained behind as a depot for recruits. The normal formation of a brigade ready for attack consisted of the first two battalions of the first and second regiments positioned to the left and right of the flanks of the divisional column. The divisions of Soult and Bernadotte marched into the Battle of Austerlitz in Moravia in this order on 2 December 1805, defeating the Austrian Army.

When a fifth regiment was available, it initiated the attack by fighting as *tirailleurs*, but, as the attack of the main army progressed, it withdrew to the rear as reserve. Behind it stood divisions in battalion columns divided into three column formations. At the Battle of Borodino on 7 September 1812, the army corps under Marshal Ney attacked in the following basic form: two battalions in the center deployed with a battalion column on each wing, followed by four battalions in column formation as reserve. From 1808 the regiments comprised only four field battalions, each battalion having four infantry companies. These companies had double the strength to those of the Revolutionary army of 1791 and did not change column tactics.

In the Battle of Wagram on 5–6 July 1809, Napoleon preceded his attack with a cannonade from 100 pieces of artillery and then, for the first time, combined 20 battalions into one mass column, eight following one another and six on each flank, a grand total of 20,000 men. It was a size, however, which transcended the possibilities inherent in column tactics; the sheer mass impeded mobility and increased the losses sustained by the defensive fire of the Austrians. Because of that relative immobility, Napoleon protected his flanks with cavalry, but his attacking infantry was decimated before the stage of close combat had been reached. This measure had, however, been taken as a result of particular circumstances. The great successes of column tactics had been based on its ability to change direction and re-form quickly, for which purpose a great number of highly experienced officers, NCOs and soldiers were needed. By 1809, however, after a series of campaigns lasting over 10 years, most of his experienced officers and subalterns were already in the grave. What Napoleon tried to do was to compensate quality with quantity. He used his columns like a medieval ramming block to increase their destructive effect. At Waterloo he used very much the same tactic, though without success.

Napoleon established a way of integrating *tirailleurs* with columns; from 1804 he attached to every light regiment, and to every line regiment from 1805, a *voltigeur* company to act as *tirailleurs*, while the fusiliers formed the battle columns. These companies formed an elite and were also called *flanqueneurs*. While on the march, they were at the rear. If the battalion led the attack, they rapidly advanced to the left and right, overtook it and engaged the enemy. As soon as the battalion itself was involved in the attack, the *flanqueneurs* moved to secure the flanks. In the case of the second column behind, the *flanqueneurs* accompanied the attacks so that they were always in touch with one another as well as with the main column, always ready to secure the flanks at critical moments. When the battle developed so that the column was firing in line, both *flanqueneur* companies, each divided into two sections, took up position about 20 yards behind their column's wings, ready to act as quick reinforcements. What previously had been a wildly improvised form of combat had been transformed into clearly ordered tactics, the movements of the *tirailleurs* being fully integrated with those of the column.

All this would have been impossible if the armies had been burdened by excessive trains. The efficiency of a mass army depends on its supplies. The Revolutionary army lived off the land when operating abroad. Every infantry battalion had only two

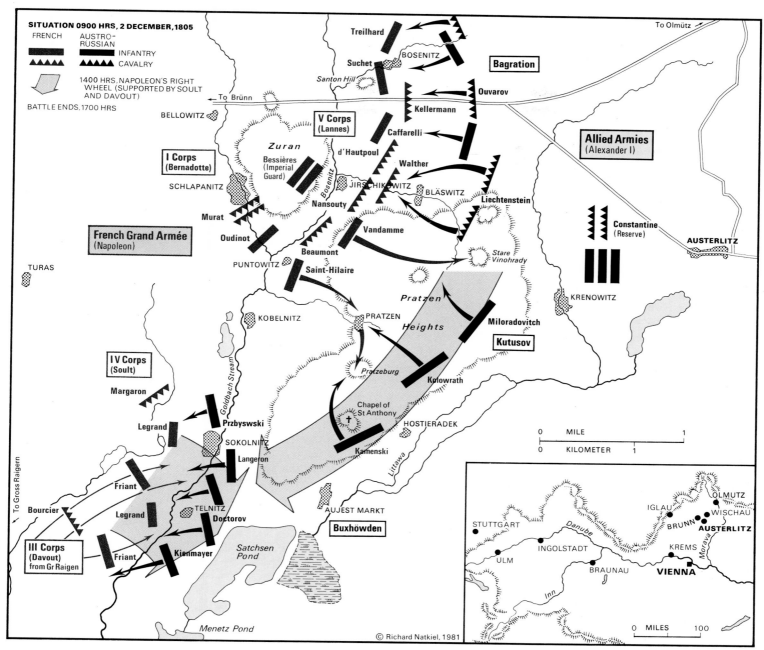

SITUATION 0900 HRS, 2 DECEMBER, 1805

FRENCH	AUSTRO-RUSSIAN	
		INFANTRY
		CAVALRY

1400 HRS, NAPOLEON'S RIGHT WHEEL (SUPPORTED BY SOULT AND DAVOUT)

BATTLE ENDS, 1700 HRS

To Olmütz

Treilhard

Suchet
BOSENITZ

Santon Hill

Bagration

To Brünn

Ouvarov

Kellermann

BELLOWITZ

V Corps (Lannes)

Caffarelli

d'Hautpoul

Walther

Allied Armies (Alexander I)

Zuran

I Corps (Bernadotte)

Bessières (Imperial Guard)

Bosenitz

JIRSCHIKOWITZ

BLÄSWITZ

Liechtenstein

SCHLAPANITZ

Nansouty

Constantine (Reserve)

AUSTERLITZ

Murat

French Grand Armée (Napoleon)

Vandamme

Oudinot

Stare Vinohrady

Beaumont

Saint-Hilaire

TURAS

PUNTOWITZ

KRENOWITZ

Pratzen

KOBELNITZ

PRATZEN

Heights

Miloradovitch

Kutusov

IV Corps (Soult)

Pratzeburg

Margaron

Goldbach Stream

Kolowrath

Legrand

Przybyswski

Chapel of St Anthony

HOSTIERADEK

SOKOLNITZ

Langeron

Kamenski

Littawa

Friant

Legrand

TELNITZ

Doctorov

Bourcier

AUJEST MARKT

III Corps (Davout) from Gr Raigen

Friant

Kienmayer

Satschen Pond

Buxhöwden

To Gross Raigern

| 0 | MILE | 1 |
| 0 | KILOMETER | 1 |

Menetz Pond

© Richard Natkiel, 1981

STUTTGART

IGLAU

OLMUTZ

BRUNN

WISCHAU

Danube

INGOLSTADT

AUSTERLITZ

ULM

KREMS

Moravia

BRAUNAU

VIENNA

Inn

| 0 | MILES | 100 |

Previous spread. *Catastrophe in the snow – the French army on the retreat from Moscow, 1812.*

Above left. *Napoleon and the Emperor Francis I of Austria meet after the Battle of Austerlitz.*

Far left. *Marshal Nicholas Soult, Duke of Dalmatia, 1769–1851. Appointed marshal in 1804, Soult delivered the decisive blow against the Austrians and Russians at Austerlitz in December 1805.*

Right. *A vivid contemporary engraving of the Battle of Austerlitz. Although the artist has exaggerated the height of the hills, he gives a good idea of the massive scale of 'The Battle of the Three Emperors.'*

Above left. *An allegorical print shows George III championing peace.*

Below left. *The Battle of Marengo, 14 June 1800. A hard-fought battle, won for the French by the timely arrival of General Desaix.*

Above. *Jacques Louis David's magnificent painting of the coronation of Napoleon.*

Right. *Napoleon's sister-in-law, Queen Hortense of Holland.*

Below. *Napoleon crossing the Great St Bernard Pass, 1801. (Jacques Louis David).*

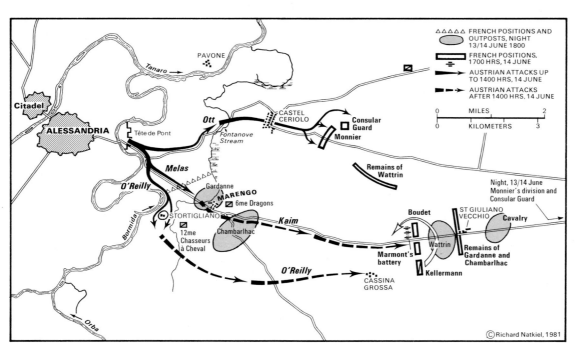

FRENCH POSITIONS AND OUTPOSTS, NIGHT 13/14 JUNE 1800

FRENCH POSITIONS, 1700 HRS, 14 JUNE

AUSTRIAN ATTACKS UP TO 1400 HRS, 14 JUNE

AUSTRIAN ATTACKS AFTER 1400 HRS, 14 JUNE

MILES 0 — 2
KILOMETERS 0 — 3

© Richard Natkiel, 1981

Above. *An English cartoon of 1807 shows French conscripts being taken to the army roped together to prevent escape.*

Below. *The French army crosses the Danube on 5 July 1809, the day before the Battle of Wagram.*

Below right. *A French sapper (left) chats to a gunner of foot artillery.*

Below far right. *The mailed fist whose impact decided many battles: a French cuirassier in full dress, 1805.*

transport wagons carrying food supplies, representing two full days' rations or four days on half rations. In addition, one wagon carried the tools necessary for entrenchment and field works. The supply of ammunition had absolute priority and provided no problem, and the officers carried the same baggage as their men. A wagon was also stocked with tents but, as they deteriorated, no new supplies were delivered and the soldiers had to bivouac under the open sky. Mobility was increased by living off the land, and the more ruthlessly it was exploited the greater distance could be covered. Certainly, the generals Pichegru and Jourdan would hardly have been able to win their victories in Belgium and Holland so decisively in 1794 had their movements been impeded by the magazine or depot system.

It was relatively easy to live off the land in central Europe, where the agricultural output was high. It was a different matter, however, in Spain and Russia; supply depots were established, but dependence on them would have limited speed and depth of penetration. For this reason alone, the armies had to live off the produce of the countries they invaded. To provide a graphic picture of the requirements of an army of about 250,000 men and 100,000 horses, the figures for the daily needs of such an army will suffice: 225 tons of bread, 550 tons of oats, 550 tons of hay, 450 tons of straw and 2800 tons of fresh fodder. To supply these quantities, 4100 vehicles or carts were required. The policy of requisitioning in enemy territory, therefore, reduced one's own train and gave greater mobility to the forces. No one knew how to live off the land as expertly as Napoleon did. The campaign and speedy conquest of Italy showed that, in well-populated areas, requisitioning could be carried out independently without actually reducing the numbers of troops in the field.

Napoleon did not only requisition food – he also filled the treasury in Paris with valuable war booty. This naturally contradicted the principle of preserving as much as possible when campaigning, as was widely practiced in the eighteenth century by the standing armies of the absolute monarchs. The full exploitation of all the available resources in enemy country was part and parcel of this new way of conducting hostilities. It did raise the question, however, of how far one could go. Every misuse, every excess, ultimately operated against the aggressor's military interests if requisitions reached a point at which the inhabitants took up their own arms to defend themselves or even drive out the invader. Napoleon paid the price for five long years in Spain; he paid it in 1809 in the Tyrol and in Germany in 1813.

Napoleon did not exploit resources according to any plan, and how food supplies were obtained was a matter of indifference to him as long as the quick pace of his operations was not impeded, and success on the battlefield was ensured, thus providing him with additional supplies. With that principle in mind, he had his armies march across Europe generally without establishing supply depots.

In the autumn campaign against Austria in 1805, the lack of any supply trains proved a great advantage; the troops simply requisitioned what they needed, and more, from the territories through which they marched. There had been a good harvest and, besides wheat, ample stocks of potatoes existed throughout southern Germany. The army could afford to live hand to mouth. Although the areas of requisition were divided between the army corps, almost chaotic conditions ensued as no firm rules of priority were established. Even requisitioning for an army required a carefully-thought-out system. Discipline was affected, and the old habits of plundering and marauding emerged as soon as shortages occurred. The absence of any system also led to wastage. If Napoleon's brilliant tactical victories, culminating in Austerlitz, had not been achieved with such unexpected speed, his army could well have become the victim of a major supply catastrophe. Napoleon realized this and immediately ordered the establishment of a great supply depot for biscuits, flour, oats and spirits.

The French army conducted the unexpected war against Prussia in 1806 again without supply depots at hand. It carried a supply of bread for 10 days. As before, operations developed with unforeseen speed and, after the victories at Jena and Auerstädt, the army moved in good agricultural country and therefore had no problem in feeding itself. Matters changed, however, when the army crossed the Vistula and the weather changed; winter was upon them and the supply system collapsed completely. There was not enough food to requisition, disease ravaged the army and supply trains got bogged down on the bad roads east of the Oder. Marshal Lannes reported to Napoleon on 11 November 1806 that, within a radius of 10 miles, there was no longer any bread for his army corps. Hunger became the constant companion of Napoleon's armies.

By the beginning of 1807, the main theater of war had shifted to East Prussia, where Napoleon had a force of approximately 600,000 men. Upon encountering the first Russian forces, who were fighting in alliance with Prussia, he forced them back to the Lithuanian border districts. On 7 and 8 February 1807 he met them again at Preussisch-Eylau in the first major battle in East Prussia. The Russians were under the command of General Bennigsen and were supported by the Prussian Corps L'Estoq, whose chief of staff was Gerhard von Scharnhorst. It was the first battle which Napoleon did not win, mainly because, in spite of superior numbers, he fought a winter campaign with a physically weakened army and with little prospect of successful requisitioning. He therefore preferred to move into richer provinces such as Silesia and Pomerania. Napoleon himself stated that it would have been a child's game to beat the Russians, but the fate of Europe depended on the question of food supplies.

For the spring of 1807 Napoleon made more thorough preparations. He considered a supply line stretching from the Rhine to the Vistula too risky in view of the primitive transport and

lines of communication of the time, and exploited Prussia instead. Quarters and food for his troops had to be supplied by the Prussian burghers, and all existing arsenals, depots, magazines and manufacturing installations were taken over; all available sources of revenue were tapped. Berlin alone had to pay two and a half million thalers. All sources of economic productivity were turned to the service of the French war effort. Prussia had to supply all the uniforms, and even the army stationed in Poland was supplied with bread and meat from Silesia. For the first time the entire system of requisitioning, financial and food supplies, was put under the central direction of the Intendant General Drau, who established a military administration whose commissioners acted according to strict rules and instructions.

France herself supplied the least – her financial burden was no greater than would have been required for the upkeep of a

Left. *British infantry charge the French during the Peninsular War.*

Right. *Marshal Ney.*

Below left. *French household troops, before the Revolution and after the Restoration.*

Below. *French engineer officers, 1732–1845.*

Below far right. *French chevaux-légers, 1690–1814.*

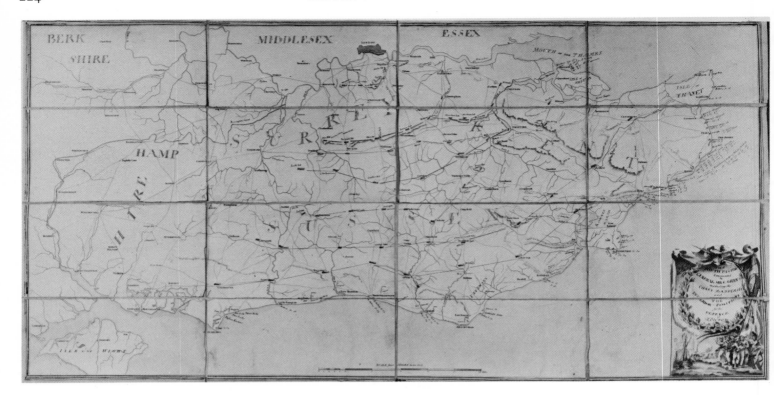

peacetime army. For France the real cost was in the number of human lives lost, especially from 1808 onward. Despite all the drawbacks of the continental blockade against Britain, in general France mobilized the entire continent's export resources which in turn had highly beneficial effects on French industry.

The near disaster with supplies in late 1806 and early 1807 led to a complete reorganization. On 26 March 1807 Napoleon ordered the establishment of eight train battalions, each divided into four companies. By 1811 the train had increased to 13 battalions, each with six companies. When he invaded Russia in 1812, the supply train consisted of 360 wagons, each army corps having its own train battalion. The supplies carried by them were to last 14 days.

The more the area of operation was extended, the more carefully had logistics to be considered. Taking recourse to methods already used in the previous century, Napoleon established supply stations every 10 to 20 miles along the route of advance. They ran along the Rhine from Wesel to Strasbourg and across central Germany. Each base was under the command of a general or a head commissioner. Their function was to obtain supplies, supervise local administration, carry out police functions and control all postal transport traffic, as well as to ensure that roads and bridges were maintained in good order. As long as the rear was peaceful, there was no need for large occupation forces and the bulk of the army served on the battlefield. In 1811 there were no more than 1000 gendarmes, who supervised the entire area between the Rhine and the Vistula. The widespread network of roads in central Europe aided this task. This was in direct contrast to Spain, where the line from Bayonne to Madrid could be secured only by the deployment of strong military forces against guerrilla attacks. Russia was another vital exception.

The Russian campaign provides a classic example of the interdependence between army leadership and supplies. The Emperor envisaged difficulties and had made preparations which he considered adequate. Supplies were accumulated in the area east of the Vistula sufficient for the needs of 600,000 men for one year. The only question that remained unanswered was how to defeat the enemy in the depths of Russia. If the Russians evaded battle, which they frequently did, then the pace of the

Above. *A map belonging to Lieutenant General Sir Eyre Coote, showing the lines of defense around London in 1803.*

Above right. *A Russian painting showing French troops in Smolensk in October 1812.*

Right. *On 17 August 1812 the Russians put up a fierce resistance at Smolensk, and eventually withdrew having set fire to the town.*

Overleaf. *In September 1807 Copenhagen was captured by a British force under Lord Cathcart, after a bombardment of the forts and citadel lasting four days.*

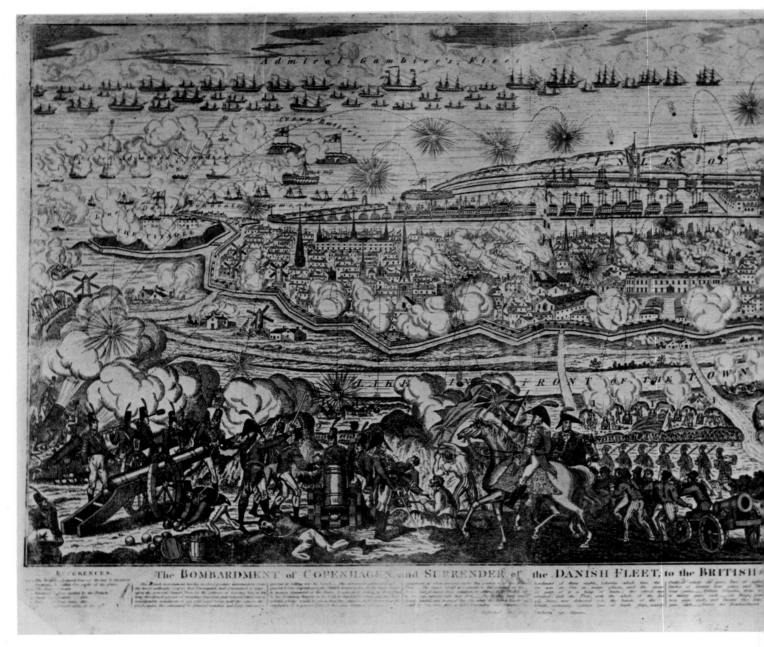

The BOMBARDMENT of COPENHAGEN, and SURRENDER of the DANISH FLEET, to the BRITISH

Left. *A popular print shows the bombardment and capture of Copenhagen.*

Below far left. *Field Marshal Augustus Wilhelm von Gneisenau, 1760–1831, a Prussian military reformer who served as Blücher's chief of staff at Waterloo.*

Below left. *General Karl Maria von Clausewitz, 1780–1831. Captured after Auerstadt in the 1806 campaign, Clausewitz decided to defect to Russia in 1812 rather than assist in the collaboration between France and Prussia. He rejoined the Prussian army in 1814, and served with distinction in the Waterloo campaign. He is best known as a philosopher of war, and his writings on strategy retain lasting importance.*

Below. *Russian helmets of the 1812 campaign.*

advance could not be increased without risking the collapse of the supplies system; to establish a line of supply from East Prussia to Moscow was impossible. Also, there was bound to be a serious shortage of horse fodder. Napoleon's intention to campaign in Russia lacked a coordinated plan. He hoped to beat the Russian army decisively near the frontier at Vilna. But the Russians evaded battle; even penetrating as far as Vitebsk brought no conclusion. Originally he had planned to leave the conquest of Moscow until 1813, but his army had reached the limits of its supply line. There were only two choices open to him: to give up and withdraw, or to march on to Moscow. Believing that supplies would be found in the agricultural regions around Smolensk and in Moscow, he opted for the latter decision.

The results were catastrophic even before Moscow had been reached. When crossing the Memel on 22 June 1812, the main army was 300,000 strong; in the course of the next few months while still on the march, hunger, exhaustion, disease and desertion had reduced it by 130,000 men, while 70,000 were combat casualties. The Russians' scorched earth policy left very little to be requisitioned, and when Napoleon reached Moscow, he conquered a burning city, not a storehouse. In the course of its retreat, the French army lost even more of its original strength. The question of supplies was not the only factor which defeated Napoleon's Russian venture, but it was a vital one.

It was virtually inevitable that the organizational, tactical and logistical changes, in conjunction with political driving forces, would revolutionize strategy. The *levée en masse* forced the entire population into arms, something which the *ancien régime* had always avoided, because a people in arms also represented a potential danger to its own rule. War was never an affair conducted according to entirely rational principles; the power of the French Revolution increased its destructive potency. Armies could be quickly organized and sent to the battlefield in great numbers. The art of maneuver, previously preferred because of the high cost of a standing army, was abandoned; the new state possessed the human resources to match even a partial defeat by quick regeneration through the supply of new troops. Human life had become cheaper. Moreover, the Jacobin army entered war with the motto of total victory. Whereas formerly operations had in the main been conducted to cut off the enemy from the rear and deprive him of his supplies, the main forces of the enemy were now the objective; the battle had become more important than the maneuver.

It is unlikely that a much shaken France would have overcome the defeats of the first two Revolutionary wars had not Napoleon come to the fore. By his superior use of the forces available to him and realizing the new requirements of the time, he became the master of the strategy of annihilation. Its practical application was the result of the restructuring of the army into divisions and army corps, of the use of troops *en masse* and the increased tactical effectiveness of the arms deployed. His forces possessed all the characteristics needed for mobile operations and his superb generalship produced the quick advance in the decisive direction. Furthermore, his ability to concentrate all available forces at the right time on the battlefield ensured victory, followed by strategic and relentless pursuit. In that way, Napoleon, in whose hands military and political leadership were united, did not only change the map of Europe but also the conduct of war. His strategy was based on the full exploitation of superior numbers, space and time. As long as the system of supplies functioned adequately, and kept pace with the swift advance of his military operations, the Napoleonic method of combined speed, mass and annihilation achieved extraordinary successes. As always, however, this new strategic concept also remained dependent on political, economic and technical factors. It presupposed a superior instrument of war, which, by 1813, no longer existed.

The war fortifications became less important. The aim of warfare was the complete annihilation of the enemy, for which all available forces were concentrated; since the cavalry had become a decisive branch, fortifications lost their operational value. Even strongly fortified cities such as Kolberg in Pomerania, which defended itself from 1806 until the Peace of Tilsit in 1807, did not seriously impede Napoleon's operations. In most cases it was quite sufficient to detach small units to keep them in check and under observation. His enemies were to learn from him: Blücher's chief of staff, Gneisenau, conducted the 1814 campaign in France in much the same manner. The more soldiers were detached for siege purposes, the fewer could be put on the battlefield. Still, Napoleon utilized the existence of strong fortresses in minor theaters of war, such as in upper Italy, for his own purposes, and in conquered territory existing fortifications were improved, such as Mantua in 1796 and Danzig in 1807. The fortifications built along the River Elbe also played an important role in 1813 as the basis for the strategic defensive line of Napoleon's forces.

Napoleon's strategy of annihilation was emulated throughout Europe. General von Clausewitz, in his work *On War*, paid great attention to it and clearly defined it. When the aim is the total annihilation of the enemy, this does not mean attacking and killing recklessly, but making the opponent defenseless, breaking his will to resist and eliminating the sources of aid and supply. The strategy of annihilation was not devoid of humanitarian principles: the horrors of war could be reduced by a quick and decisive battle which shortened the war.

Statistics show that, in its initial phase, this strategy caused fewer fatal casualties than the battles of the eighteenth century, primarily because of the increased mobility of the armies. However, the more frequently this strategy was applied, the larger were the masses on the battlefield and the greater the losses became. One of Napoleon's critics maintained that the life span of the average soldier in Napoleon's army was between 33 and 36 months. As the theater of operations of Napoleon's armies increased in size, so did the manpower requirements. Soldiers became no more than 'cannon fodder.' Napoleon's campaigns cost some 3,500,000 dead and wounded.

However, a major improvement of the time were doctors provided with horses and a military medical service, which was extended under General Larray into a network of mobile field hospitals. At the Battle of Aboukir in Egypt in 1798, it was said that none of the 800 wounded had to wait longer than a quarter of an hour for treatment. However, with the spread of Napoleonic warfare and its immense territorial operations, the development of the field hospitals could not keep pace – hospitals could be provided but not sufficient personnel.

A vital component of Revolutionary and Napoleonic warfare was propaganda, that is to say the dissemination of the new principles of liberty, equality and fraternity, in France and then throughout Europe. In France it had sustained the Revolutionary armies and carried them forward to victory; counterrevolutionary risings, such as in the Vendée, could be mercilessly crushed, and the armies could range themselves against princely despotism beyond the frontiers of France. The *citoyen armée* believed it upheld the dignity of revolution, a dignity destined to proclaim to the world at large the principles of human rights and the recovery of allegedly inalienable natural rights of man. The Revolution had therefore not only to succeed in France, but to conquer and remove the entire *ancien régime* in Europe; it claimed to fight for the liberation of Europe from the 'world enemy.' The transformation of an ideology for domestic consumption to an expansive missionary ideal was complete. Scharnhorst says in his account of the campaign of 1794, the *Development of the General Causes for the Fortune of the French in the Revolutionary War*: 'They considered themselves enlightened, clever, free and happy and that all other nations were uneducated, akin to animals and unhappy. . . . They believed not only in their further existence and good fortune, but that they were fighting for the welfare of all mankind. Such effective motives for self-sacrifice of all kinds have not been found among any other nation.'

The French army fought with ideological weapons. Already in 1792 every allied deserter was promised naturalization and a lifelong pension, irrespective of whether he would serve France as soldier or civilian. While in combat, French guards always endeavored to come into contact with their opposite numbers to convince them of the righteousness of the French cause. Masses of leaflets proclaiming the new principles were printed in all European languages in Paris and found their way into the

Left. *The Battle of Aboukir, 25 July 1799. Napoleon completely defeated a superior Turkish force under Mustapha Pasha. Treatment of the French wounded was remarkably efficient.*

Above right. *General Gerhard Johann Scharnhorst, 1755–1813. After service in the Hanoverian army, Scharnhorst transferred to the Prussian army in 1801, and played a leading role in rebuilding it after Jena. He was mortally wounded at Lutzen in May 1813.*

Right. *King Frederick William III of Prussia, who reigned from 1797–1840.*

allied armies. They were not without effect: few Germans could be enthusiastic about fighting on behalf of obsolete feudal rule, or few British for the naval supremacy of Britain. Even Scharnhorst, while still an artillery captain in the service of Hanover, could see little purpose other than that of simply doing his duty. Confronted with the Revolutionary propaganda, the allied officers often felt rather helpless; it was a dimension of warfare they had not encountered before and for which they had not been prepared.

Nevertheless, the allied armies did not simply dissolve and the number of desertions was no higher than usual; there was also the element of historic consciousness, the memory of how France a century before had ravaged the Palatinate and of how Louis XIV had robbed ancient German territory and annexed it to France; the rape of Strasbourg had not been forgotten. These memories provided an active antidote to the revolutionary and humanistic visions of the French. Also the lack of success of French propaganda was evident when the *Sans-Culottes* confronted traditional, professional armies. The two were irreconcilable. 'One must not imagine the French Army of that time as having the appearance of its later period of glory. The *Carmagnoles*, clad in rags, without any real military spirit and countenance, who daily sent abuse and weak shots across the Rhine, hardly excited respect,' wrote one contemporary. Another, however, who had been a prisoner in France, saw it from a different perspective: 'What among us is the product of . . . exercise as well as fear, is done here upon one word naturally and without inhibition. While among the French we had acquired a free and easy way of life, now, *after return to the Austrian lines*, we were again confronted by the stiff puppet theater. I was shocked as soon as I met the first comrades on guard in their powdered wigs.'

The change from cabinet warfare to warfare accompanied by missionary, ideological propaganda only exacerbated the barbarity of warfare. The enemy was equated with the devil and the promise was to clear out hell. It resulted in a fury of national passions on all sides, which, for instance, gave the Prussian campaigns in 1813 the fervor and passion of a crusade, once they had learned their lessons from the French. Schiller summarized the French argument of liberty, equality and fraternity in the rhyme: '*Und willst Du nicht mein Bruder sein, so schlag ich Dir den Schädel ein*' – 'If you don't want to be my brother, I shall break your skull!' The National Convent ordered that no more prisoners be taken, an order largely ignored in the field.

Once Napoleon had taken over the helm of the state and army, more orderly ways were introduced in the army, but propaganda still played a major part. He raised Polish hopes of regaining their state, and his addresses to his soldiers were masterpieces of military and political rhetoric. Until the very end he managed to keep morale high, at least in France. Propaganda successes were also achieved in the fragmented German states along the Rhine and in Westphalia, where his administrative reforms did much to make him popular, but they were short-lived. As his armies flooded across Europe, living off the land and bringing oppression and disruption, the impact of his propaganda was lost – indeed it turned against him. What liberties he allowed were also strictly limited, and, master of propaganda that he was, he also feared this weapon when it was deployed against him. The entire German press was subject to French censorship, and no book could appear without being licensed first by the French. Obstinate writers landed in prison, and the Nuremberg bookseller Johann Philipp Palm was executed by firing squad at Braunau on 26 August 1806 because he had ventured to publish an anonymous pamphlet under the title *Germany in its Lowest Degradation*.

Napoleon employed an unknown number of writers and cartoonists to fill the German gazettes with whatever pleased him. The import of British newspapers and books was prohibited, which, however, did not prevent Burke's *Reflections on the French Revolution* turning up in Germany, to be duly translated by Friedrich von Gentz, later Metternich's adviser. Such censorship also extended to France and its own publications. In other words, the press became an instrument of psychological warfare as well. As Napoleon approached his military and political end, however, the truth could no longer be hidden. Even the most inspiring press appeals could not obscure the reality of being unable to pacify Spain and conquer Russia, or his failure to resist the military onslaught of Prussia, Russia and Austria, aided by those German states who were former members of the Confederation of the Rhine.

The French Revolution, at first so enthusiastically received by many Germans, later, ironically, regenerated German national consciousness in response to the Napoleonic invasions. In reacting to the Revolution, they modified the lessons taught by Napoleon and developed a type of psychological warfare which was not to be seen again in central Europe until the twentieth century. Militarily and psychologically, Napoleon was beaten with his own weapons.

By 1806 Prussia had withdrawn from the Revolutionary wars, mainly because its priorities lay to the east. Frederick William III ascended the Russian throne in 1797 and, in view of the shaky state of Prussia's finances which his predecessor Frederick William II had left, was anxious to keep out of all foreign entanglements. While Austria battled on with short interruptions until 1805, leaving Britain on her own, Prussia hoped to maintain her neutrality. When French troops violated this neutrality, however, Frederick William III mobilized his army on 6 August 1806. Napoleon demanded their withdrawal, Frederick William refused and war ensued.

The Prussian army expected to meet Napoleon west of the Thuringian forest, and, totally underestimating the rapidity with which Napoleon could move his forces, they moved into the region. However, the Prussian vanguard was defeated by the French at Saalfeld on 10 October 1806, and Prince Louis Ferdinand, a nephew of Frederick the Great, was killed. In their rapid advance the French forces bypassed the Prussians on their flank, penetrating to the rear. On 14 October the battles of Jena and Auerstädt were fought, which for Prussia were absolutely disastrous. At Jena the Prussian army under the command of Prince Hohenlohe-Ingelfingen confronted a force three times its size, while a few miles away to the north near the village of Auerstädt stood the bulk of the army, where it enjoyed numerical superiority over the French. The army's commander, the Duke of Brunswick, was wounded early in battle; this put the king directly in charge of operations but, while not lacking in personal bravery, he lacked the gift of command, the capacity and vision necessary for quick and momentous decisions. At Auerstädt the Prussian army was beaten as soundly as at Jena. The old linear tactics proved of little use against Napoleon's columns. The fact that the Prussian troops had been bypassed and taken from the rear meant that the French fought with their backs to the River Oder, while the Prussians faced east. Their communications cut, they lacked any base to withdraw to; having been defeated, they were then also routed, the army being in complete disarray. Unit after unit capitulated, fortress after fortress surrendered.

Frederick William III immediately attempted to enter into negotiations with Napoleon, but these were rejected outright; Rossbach was to be avenged to the full. On 27 October the Corsican entered Berlin. One of his first visits was to the tomb of Frederick the Great at Potsdam; deep in thought before the sarcophagus, he turned to his attending generals and said: 'Gentlemen, if this man were still alive I would not be here.'

Frederick William and his family, together with his government, fled beyond the River Oder. Now Napoleon put forward his demands: the cession by Prussia of all its territory west of the Elbe. Frederick William tried to negotiate better terms but without success, and, against the advice of his councillors, decided to continue the war. This decision separated the wheat from the chaff among his advisers; men like Stein and Hardenberg now came to the fore to direct Prussia's fortunes. By that time Frederick William and his court had moved to Königsberg, the French close on their heels. The Battle of Preussisch Rylau and Napoleon's failure to conquer caused the latter to repeat his peace terms. Frederick William, now counselled by Hardenberg, refused in the hope that Russia's strength would soon make itself felt and change the situation in Prussia's favor. The war continued and, when Napoleon beat the Russians at the Battle of Friedland on 14 June 1807, Czar Alexander asked Napoleon for an armistice. Eleven days later, on 25 June, the two emperors met on a raft on the River Memel and concluded an agreement at the expense of Prussia. While Russia was not to sustain any losses, Prussia was to pay the bill, its continuing existence suffered by Napoleon only as a personal favor to Czar Alexander. On 9 July 1807 at the Treaty of Tilsit, Prussia lost all its territories west of the Elbe, including the city of Magdeburg, and her Polish provinces to the Duchy of Warsaw under the king of Saxony. Prussia was reduced to an area of 7311 square kilometers with a population of 4,500,000. From the western provinces which Prussia lost, the Kingdom of Westphalia was formed, on the throne of which Napoleon put his youngest brother Jerome. The Treaty of Tilsit was supplemented by the Convention of Königsberg of 12 July 1807, in which Napoleon stipulated that he would withdraw his occupying forces from Prussia only when the reparation payments demanded had been paid; no figure had then been determined.

In the course of time, however, Napoleon found himself compelled to withdraw troops from Prussia earlier than he had expected, due to a major mistake. During the same year, under dubious pretexts and to further a campaign against Portugal, Britain's oldest ally, Napoleon first subjected the northern part of Spain to his control, then forced the Bourbon King Charles IV to abdicate early in the following year and put his brother

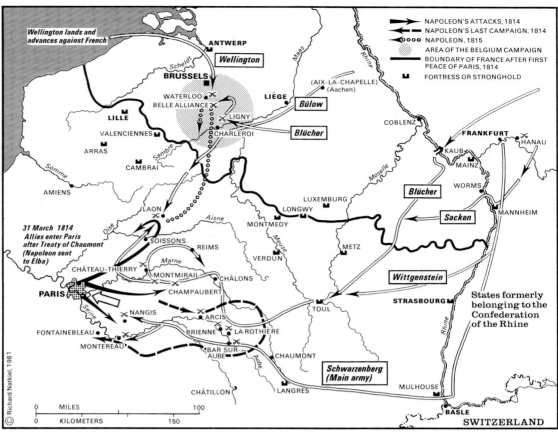

Above. *Field Marshal Gebhard Liberecht von Blücher, 1742–1819. A dashing cavalry leader, Blücher commanded the Prussian rearguard after Jena and led the Prussian army at Waterloo.*

Below. *Napoleon's brother, Jerome Bonaparte, King of Westphalia (engraving after Antoine Gros).*

Joseph on the Spanish throne. Napoleon had reached the zenith of his power.

His action in Spain, however, precipitated something he had not expected – a people's war conducted by guerrilla tactics. By comparison with guerrilla conflicts in the Vendée, the irregular forces in Spain managed to resist the most powerful military might of Europe. The almost inaccessible mountainous landscape, the poor state of the roads, the extensive coastline and the relatively mild climate provided the guerrillas with sufficient advantages to match France's military power. Charged with wild fanaticism, they conducted a war of attrition accompanied by an unexpected series of insurrections in the urban centers. Guerrilla means 'little war,' but its effects in this instance were considerable. It became fully effective after 1807, when Napoleon, with forces drawn from Germany, had defeated the regular Spanish army in his campaign of 11 November to 4 December 1808. While the Duke of Wellington, as supreme commander of the Anglo-Portuguese forces in Portugal and Spain, conducted his campaigns in accordance with the old strategic rules, aiming to cut off the French from the rear and conquer Madrid, bands of small guerrilla units, each no more than 300 to 500 men strong, kept the occupying army of 300,000 soldiers continuously out of breath, and for years decisively tied it down and weakened it. The Spanish militia units supporting Wellington's army were, on the other hand, of very low combat value.

The bands of guerrillas consisted only of volunteers, mostly peasants; there were also many former regular soldiers. Sufficient weapons were available, but uniforms were not worn. Without strict central direction, each guerrilla leader operated more or less independently. The Junta-Central, however, called into being on 25 September 1808, formed a government committee 35 members strong in place of the deposed king and raised the call for the defense of Spain's sacred soil against the foreign invader. But it was no revolutionary government, and was in no way the spiritual driving force of the people's war.

The proud Spaniards, in spite of the primitive military means available to them, carried the burdens of their war with admirable patience. They fought without knowledge of organizational military principles but with guile and endurance, ignoring the cost of blood with which they had to pay. Their motives are to be found in religious and patriotic sources as well as in their allegiance to the monarchy. The social reforms which Napoleon intended and partly implemented in a very hasty fashion found little favor because the country lacked an 'enlightened' bourgeois society. On the contrary, the measures further increased the hatred of the foreigner and released passions without bounds; prisoners were hanged on the nearest tree and women butchered the wounded, in many cases taking recourse to refined methods of torture. Only those who managed to escape to monasteries or convents could be sure to remain alive, for even a short time. After the bloody suppression of the Madrid rising during the night of 3 May 1808, French courtmartials had numerous citizens executed, many of whom were innocent. Goya has provided us with a horrifying pictorial record of these executions, his victims displaying impotent defiance, resignation and despair in the face of inevitable death.

This bloodbath was followed by a series of repressions. They did not cause the Spanish people to submit; as every French prisoner was hanged, so every captured insurgent was shot on the spot, both sides operating outside the existing rules of war. The Spanish guerrilla was the national resistance fighter, the underground activist; he was a partisan within the modern meaning of the term. The differences between the regular armed forces and civilians became completely blurred – they became between combatants and noncombatants. That the guerrillas also harbored criminal elements among them goes without saying, though it did little to further their cause. In cases where inhabitants were reluctant to aid the guerrillas or, worse, collaborated with the enemy, their fate was as final as was that of the invader, sometimes even worse.

The Junta attempted to organize the struggle, but without success. The partisans could not afford combat in the open; guerrilla warfare required efficient forces under a very flexible leadership. Tactical successes could have been achieved only if the bands of guerrillas, instead of fighting in independent groups, had possessed the ability to support one another. The rising had been a spontaneous one, however, lacking any military preparations whatsoever. The particularist-inclined provincial juntas were only able to rally large armed mobs, strict military discipline, in view of the prevailing chaotic conditions, being impossible. No single guerrilla leader managed to combine under his command all the other guerrilla units. They therefore had to avoid major engagements with the enemy, concentrating on ambushes and assassination wherever possible; the geography of the country favored this mode of warfare. As a result of the Anglo-Portuguese intervention, the guerrillas obtained firm support and Napoleon's troops faced hitherto unknown problems. They had to fight Wellington offensively in the first instance, but more than two-thirds of their combat troops had to be detached to secure the fortified cities. The guerrillas continuously interrupted the lines of communication, ambushed supply columns, captured couriers and successfully attacked and conquered fortified posts. No pardon was given to guerrillas, but that made no difference – for every one killed, two or three stepped in his place. Meanwhile, matters were getting more difficult for Napoleon, and he had already withdrawn 25,000 men from Spain in the spring of 1812 to strengthen his position in central Europe. It cannot be said that the Spanish guerrillas decided the issue in Spain – that decision was brought about by Wellington, who, on 21 June 1813, com-

pletely routed King Joseph's army at Vitoria. But without the aid of the guerrillas, Wellington's forces in the previous years would have had a rather more difficult stand and may not have established themselves at all in Spain.

The impact of the Spanish guerrilla movement was not limited to Spain – indeed, the Spaniards carried the torch of liberty and set aflame the emotions and passions of all those suffering under Napoleon. It strengthened the faith of those who believed that the moment was at hand to overthrow Napoleonic rule in central Europe. As elsewhere, the war in Spain was fought by means of press and pamphlet propaganda. Within a few months of its beginning, the widely distributed Spanish pamphlet literature inciting the population to resist the French had reached the German states. Here it served the same purpose, sometimes as a model, but more often in direct adaptation. The literature made its way from Spain in two directions, to London and Vienna, subsequently finding its way back into the German heartland.

The Austrian Chancellor, Count Johann Phillip von Stadion

Above. *In April 1799 Kléber's division was assailed by a large Turkish force at Mount Tabor. The Turks failed to make any impression on Kléber's squares, and late in the afternoon, when ammunition was running low, Napoleon arrived with reinforcements and drove the Turks off with heavy loss (contemporary engraving).*

Above right. *Napoleon at the Battle of Friedland, June 1807 (painting by Horace Vernet).*

Right. *General Sir Ralph Abercromby (center) is mortally wounded as his troops defeat General Menou's French at Alexandria, 21 March 1801.*

thought that the moment had come, provided that Prussia could be rallied to Austria's side, thus restoring not only unity of action but also continuity of German history by abolishing the recent Austro-Prussian dualism. Stadion was, like von Stein, the scion of an old German family of *Reichsritter* and found in Stein a man from the same mold and of like mind. Stein, who had failed to obtain any concessions from the French by negotiation, expressed himself in favor of taking action. Frederick William III was prepared to move but only if Russia would take the same course, and of that there was no sign at the time. Spain now achieved by force what Stein had failed to obtain by negotiation: Napoleon had to move substantial forces from central Europe into the Iberian peninsula, the French occupation of Prussia was reduced to a minimum, and Frederick William III could return from Königsberg to his capital, Berlin.

Czar Alexander advocated peace; in Prussia, too, the peace party advised moderation, while Stein recommended that Prussia join Austria against Napoleon. However, a letter of his containing strong anti-Napoleonic sentiments was intercepted

by the French and Napoleon, who now realized the danger, demanded that Stein be dismissed. Stein formally resigned on 24 November 1808; he first found refuge in Vienna, then in St Petersburg.

Austria decided to make the most of the favorable circumstances that seemed to have presented themselves, hoping that, by its example, it would ultimately carry Prussia as well. The year 1809 saw the Habsburg dynasty at the head of the first attempt of the re-forming German nation to obtain its liberty by means of a national rising. The Spanish example was to be emulated in Germany. By the combined weight of popular risings along both the Danube and the Ebro, Napoleon was to be toppled. Friedrich von Gentz, Friedrich Schlegel and a host of other writers penned pamphlets and proclamations appealing to German patriots everywhere. Archduke Charles, in a public proclamation to the German people and his troops, announced: 'Your victories will free them from their chains, and your German brothers, still in the ranks of the enemy, are waiting for their liberation.' Vienna became the center for a systematic propaganda campaign – they had learned from the French! – for the rest of Germany, with branches run in Munich by Stadion's brother Friedrich Lothar von Stadion, in Dresden by the Austrian envoy Buol, and in Prussia by Adam Müller and the poet Heinrich von Kleist. The feeling of certainty that these efforts would result in a general rising of the Germans against Napoleon was the critical factor in Austria's final decision to go to war, a decision already reached in principle by the end of 1808. War began in April 1809 with an appeal written by Friedrich Lothar von Stadion and Schlegel and signed by Archduke Charles, addressed 'To the German Nation.' In Prussia Scharnhorst and Gneisenau were in favor of joining Austria, and Queen Louise said that, if Prussia's downfall were inevitable, then it would be better if it were to happen with honor.

However, the forces of Archduke Charles moved too slowly, allowing Napoleon to concentrate his army. Charles was pushed back into Bohemia and Napoleon advanced toward Vienna. At Aspern on 21 and 22 May 1809, however, Charles succeeded in inflicting the first defeat Napoleon had suffered. However, success was again not followed up and Napoleon

regained the initiative, defeating the Austrians at Wagram on 5 and 6 July. Six days later Napoleon and Emperor Francis decided to conclude an armistice, culminating in the Peace of Schönbrunn on 14 October 1809. Austria was reduced to a second-rate power, it had to participate in the continental blockade against Britain and reduce its armed forces to 150,000 men. Count Metternich, who had negotiated the treaty, now replaced Stadion as Austria's leading minister.

The battles between the regular forces of the Austrian and French armies were, however, only one aspect of the war; the other was a mass popular rising of the Tyrolean peasants. After her defeat by the French in 1805, Austria was compelled to cede the Tyrol to Bavaria. Immediately it was occupied by a mixed force of Bavarian and French troops, and France levied heavy contributions to finance its army, as did Bavaria. In addition the Roman Catholic Church in the Tyrol was to be secularized by Bavaria, whose government both at home and in the Tyrol claimed to pursue an 'enlightened policy.' Like the Spaniards, the Tyroleans were motivated by religious and patriotic causes and by their allegiance, in this case, to the House of Habsburg. Unlike the Spaniards, they already had previous experience in guerrilla fighting; a century before, in 1703, they had expelled the Elector of Bavaria and his forces, and between 1796 and 1797 had successfully defeated the French invasion until the conclusion of the Peace of Campo Formio. Another important difference was that the Tyroleans had possessed their own form of military organization since the late Middle Ages, put into proper shape by the so-called *Landlibell* of Emperor Maximilian I in 1511; it meant that, for every part of the Tyrol, a defensive force could be raised if the need should arise. The numbers depended on the size of the population in each area. More specific requirements were made in 1605 and also in 1703 after the Bavarian invasion. In case of attack the province had to provide 20,000 men in all, but only to defend the Tyrol. The province was poor in agriculture because of its climate and mountainous terrain, and was dependent on wheat imports. It was suitable only for dairy farming and hunting. The Tyroleans were natural hunters and, when supplied with weapons, could quickly form a ready force in an emergency.

Increased taxation, attacks against the Church and, finally, the introduction of conscription drove the Tyroleans into rebellion. The geography of the country was an advantage: with the exception of the *Ausserferner*, the region lying north of the Mieminger mountain chain containing the Lech Valley, the *Innerferner* or Tyrol consisted of the Inn Valley stretching from Kufstein on the Bavarian frontier down to Switzerland. To the south was another mountain chain, including the Zillertaler, Stubaier and Ötztaler Alps, crossed by several passes, the main one being the Brenner. South of it was the southern Tyrol with its provincial capital of Bozen, to the east of which was the Pustertal and, ultimately, eastern Tyrol with its provincial capital of Lienz near the Carinthian border. Access from Bavaria to the north was difficult because of the mountainous terrain, and the Inn Valley was therefore preferred – it could be reached from Austria via the Pustertal from the Lower Inn valley at Kufstein, and directly from the south, from Italy.

The rising in the Tyrol had been planned for some time by Archduke Johann. He appointed an intendant, General Hormeyr, a native of Innsbruck but serving at the court of Vienna. An Austrian army advanced up from Lienz through the Pustertal and, when they received this piece of news, the peasant leaders leapt into action, the most prominent among them being Andreas Hofer, trader and innkeeper in the Passeier Valley. Bonfires on the mountain summits signalled the attack, and the peasants expelled the Bavarian and French troops from

the Inn Valley. However, they failed to take the fortress of Kufstein. They avoided fighting in the open and instead attacked from the forests along the marching routes. On the mountainous heights they built stone avalanches which, upon the cutting of ropes, thundered down with deadly accuracy. Along the Inn Valley, city after city was liberated under the able leadership of Josef Speckbacher, and, by 11 April 1809, they had liberated Innsbruck. The peasants were jubilant over their success. But news of any victories by Austria's main armies against Napoleon was still outstanding. The Austrian army under Chasteller then arrived in Innsbruck and, moving down the River Inn, was defeated by newly arriving French forces commanded by General Lefebvre. The Austrian forces withdrew across the mountain passes, leaving the field to the French and Bavarians, who reoccupied Innsbruck. At that point Andreas Hofer assumed supreme command over the peasants, assisted by Speckbacher and the Capuchin monk Haspinger. Again they rallied their forces at the Isel Mountain, which overlooked

Above left. *The Tyrolean patriot Josef Speckbacher, 1767–1820.*

Above right. *Prince Klemens Metternich, 1773–1859, an Austrian statesman and diplomat whose conservative policies held sway for half a century.*

Right. *Wellington defeats the French at Vittoria, 21 June 1813.*

Innsbruck, and provoked the enemy to attack; by 29 May General Deroy's forces had been reduced to a point where they had to evacuate Innsbruck and withdraw down the Inn Valley. In the meantime the news of the Austrian victory at Aspern reached the Tyrol and liberation seemed at hand. The news of the defeat of Wagram and of the armistice concluded between Napoleon and Emperor Francis did not get through.

It seemed as though the armistice did not apply in the Tyrol. Generals Lefebvre and Beaumont led exclusively French forces from the north up the Inn Valley and from the south across the Brenner Pass upon Innsbruck and retook it. And again, under Hofer's leadership, the peasants rallied for a third time. Between 11 and 13 August 1809 the most ferocious battle raged at the Isel Mountain between the French and the Tyroleans, both fighting to the point of exhaustion. Indeed Lefebvre decided to retreat down the River Inn, burning towns and villages on the way. Innsbruck was spared because the Tyroleans immediately occupied it, for the third time. Hofer took over the government in Innsbruck, but Napoleon declared him an outlaw who had broken the armistice. As new French and Bavarian forces were in the process of returning, Haspinger and Speckbacher argued in favor of fighting it out, while Hofer thought the country was exhausted. Individual actions were still fought in all parts of the province, but the Tyrol could no longer rely on Habsburg support. By the Treaty of Schönbrunn, Tyrol was again confirmed a possession of Bavaria. The French now mounted a punitive expedition throughout the Tyrol, and memorial tablets on the churches still tell the bloody tale. At first Andreas Hofer escaped, hiding in a mountain hut near his inn; betrayed, he was taken prisoner by the French, perfunctorily tried, and then, on Napoleon's orders, put before the firing squad at Mantua in 1810.

The Tyrol episode was not without its consequences. On 28 April 1809, the 2nd Brandenburg Hussar Regiment in Berlin under the command of Ferdinand von Schill, already distinguished in the defense of Kolberg, marched out of the city, ostensibly for an exercise. Schill's plan, however, was not to return but to conduct his own campaign against the French troops; in this way he would force king and government to join in a general effort. Once he left the city he told his officers and men about his plan and gave them the opportunity to return. Only a handful did so, the vast majority of officers and men pressing to take action against the French at the earliest possible moment. Schill then marched south to Dessau, which he entered with a public proclamation announcing his plans and the city's liberation. He was enthusiastically received by the city's population, but public support did not go much further. He and his troops remained isolated and the popular uprising which Schill had imagined his action would incite did not materialize. His intention had been to march to Westphalia and join up with the forces of Colonel von Dörnberg, who had planned a similar rising against King Jerome. That rising, too, proved abortive and Dörnberg escaped to Bohemia. Schill, however, decided to move north to the Baltic in the hope that he and his men would be taken and saved by the British navy. He surprised the garrison of the city of Stralsund and occupied it, hoping either to turn it into another Saragossa (where in 1808 Spanish soldiers and civilians under the leadership of José de Palafox y Melci had given a splendid account of themselves in defending the city against the French) or at least hold it until the British navy should arrive. On 31 May 1809 Dutch and Danish auxiliary forces of the French stormed the city defended by Schill and his 500 men. Schill was killed in action and 11 officers of those captured were put before a French court-martial at Wesel and shot on 16 September. From Dörnberg's forces, 14 officers were selected by lot and shot at Brunswick. The remaining prisoners were condemned to serve as French galley slaves, and those that survived regained their liberty after the fall of Napoleon.

French cuirassiers charging a British square at Waterloo, 18 June 1815 (watercolor by Denis Dighton).

CHAPTER XII

THE NEW AGE
II: THE GERMAN REACTION

The German reaction to the defeat of Napoleon was the Prussian reform movement, and Prussia was to serve as a model for the rest of Germany. Within this chapter only the military aspects of the Prussian reform movement will be examined, and their effects in the War of Liberation between 1813 and 1815.

The movement's military function was inspired by General Gerhard Johann David von Scharnhorst. He originated from a peasant family in lower Saxony, and his father had been an NCO in the Hanoverian army. Serving first Count Wilhelm von Schaumburg-Lippe, he became an officer in the Hanoverian army and fought in the first war of the coalition against Revolutionary France in the Netherlands, for which service he was ennobled. Like Napoleon, he belonged to the artillery. His most important colleagues were Gneisenau, Grolman and Boyen.

August von Gneisenau (1760–1831) had served as a young lieutenant in an Ansbach-Bayreuth regiment which, as a mercenary force, had served on the British side in North America during the American Revolution. He had experienced at close quarters the superiority of the American forces. He then joined the Prussian army and had led the defense of Kolberg. Karl von Grolman (1777–1834) was one of the youngest of the reformers. In 1809 he served on the Austrian side and then went to Spain, where he commanded a regiment of foreign guerrillas. In January 1813 he returned to Berlin and served as major on the general staff in the War of Liberation. From 1815–19 he was chief of the general staff. Hermann von Boyen (1771–1848) became Prussian Minister for War during the War of Liberation, but in 1819 resigned his post in protest against the policy of restoration, which tried to undo some of the reformers' work.

Scharnhorst displayed a great talent for education from the early days of his career. Besides Gneisenau, he was also one of the few German officers fully to realize the implications of the colonial militia of the North American settlers, and the important part they played in the defeat of Britain's mercenary forces. They enjoyed the advantage of knowing their country's geography and being able to exploit it. Once they were organized into a proper army, they were victorious. What had been demonstrated in North America was confirmed by the French Revolutionary armies. In other words, Scharnhorst had realized the significance of the *levée en masse* before it was put into practice in France; before the outbreak of war between Prussia and France, he wrote his famous memorandum of 1806, in which he stated: 'We have begun to estimate the art of war higher than military virtues. This has been the downfall of people at all times. Bravery, self-sacrifice and steadfastness are the basic pillars of our independence. If our heart does no longer beat for them, then we are already lost.' He advocated the national people's war in an age which assumed that war was of no concern to the civilians. He received support in Berlin from patriotic circles, but the king wanted to know nothing of it. Even Stein, in his early phase, shrank back from what was bound to become a war of extermination, though later he became one of its supporters. Scharnhorst, however, was supported by Prince Hardenberg, Stein's successor as chief minister in 1809, when Scharnhorst entertained the plan of turning the whole of western Germany into an area of popular insurrection and combine it with similar actions in Pomerania and Silesia. However, it would have needed strong British support, which was not forthcoming, and the support of the czar, who counselled peace.

Prussia possessed the resources to conduct such a war even in 1806, but it would have required revolutionary political and social impulses which, in its *ancien régime*, were lacking. How could peasants living in a state of servitude and burghers almost devoid of political rights know what they were risking their lives for? The closer the ties between the population and state on the basis of a liberal constitution, the greater the impetus for

Left. *General Gerhard von Scharnhorst.*

Right. *Field Marshal Augustus Wilhelm von Gneisenau.*

Far right. *A contemporary German engraving shows French troops on the march.*

Below. *Prussian landwehr infantry, 1813. Note the distinguishing landwehr cross on their caps.*

sacrifice. Gneisenau wrote in 1808: 'It is self-evident and clever, at the same time, to give to the people a fatherland, if they are meant to defend it strongly . . . a free constitution which allows the burghers to elect their own superiors who are accountable to them. . . . If we begin first with a new municipal constitution, then this is more effective for the people who understand its benefits immediately before they understand the benefits of a new constitution for the state. If the state is given freer forms, then this satisfies the thinking heads, carries the enthusiasts, converts the pro-French and frightens the traitors.' Such reforms were carried out by Stein and Hardenberg, and the king, at the time, gave them his blessing. A people's army first required a people's state.

Scharnhorst recognized, along with others such as Stein, the need for thorough reform of state and army even before Jena and Auerstädt, and dedicated himself to this purpose. Time and again he called for new strategies and tactics, and, as director of the War Academy, which was founded on his initiative, he developed a new theory for the conduct of war. One of his most dedicated pupils was Carl von Clausewitz. All his calls for reform, however, were turned down time and again, till the defeats at the hands of Napoleon created a more favorable climate of opinion. Clausewitz summarized the ideas of Scharnhorst and his fellow-reformers in four requirements:

1 'A new structure, new armaments and equipment in accordance with the new methods of warfare.' Mercenaries and the hiring of foreigners were abolished. According to the French example, Scharnhorst reorganized the Prussian army into brigades, which combined all arms.

2 'Ennoblement of its constituents and general lifting of the spirit.' Since the mercenaries had been abolished, the severity of discipline could be reduced, since the number of deserters would be much lower. Corporal punishment was abandoned so that the army was no longer greatly feared by the people, and service

in arms was respected. The proclamation of liberty had to precede national conscription. Running the gauntlet was also abolished. The Prussian army had to be carried by a spirit of conscious voluntary discipline.

3 'A careful selection of these officers commanding larger formations.' In principle, 'in peace they should display knowledge and education, in war bravery and vision.' These were the qualities required in the new officer corps. In fact, until the end of the War of Liberation, the privileges of the Prussian nobility in holding the upper ranks were effectively removed.

4 'New types of military exercises in accordance with the new methods of warfare.' One of the most important aspects of army reform was the abolition of linear tactics and the introduction of *tirailleur* and column tactics; this changed the entire training system. Drill on the parade ground was replaced by exercises in the field, and target practice was introduced in place of mere musket drill.

By these means the Prussian army managed to draw level with the French in the tactical field and the way was paved for the victories in the War of Liberation. 'The entire military system . . . which was introduced in Prussia was the attempt to organize a popular resistance against the enemy, insofar as this was possible within the framework of an absolute monarchy,' wrote Friedrich Engels, although, through the political reforms introduced by Stein and Hardenberg, the Prussian monarchy was much less absolute than Engels would have it; it was on the road, albeit a long one, to becoming a constitutional monarchy.

A fundamental change in the relationship between army and state resulted. So far the middle class, the burghers of the towns and cities, had been exempted from military service; now they were gradually drafted into the army, though not without protesting the infringement of their 'ancient privileges.' Scharnhorst argued in favor of opening up all the ranks of the army to members of the middle class, from which he himself had come,

Left. *Prussian generals, 1750–1850.*

Below left. *Prussian lancers, 1786–1845.*

Below far left. *The Emperor Alexander I of Russia, 1777–1825.*

Below left. *Field Marshal Gebhard von Blücher.*

Below. *The liberal Prussian statesman Baron Karl von und zum Stein, 1757–1831.*

Right. *The French army withdraws from Leipzig, October 1813, under heavy pressure from the Prussians.*

and this proved a step of considerable long-term significance. Hitherto, the commissioned ranks had almost exclusively been the preserve of the nobility, while peasants constituted the rank and file. Scharnhorst's aim was to make the members of the middle class eligible for commissions, and introduced higher education as the prerequisite for advancement into the upper echelons.

The relations between army, state and society were to be reformed in such a way that the army would adopt the values and political consciousness of the middle classes. Thus the army became an institution which was to play a vital role in the process of political and social integration in the Prussian state. In July 1809, when many of the reforms had already been carried out, Scharnhorst answered objections against the entry of commoners into the Prussian officer corps in a memorandum, in which he wrote: 'If only children of noblemen possess the privilege to be employed as officers, and despite their gross ignorance and tender age, men are made subordinate to them who have knowledge and courage, then this will help the noble families, but the army will rot and never obtain the respect of the nation – it will become an object of derision for the educated.'

Education was a vital factor in Scharnhorst's reform program: 'If the education of the nation is to prosper, then the entire school system of a nation must originate from one source. . . . The same concept of the nation must predominate in all educational institutions; the same organic connections must embrace the entire education of youth and all be directed to the same goal. There is only one humanity, and every nation represents on entity within it; therefore the national educational institutions should not educate individuals or classes, but the nation as a whole, and all schools must represent one school of the nation.' Two features are fundamental to this concept: a national goal and a democratic aim, interrelated with one another. The school should not be an institution for the state, nor for the education of a particular class, nor for the preparation for a particular profession – this would only serve particularist interests and, as such, be in opposition to his views of national education. Specialization, too, at school level would breed separate interests and would not lead to the unity of all citizens in one nation. For this reason as well, all citizens had to serve in the army. 'Only by arming the whole of the people will the smaller establish a kind of equilibrium of might in a defensive war conducted against a larger who carries on a war of subjugation by aggression.'

The new army was to be based upon honor and bravery, with opportunities for anyone with ability. Wars of conquest, so Scharnhorst argued, are always dependent upon the man who has the ability and charisma to lead and inspire his army, but wars of defense depend to a much greater degree on the character of the individual soldier.

After Jena and Auerstädt, Scharnhorst was called to head a military commission. Gneisenau was also a member because of his brilliant defense of Kolberg. The commission was to enquire into the causes of the defeat and weed out those who had proved themselves incapable; it was also to submit and carry out the reforms considered necessary: 'One must give the nation the feeling of independence; one must provide the opportunities for it to become familiar with itself, so that it looks after itself, for only then will it respect itself and know how to compel others to respect it. To work toward this aim is all that we can do. To destroy the old ways, remove prejudice, lead the rebirth, watch over it and not stop its free growth, more than that we cannot effect.'

In many ways one can argue that the principle of general

military service had existed in Prussia since Frederick William I's *Cantonal Règlement* of 1730, but any such view would not take account of the vast numbers of exemptions, which included all towns and cities and which necessitated the continued recruitment of mercenaries. During the Seven Years' War, especially in its later stages, forcible recruitment had been carried out; few had conceived of the 'citizen soldier,' of the duty of every citizen to carry arms for this country or to prepare for the day when he should need to use them. But then the citizen did not yet exist in Prussia, only the subject, and among the royal subjects of Frederick the Great the burghers were important chiefly commercially and were essentially unmilitary.

Stein fully supported Scharnhorst's demand for the introduction of general conscription. One of the first obstacles was financial, namely what would any army based on general conscription cost? The figure proved staggering, bearing in mind the financial obligations of Prussia toward France. It was therefore necessary to accept what already existed, namely the standing army, reform it from within and add to it an inexpensive component – the *Landwehr* or militia. Forcible recruitment was adapted and turned into a general duty of all citizens to serve in the army. In these ways the Prussian army experienced its most thoroughgoing transformation since the days of the Great Elector.

The standing army was badly in need of improvements, especially its senior officer corps. Scharnhorst's commission purged it to the extent that, of 143 generals who were still on the active list, only two remained on the eve of the War of Liberation: Blücher and Taunzien. Scharnhorst wanted to turn the army into the school of the nation, but in practical terms he

had to form a small, efficient but cheap military force for an impoverished state. The solution he envisaged was firstly to draft all who were able to carry arms. Because the Treaty of Tilsit limited the Prussian army to 42,000 men, this could not be put fully into effect until 1813. The national servicemen were to serve for a limited but uninterrupted period of time, and then were released, but remained in the reserves. The standing army and reserves were to constitute the regular army. However, to ensure that everyone served in the army, the *Landwehr* was to be called into being to act as reinforcements.

Scharnhorst devised methods of evading Napoleon's limitations on the size of the Prussian army, introducing the *Krümper* system. *Krümper* was already a popular expression in the old army for those soldiers who belonged to a particular regiment, but were on leave because of a small regimental budget; in case of war, however, they rejoined. Boyen reintroduced this 'rejoining' to obscure the real intention behind the move and, after the evacuation of Prussia by the French, the system was extended. It amounted to five men per company, later to eight, plus 15,200 Prussian prisoners of war who returned in 1809. At first they were intended to serve for one month only, immediately to be replaced by an equal number of *Krümpers*, but one month was too short a period to produce soldiers efficient in field exercises. Ultimately the period of service was extended to six months. Once released, they became part of the reserve of the line regiment, and their training continued in their home districts under the supervision of officers on half-pay. As one report put it: 'The exercises of those on leave proceed very well here. The mild treatment of the soldiers had reduced the dread non-soldiers had of military service. Young and old watch the exercises and the targets are carried by a great procession. The warlike spirit is especially kindled among the youth, whose fondest game is now playing soldiers.' At its peak the *Krümper* system produced between 60 and 80 soldiers per annum for each company.

Scharnhorst's reforms faced serious opposition, particularly from the Prussian nobility, who resented the erosion of privileges. They rejected the argument that Prussia had failed because the army had been allowed to grow weak and lazy. Scharnhorst and his fellow military reformers could see only one option open to them: thorough reform or none at all. Their opponents maintained that it could have been carried out within the established framework; they were blind to the new national currents which played so large a part in the motivation of the new military forces. They either failed to see the significance of the popular risings against Napoleon in Spain and the Tyrol, or else feared them. Nothing was more dangerous to their concept of state than an army consisting of the 'emancipated masses.' 'To arm the nation means merely to organize and facilitate opposition and dissatisfaction,' wrote Prince Wittgenstein.

Certainly the democratic trends evident in the rule that allowed the *Landwehr* to elect its own officers, and in the growing demand for the introduction of a constitutional monarchy, were ultimately the stumbling block for the Prussian reform movement after 1815. It was the middle class which was most receptive to the ideas of the French Revolution, and which most vociferously expressed the opinion that the time had come to apply its lessons to Germany.

Frederick William III did not make things easy for Scharnhorst. He could not deny that Scharnhorst was right, but he remained emotionally tied to the legacy of his granduncle, and this made him vulnerable to the arguments of those who opposed Scharnhorst. He, too, wondered what forces would ultimately be unleashed by the introduction of military conscription. He saw a need for the abolition of noble privileges in

the army and therefore approved of the introduction of formal examinations for ensigns and officers. However, he obstinately refused to close down the cadet institutes, which Scharnhorst saw merely as training schools for the nobility and unlikely to produce the necessary national elite. In the long run, however, the pressure of the growing middle class proved too strong even for the conservatives in Prussia, and the cadet institutes were opened to all suitable applicants.

It is important to note that Scharnhorst's reforms, with a few exceptions, can be discerned only in the army regulations. For instance, compulsory military service was never publicly proclaimed. *De jure* the old cantonal system of Frederick William I remained in force until March 1813, although *de facto* it had been abolished for five years. Only the tactical reforms of the army found expression in a general revision of the military manual. Of course attitudes established over a century could hardly be eliminated within nine years. After the death of Scharnhorst, and later the departure of Gneisenau and Boyen, the results of the military reforms were still visible, but the changes in attitudes that had motivated them had apparently sunk into oblivion.

Still Frederick William III was reluctant to join Austria, not only because of the czar's advice against it but because he also feared the consequences of a people's war. The reformers were disgusted: Grolman joined the Austrians and then went on to Spain, Gneisenau travelled to London and then to St Petersburg for the duration of the peace, and Scharnhorst, as a result of Napoleon's pressure, had to resign his post, although he still managed to act as an adviser. He then went on to St Petersburg and Vienna, where Metternich informed him that it was not his intention to replace French hegemony in Europe with Russian hegemony. Clausewitz went to St. Petersburg as well, where Gneisenau and Stein had set up a Committee for German Affairs.

The time for action against Napoleon would not come until Napoleon's army had been defeated in Russia. Prussia, as well as the other German states, had to provide auxiliary forces, the Prussian contingent being commanded by General von Yorck. After Napoleon's debacle, when the Prussian corps was cut off by Russian forces under General Diebitsch, the Russians refrained from attacking the Prussians and instead asked them to change sides, or at least declare their neutrality. On the Russian side, the negotiations were conducted by Clausewitz and Scharnhorst's brother-in-law, Count Dohna. The Czar dispatched a personal letter to Yorck in which he undertook not to lay down arms against the French until Prussia's former position among the powers of Europe had been fully restored. This letter was crucial; it decided Yorck to resume personal negotiations with Diebitsch. At the same time he informed Frederick William of the development, sending a Major von Seydlitz to Berlin, and hoped for definite instructions from the king. When Seydlitz returned, he had no explicit orders from the king, only evasion; by word of mouth, however, Seydlitz was to relate that negotiations with the Austrians had already begun and that Yorck should act according to the circumstances. Taking this as a blank check, Yorck met Diebitsch again on 30 December 1812 at the Poscherun mill outside Tauroggen, and they signed the Convention of Tauroggen, by which Yorck separated his forces from the French and promised to maintain neutrality.

The Russians advanced, followed by Stein, Dohna, Clausewitz, Gneisenau and Boyen. Boyen was sent to Prussia, Stein to Breslau, where Frederick William had withdrawn, while, in the meantime, Yorck's forces had already joined the Russians. By the end of February no French soldier was left east of the River Oder. On 3 February 1813 Frederick William issued an

Above. *French infantry in action in Saxony in 1813. The nearest soldier is biting off the end of a cartridge, before loading his musket.*

Above right. *The Emperor Francis I of Austria, 1767–1835.*

Right. *Wellington enters Toulouse after his defeat of Soult, April 1814.*

Below. *The Prussian Field Marshal Yorck von Wartenburg, who negotiated the Convention of Taurrogen (December 1812) which effectively swung the Prussian army away from its alliance with the French.*

in favor of attacking again but, being under Russian supreme command, he was held back. At Bautzen Napoleon forced a crossing over the River Spree.

Two battles had now been lost by the Prussians, but they were fought with such fanaticism and enthusiasm that Napoleon concluded that his opponents were rather stronger than they really were. Since he himself knew best the weaknesses of his own army, he offered an armistice which was concluded on 4 June 1813. Napoleon later described it as the greatest stupidity of his life – the French were at Prussia's frontier and the Russians were already considering withdrawing into Poland. The duration of the armistice was also well used by the allies; apart from improving both the numbers and equipment of their forces, their main effort was spent in bringing Austria into the coalition, an endeavor in which they ultimately succeeded. The armistice came to an end on 4 August 1813 and, on the 11th, Austria joined the coalition. Prior to this, Sweden had also joined and landed an army on the shores of the Baltic. The Allies now numbered 480,000 men against Napoleon's 450,000, though this superiority in numbers was in effect reduced by their disunity; only Prussia and Russia were decided upon terminating Napoleon's days as Emperor. Austria on the other hand feared that Prussia and Russia might grow too strong, and Sweden wanted to annex Norway, which at that time belonged to Denmark.

The allied autumn campaign of 1813 planned to encircle Napoleon's central position in Dresden. The main army in the south under the command of the Austrian Prince Schwarzen-

edict calling to arms all citizens from 17 to 24 years old and, on 9 February, removed all exemptions to military service which still existed, for the duration of the war. General conscription had been introduced. Under Stein's guidance the Treaty of Kalisch was signed on 27 February between Prussia and Russia. It was a risky venture for the Prussians, as it was soon apparent that the Russian forces were not as numerous as had been imagined, while the French still held considerable contingents in Germany. Austria was in favor of a new coalition but, for the time being, adopted a wait-and-see policy.

On 11 March Frederick founded the Iron Cross decoration. Five days later the Czar entered Breslau, the next day Prussia declared war on France and, on 16 March, Frederick issued his famous proclamation *An mein Volk*, which was enthusiastically received by the population. Volunteers from all over Germany, even from the Tyrol, poured into Prussia and, in the 12 months from March 1813 to March 1814, the Prussian army received more than 50,000 volunteers. For them it was a crusade against Napoleonic despotism. On the same day on which Frederick William issued his proclamation, General Yorck and his corps entered Berlin; Russian Cossacks ventured even as far as Hamburg, where they were received enthusiastically.

Napoleon had now begun to rally his forces, building a new army from the remnants that had returned from Russia supplemented by troops from the German states of the Confederation of the Rhine. Only Bavaria wavered in its support: it had lost 30,000 men in Russia and Crown Prince Ludwig advised joining Prussia. Austria was still indecisive. The first encounter between the Prussians and the French took place on 2 May 1813 at Grossgörschen. Napoleon's forces fought off the Prussian and Russian attack, but he immediately realized that this was no longer the army which he had defeated in 1806. The loss of this battle was Scharnhorst, who, though wounded, nevertheless made his way to Prague to persuade the Austrians to join Prussia. His wound developed gangrene and he died on 28 June. Blücher, whose chief of staff was now Gneisenau, was

Above left. *The Austrian Field Marshal Karl Philip, Prince Schwarzenberg, 1771–1820.*

Right. *A Meissen plate depicting the Battle of Toulouse.*

Far right. *The Allies meet at Leipzig, October 1813.*

Below. *Marshal Etienne Macdonald, Duke of Tarentum, 1765–1840.*

berg, and consisting of Austrians, Russians and Prussians, together with Blücher's Silesian army, was to force Napoleon into decisive battle. The allies achieved initial successes at Grossbeeren and Bad Hegelberg, south of Berlin, in which the *Landwehr* formations particularly distinguished themselves; the southern army, however, suffered a reverse at Napoleon's hand near Dresden. Blücher, on Gneisenau's advice, decided to escape the shackles of the high command which shunned any risk and, on 26 August 1813, attacked Macdonald's forces at the Katzbach River and inflicted a heavy defeat. As Blücher wrote to his wife: 'Today was the day for which I have wished for so long. We have completely beaten the enemy. The fighting lasted from 2 o'clock in the afternoon until the evening. Not many prisoners were taken; the troops were too embittered and killed everything. It rained the whole day and guns would not fire any longer. My infantrymen fought with the bayonet. After the battle everyone wanted to rest, but I ordered that the men and horses summon their last reserves of strength in the pursuit of the enemy.' As at Grossbeeren, Blücher's infantrymen were mainly *Landwehr* men.

Napoleon continued to concentrate his forces around Dresden, seeking to defeat his opponents one by one. The Allies' main objective was to combine their armies while Napoleon still stood between them. Bernadotte and his Swedish troops declared themselves ready to have Blücher's army move toward them and join forces; when they met they moved toward Leipzig, while Schwarzenberg's army approached from the south. Napoleon now saw the danger of being cut off in the rear

and having to fight with reversed fronts like the Prussians at Jena. To counter this danger he moved the bulk of his forces against Bernadotte and Blücher with the intention of beating them. Bernadotte was, in fact, ready to withdraw, but Gneisenau suggested that any withdrawal be achieved without crossing the River Elbe, thus not only threatening Napoleon's rear but also making it possible to combine with Schwarzenberg's forces. Napoleon's army could not find an enemy to attack. Near Merseburg the Allied armies joined and Napoleon now decided to force battle, if only because a decision in his favor would open the way to the west; he had to seek a battle in order to win an opportunity to retreat.

The Battle of Leipzig raged from 16 to 19 October 1813 and was one of the greatest battles fought in the nineteenth century. Napoleon had positioned his army around Leipzig, 190,000 men in all, against an Allied force which initially numbered 200,000, but which in the course of the battle increased to 300,000. On the 16th the Allies fought their way in to the approaches of Leipzig, on the 17th the Prussians entered the suburbs, and the battle for the city commenced the following day. Heavy street fighting raged throughout the city, the French and their allies trying to fight their way out to the west. When, however, a French corporal blew up the Elster bridge over the Elbe, a vast number of French and Confederation of the Rhine troops had their escape route cut off. Marshal Poniatowski, Polish prince and Marshal of France, tried to swim across the river and perished, as did thousands of others; the French were defeated. The Allied forces met in the market

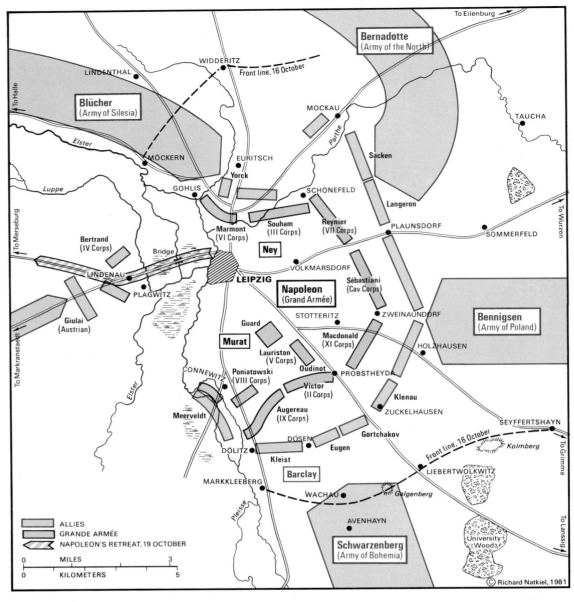

Bernadotte
(Army of the North)

To Eilenburg

WIDDERITZ

Front line, 16 October

LINDENTHAL

To Halle

Blücher
(Army of Silesia)

Elster

MÖCKERN

Luppe

EURITSCH

Yorck

GOHLIS

MOCKAU

Parthe

SCHÖNEFELD

Sacken

Langeron

TAUCHA

To Wurzen

PLAUNSDORF

SOMMERFELD

To Merseburg

Bertrand
(IV Corps)

Bridge

Marmont
(VI Corps)

Souham
(III Corps)

Reynier
(VII Corps)

Ney

LINDENAU

PLAGWITZ

LEIPZIG

VOLKMARSDORF

Napoleon
(Grand Armée)

Sébastiani
(Cav Corps)

Giulai
(Austrian)

STOTTERITZ

ZWEINAUNDORF

Bennigsen
(Army of Poland)

To Markranstaedt

Guard

Murat

Macdonald
(XI Corps)

HOLZHAUSEN

Elster

Lauriston
(V Corps)

Oudinot

PROBSTHEYDA

CONNEWITZ

Poniatowski
(VIII Corps)

Victor
(II Corps)

Klenau

Meerveldt

Augereau
(IX Corps)

ZUCKELHAUSEN

SEYFFERTSHAYN

To Grimma

Gortchakov

DÖSEN

Eugen

Front line, 16 October

Kolmberg

DÖLITZ

Kleist

Barclay

LIEBERTWOLKWITZ

To Lanssig

MARKKLEEBERG

WACHAU

Galgenberg

ALLIES

GRANDE ARMÉE

NAPOLEON'S RETREAT, 19 OCTOBER

AVENHAYN

University
Wood

0   MILES   3

0   KILOMETERS   5

Schwarzenberg
(Army of Bohemia)

Pleisse

© Richard Natkiel, 1981

Above. *Bashkir soldiers, tribal horsemen in Russian service, survey the ruins of Hamburg, 1814.*

Below left. *Austrian troops, 1814.*

Below. *Off-duty Austrian infantry enjoy a game of cards among the baggage wagons.*

Below right. *An Austrian carpenter at work in camp, 1814.*

achieved, however, when news arrived that, on 1 March 1815, Napoleon had returned to France and that most of the army of the Bourbon king had joined him. The Bourbons had only just vacated Paris when Napoleon entered the city in triumph on 20 March. Among the Allies, only the Prussian and British forces were on an immediate war footing. The British army was in the Netherlands, having made its way across France from Spain, while the Prussian army under Blücher was in the Rhenish provinces. Once again Gneisenau was Blücher's chief of staff, though he had hoped for an independent command; in fact it was under Gneisenau that the office of chief of staff attained the significance it has enjoyed ever since.

At first the Prussian campaign suffered a setback near Liège: Saxon formations mutinied upon hearing that they were to be split up as a result of territorial changes which had been made to their country; they were disarmed and the ringleaders shot. Napoleon moved onto the offensive with the aim of splitting the coalition. While the center of gravity of the Prussian army was Liège, that of the British was around Ghent, their vanguards meeting in the Charleroi region. Napoleon realized that these two armies could fully join forces only if one or the other would give up its main base, and therefore believed he could beat each separately. With surprising speed he attacked Blücher at Ligny on 16 June 1815; Blücher accepted battle because Wellington had promised aid, but the Prussian and British forces were still too far apart for this assistance to come in time. Moreover, once Wellington was himself under attack by Marshal Ney at Quatre Bras, he was soon in need of all his forces himself. The Prussian lines became overextended, stretched in one direction in order to cover their rearward communications, in the other in order not to lose touch with Wellington. For hours the Battle of Ligny raged on a hot June day until, as evening approached, Napoleon used his Imperial guards to capture the town. Blücher was wounded and only the onset of darkness put an end to the battle. Retreat was now unavoidable, with Wellington likely to do the same in the direction of Antwerp.

At that moment Gneisenau issued the instruction that the

square but, although the possibility of routing the French forces existed, the Allies were exhausted. Napoleon, attacked only once during his retreat by Bavarian forces, and managed to escape beyond the Rhine.

On New Year's Day 1814 the Allied troops crossed the Rhine. Differences of opinion about the course of operations, however, delayed them again until Blücher achieved their first victory on French soil at La Rothière on 1 February, and the general advance was resumed. However, after he had suffered three quick defeats by Napoleon, Blücher rejoined the Allied armies. The Allies again wanted to withdraw but, mainly on Blücher's and Gneisenau's urging, the advance was resumed and the Allies entered Paris on 31 March 1814. A few days later Napoleon abdicated and left for Elba.

In the meantime the Congress of Vienna had assembled and, as usual, the diplomats were divided. Solidarity was quickly

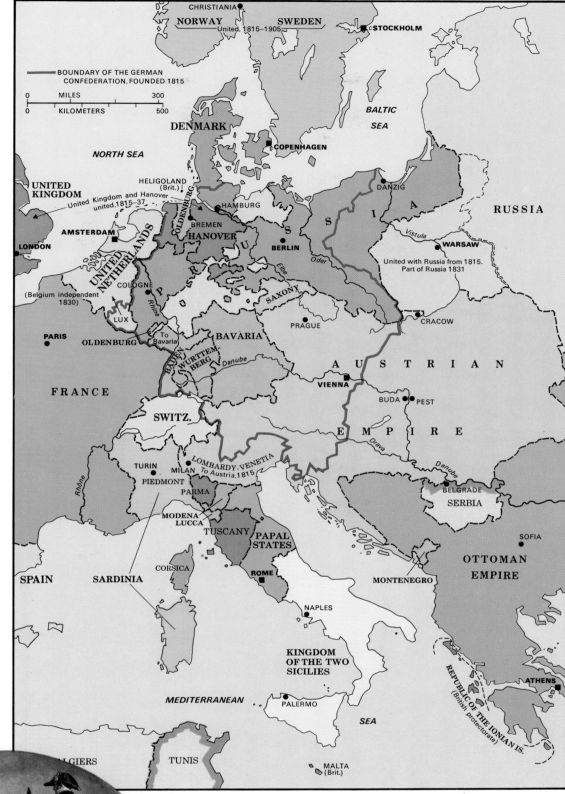

Left. On 30–31 October 1813 Napoleon, with the survivors of Leipzig, battered his way past a blocking position at Hanau (after Horace Vernet).

below left. The Battle of Waterloo (contemporary English aquatint).

below. Adolf von Menzel's painting of the meeting of Blücher and Wellington on the field of Waterloo. Blücher had been unhorsed and ridden over at Ligny two days before, and had dosed himself with a lethal brew of gin and rhubarb. 'I stink a bit,' he admitted when he met Wellington.

below right. British wounded arrive in Brussels after Waterloo.

BOUNDARY OF THE GERMAN CONFEDERATION, FOUNDED 1815

MILES 0 — 300
KILOMETERS 0 — 500

CHRISTIANIA

NORWAY   SWEDEN
United, 1815–1905

STOCKHOLM

BALTIC SEA

DENMARK

NORTH SEA

COPENHAGEN

DANZIG

RUSSIA

UNITED KINGDOM

HELIGOLAND (Brit.)

United Kingdom and Hanover united 1815–37

HAMBURG
OLDENBURG
BREMEN

Vistula

WARSAW

United with Russia from 1815. Part of Russia 1831

AMSTERDAM

HANOVER
BERLIN

LONDON

P R U S S I A

UNITED NETHERLANDS

COLOGNE

SAXONY

Oder

(Belgium independent 1830)

Rhine

PRAGUE

CRACOW

LUX

PARIS

OLDENBURG

To Bavaria

BAVARIA

BADEN
WÜRTTEM-BERG

Danube

AUSTRIAN

FRANCE

SWITZ.

VIENNA

BUDA   PEST

EMPIRE

Drava

LOMBARDY-VENETIA
To Austria,1815

TURIN   MILAN
PIEDMONT
PARMA

Danube

BELGRADE

SERBIA

Rhône

MODENA
LUCCA

TUSCANY

PAPAL STATES

SOFIA

SPAIN

SARDINIA

CORSICA

ROME

MONTENEGRO

OTTOMAN EMPIRE

NAPLES

KINGDOM OF THE TWO SICILIES

REPUBLIC OF THE IONIAN IS. (British protectorate)

ATHENS

MEDITERRANEAN   SEA

PALERMO

ALGIERS   TUNIS

MALTA (Brit.)

The battle of Waterloo from 11 am to 3 pm, 18 June

0 MILE   ¼   ½

MONT ST JEAN

Wellington
72,000 men

Lambert

de Ghigney

Vivian (K.G.L.)

Vandeleur

Tripp

Mont St Jean farm

Somerset

Ponsonby

Sir L. Cole

Pack   Best

Vincke

Brunswick

Merlen

Saxe-Weimar

Perponcher

Prussi (Bülow with 3 approaching)

W. Halkett

Arentshildt

Kruse

Picton

Reserve Corps

Kempt

PAPELOTTE

TER LA HAYE

Sir H. Clinton

I Corps

Kielmansegge   Ompteda

Bylandt

95th

Sandpit

Adam

Dörnberg

C. Halkett

Baring (K.G.L.)

LA HAYE SAINTE

Ⓒ   Ⓑ

Ⓑ

FRIS

Du Plat (K.G.L.)

Grant (K.G.L.)

Maitland

II Corps

Cooke

Ⓑ   Ⓒ   Ⓑ

Jacquinot

Hill

Byng

Durutte

13 Hussars

Marcognet

D'Erlon I Corps

Quiot (Allix)

St Alphonse

HOUGOUMONT

Donzelot

Delort   Milhaud

Macdonnel

Piré

Ⓐ

Ⓐ

Bachelu

Prince Jérôme

Foy

Domon   Subervie

Lefèvre - Desnouettes

Reille II Corps

Simmer

D'hurbal

Kellerman

Lhéritier

Jannin

Imperial   Guard

Guyot

Napoleon
68,600 men

Guards Corps

Young Guard

Middle Guard

Old Guard

ROSSOMME

ALLIES   FRENCH

	ALLIES	FRENCH
INFANTRY	▬▬▬	▬▬▬
CAVALRY	▲▲▲▲▲	△△△△△
ARTILLERY	ⅢⅢⅢ	ⅢⅢⅢ
SKIRMISHERS	▬▬▬	

Ⓐ FRENCH ATTACK ON HOUGOUMONT, 11.30 AM
Ⓑ D'ERLON'S ATTACK, 1.30 PM
Ⓒ PONSONBY'S CHARGE, 2 PM

© Richard Natkiel, 1981

Prussian retreat should not be in the direction of the Rhine but to the northeast toward the village of Waterloo, joining up with the British there. The Prussians therefore made the sacrifice of their own main base. This went against Napoleon's calculations and proved disastrous for him; he did not believe that a defeated enemy would accept a second battle immediately, and assumed that the Prussians and the British would retreat in different directions. Marshal Grouchy was dispatched with his forces toward Liège to harass the Prussians, but there were none there to be harassed. Believing that he had only one enemy to fight, Napoleon made ready to fight the British at Waterloo.

Wellington moved into defensive positions and determined to hold them: 'Our plan is simple: the Prussians or the night.' Napoleon calmly reviewed his troops in full view of the British contingents and then attacked, three major attacks being repelled by the British and their defensive fire. Nevertheless, the British position was becoming very precarious when, toward the late afternoon, the Prussian army driven on by Blücher – 'Marshal Forward' as he was called – reached the battlefield; they immediately re-formed for attack from their marching columns, taking the French from their right wing and in their rear. At first Napoleon thought that it must be Grouchy, who had about one-third of the French army with him, but soon realized his error. Blücher's attack transformed the situation completely. The defensive battle became an offensive one and the French, fearful of being taken between the British and the Prussians, tried to escape *en masse*. With Wellington's forces in a state of near exhaustion, the Prussians undertook the pursuit of the enemy. Gneisenau told the troops: 'We have shown the enemy how to conquer, now we shall demonstrate how to pursue.' Almost all the French artillery was captured, as well as Napoleon's carriage and personal belongings.

Blücher and Wellington met near a farm called Belle Alliance. Not much was said – both were too moved by the awareness of how close they had been to the abyss of defeat, too grateful that it had been transformed into victory. And victory was complete, for Napoleon had been toppled, his career ended. The nemesis of power had taken him to St Helena, there to end his days.

A new age of warfare had reached its zenith, but also its end. The powers of restoration, fearful of the ultimate consequences of a people's war, returned to cabinet warfare for the rest of the century, though the industrial revolution set unforeseen forces free. Metternich, and in a way his successor Bismarck, held the doors firmly closed to mass democracy and all that this implied, politically, socially and militarily, almost to the end of the nineteenth century. Ironically enough, that door was pushed open, not in Europe, but in North America, where the American Civil War provided the first indications of what Total War could mean.

Above. *Cossacks bivouacked in Paris.*

Above right. *French* Cuirassiers *crash into a sunken lane at Waterloo. Although there were obstacles on the battlefield, the story of the 'ravine' or 'sunken lane' was exaggerated as a convenient sop to French pride.*

Left. *The tide of battle turns at Waterloo: Wellington signals with his hat for his army to advance.*

Right. *Wellington rides through his army's drenched bivouacs on the morning of Waterloo.*

INDEX

ACKNOWLEDGMENTS

Ardea London (Sue Gooders): 206(top); 210(all).

Author's collection: 122.

BBC Hulton Picture Library: 40; 48(bottom right); 58(top right); 85; 87(top and bottom right); 144(right); 150(top right); 196(both); 236(top left).

Bibliothèque Nationale, Paris: 11(left).

Bildarchiv Preussischer Kulturbesitz: 26–27; 129(both); 154; 162; 251(bottom left).

Bison Picture Library: 169; 175(top).

British Crown Copyright Reserved (Tower of London): 22(top); 46(left); 56(top left and right); 79(top).

Chateau Versailles: 194(top); 206(bottom); 219(top and bottom right).

Cooper Bridgeman Library: Cover; 22(bottom); 46(right); 47; 54(left); 58(bottom); 70(top); 71; 100–101.

Historical Society of Pennsylvania: 187.

Ian Hogg: 10(top both).

Library of Congress: 164–165; 168(bottom); 170; 176; 177(top); 179; 182; 183(bottom).

Mansell Collection: 8; 9(both); 15(top); 18(left); 32(top and bottom); 41(top); 44–45; 50(left); 51; 53(bottom); 55(bottom); 66(top); 74(top); 79(bottom).

86(both); 96(bottom); 158(center); 159(bottom); 168(top left); 181(bottom); 191; 211(bottom); 218(top); 220(top); 234; 251(bottom right).

Mary Evans Picture Library: 10(bottom); 13(bottom); 15(center); 17(right); 18(right); 37; 56(bottom); 65(top); 66(bottom); 82–83; 92; 94; 123(both); 126; 128(top); 134(top); 142(right); 143(top); 146(bottom both); 148; 149(top); 150(bottom); 156(top); 157; 158(top); 190(bottom); 193(both); 194(bottom); 195; 205(top); 208; 228(bottom right); 246(top left).

Musée de l'Armee: 223(top).

National Archives: 171(bottom); 172(left).

National Army Museum: 39(top left and right); 48(top left and right); 49; 50(right); 52; 53(top); 54(right); 55(top); 56(top center); 57; 58(top left); 59(both); 60; 61; 64; 68(top left and right); 69(both); 70(bottom); 72(all); 73(both); 74(bottom); 76; 77; 90(left); 91(right); 97(bottom); 98; 99(both); 130; 131; 133(right); 142(left); 143(bottom); 151; 161(bottom); 167(all); 171(top right); 172(right); 173; 174(both); 175(bottom); 177(bottom); 178(all); 181(top); 183(top left and right); 186(bottom); 190(top); 198(top); 200(both); 201; 204(both); 205(bottom); 207(both); 211(top right); 212; 213(both); 217; 218(bottom); 221(both); 222(both); 223(bottom both); 224; 226–227; 228(top); 235(bottom); 237; 238–239; 240(bottom right); 242(top and center); 245(top left and bottom left); 246(center right); 247; 248; 249; 250(bottom); 252; 253(top left, bottom).

National Gallery: 21(bottom).

National Maritime Museum: 65(bottom); 115(bottom).

Novosti Press Agency: 102; 103(both); 104(bottom both); 105; 107(both); 108(both); 109; 110(both); 111(both); 112(both); 113; 114; 115(top); 116; 117(left); 118; 119; 214–215; 225(both); 229.

NTE: 117(right).

Peter Newark's Historical Pictures: 6–7; 14; 15(bottom); 19(top and bottom left); 23(bottom right); 31(right); 34; 104(top); 125; 127(bottom); 128(bottom); 158(bottom).

Peter Young: 41(bottom); 199; 209(all); 216(top); 233(bottom); 243; 246(bottom); 250(top); 253(top right).

Photo Bulloz, Paris: 198(bottom); 202–203.

Photographie Giraudon: 30(bottom); 62–63; 67(top); 139; 155(top); 188–189; 192; 203(top); 235(top).

Robert Hunt Picture Library: 20(top); 90(right both); 138(both); 145; 155(bottom); 163; 184(top).

Rolf Steinberg: 12(both); 13(top); 16; 17(left); 28(both); 35(bottom); 84(top); 88–89; 91(left); 96(top); 97(top); 120–121; 124(bottom); 127(top); 134(bottom); 135; 140(bottom); 144(top); 146(top both); 160; 230; 233(top left); 241.

Schloss Charlottenburg: 219(bottom left).

Smithsonian Institution: 186(top).

Svenska Porträttarkivet: 30(top); 31(top left); 32(center); 33; 35(top left).

Ullstein Bilderdienst: 29; 35(top right); 36(both); 38; 39(bottom right); 42; 43; 87(bottom left); 93(right); 95; 124(top); 136–137; 140(top); 144(left); 150(top left); 152(both); 153; 156(bottom); 159(top); 161(top); 228(bottom left); 231(bottom); 236(top right); 240(left, top right); 242(bottom all three).

US Army: 180; 184(bottom); 185(both).

Wallace Collection: 10(center); 11(right); 19(right); 20(bottom left and right); 21(center); 23(left, center and right); 24; 25; 31(bottom left); 39(bottom left); 80; 84(bottom both); 132(top); 149(bottom).

Victoria & Albert Museum: 67(bottom); 68(bottom); 132(right); 168(top right); 216(bottom); 220(bottom); 231(top); 245(top right, bottom right).

The author and publishers extend their grateful thanks to Stephanie Lindsay for the picture research; to Richard Natkiel for the maps; to Richard Holmes for the captions; to Penny Murphy for the index; to Richard Crossman for reading the text; and David Eldred for the design.

Extract on page 117 from J. C. F. Fuller's *The Decisive Battles of the Western World*, published by Eyre Methuen appears with permission.

355
Koc

Koch, H. W.

AUTHOR

The Rise of Modern Warfare.

TITLE

DATE DUE

355
Koc

Koch, H. W.

The Rise of Modern Warfare.